MERIT, MONEY AND TEACHERS' CAREERS

Studies on Merit Pay and Career Ladders for Teachers

Edited by

Henry C. Johnson, Jr.

Commissioned by
The College of Education of
The Pennsylvania State University

UNIVERSITY
PRESS OF
AMERICA

LANHAM • NEW YORK • LONDON

Copyright © 1985 by

University Press of America,® Inc.

4720 Boston Way
Lanham, MD 20706

3 Henrietta Street
London WC2E 8LU England

Printed in the United States of America
Library of Congress Cataloging in Publication Data

Main entry under title:

Merit, money, and teachers' careers.

"Co-published by arrangement with the College of
Education, the Pennsylvania State University."
    1. Teachers—Salaries, pensions, etc.—United States—
Addresses, essays, lectures.   2. Compensatory management
—United States—Addresses, essays, lectures.
3. Teachers—United States—Rating of—Addresses,
essays, lectures.   I. Johnson, Henry C., 1929-
II. Pennsylvania State University.   College of
Education.
LB2842.2.M46   1985   371.1'44'0973   85-13549
ISBN 0-8191-4819-9 (alk. paper)
ISBN 0-8191-4820-2 (pbk. : alk. paper)
        Co-Published by arrangement with

The College of Education, The Pennsylvania State University

Cover design by Anne Masters

Table of Contents

Possibilities

Introduction
Stances, Stereotypes, and Public School Policy

Henry C. Johnson, Jr.

The call for new forms of professional life linked to new reward systems is being couched as a demand for a new national policy respecting the American public school teacher. But, is there such a thing as American public school policy? If there is, who constructs it, and how, and to whom is it addressed? There is no clear answer to that complex question.

It is alluring to think that in a simpler age there might have been such a thing. As historian of education, however, I have yet to find it and every reason to doubt its existence, if only because we have never had the single, coherent educational system some have dreamed about. In spite of repeated attempts to centralize and rationalize, the formation and control of public school policy remains the last stand of the eighteenth and nineteenth century liberal individualism that once characterized much of our institutional life.

Yet, things do happen; change occurs; movement in definable directions does take place, thus providing at least a semblance of policy even in so amorphous an entity as the American public school. At the moment there is a newly focused spate of anxiety about the schools. Once again, "the teachers are the problem." The situation is So Serious it demands an Official Remedy, to be quickly prescribed and administered before the nation collapses! What provokes such precipitous shifts in our attention? Wars and other calamities? Perhaps. Some vague sense of corporate guilt or national neurosis? More likely. The dark hand of big business? A useful foil. Or, one even better: The machinations of self-serving politicians. About any or all of this, no one can be sure. But, one can be sure that once again, as for the last century and a half, we address our common problems in the person of our public schools. And we can be sure that the cry will characteristically be for a "broad, new policy," clearly articulated, efficiently implemented, and responsibly monitored, in spite of the fact that there may be neither vehicle nor real object to which the policy will apply.

Who will create and carry out this desperately needed policy? Everybody and nobody. But surely somebody! There exists, however, no hierarchical authority or institutional structure to serve as the medium. American public schooling is at best a "loosely coupled system" (as the sociologists are fond of saying), functioning not through a tightly forged chain of command but through battens of bureaucracy that stifle change even while thankfully insulating us from random crises and self-appointed crusaders.

There is, furthermore, a new aspect of things — not radically new, of course, but now so well developed as to make the policy-making landscape appear very different: There is a debilitating territoriality, a hardening of lines, a polarization and politicization of what we have come to call "interest groups:" The school boards, now vigorously protecting their "grass roots" prerogatives. The professional administrators, perhaps the most vulnerable of all contemporary public servants. An army of state (and increasingly federal) functionaries, with ever more powerful financial and legal weapons. And the organized teachers, desperately trying to take charge of their lives and their long sought profession, exclusive rights to which other shareholders in the educational enterprise are unwilling as yet to grant. And, finally, the "unorganized interests," however anomalous the concept: The school users, of course, and ultimately, in a democracy, "the people!" But, who, what, are the people? How does one hear them? Obey them? Help them? Are they made tangible only in Neilsen Ratings, Gallup Polls, and voting patterns, in cultural minorities and moral majorities?

With the compartmentalization of the public educational enterprise (in the name of rational efficiency) at the turn of the century, the functional elements in the process of policy formation and implementation have become the stances adopted by these organized interests, the stereotypes with which they operate, and the myths upon which they rely. Each separate group now has its stance, its "official position" on issues, to be articulated and defended, rigidly adhered to, never compromised. How, then, is policy to be negotiated, there being no authoritative superstructure to compel arbitration? How, then, is intelligent change to be brought about, when none in this balkanized social-institutional environment has sufficient power or resources to effect it unilaterally?

Stances are made easier and more plausible by stereotypes. At this moment, with the focus once again on the teacher, we are dealing with one of America's most potent and persistent stereotypes: The Teacher as Bumbler! At least since Ichabod Crane, the quintessential incompetent, the teacher has largely been seen as the inadequate male or the passive female. (Washington Irving, one Nineteenth century educational leader remarked, may have immeasurably enriched American literature but he destroyed the American teacher!) "Those who can, do," we say, and "those who can't, teach" — and we mean it!

Also present, but far less frequently noticed, is the stereotype of the teacher as "part-timer." Teachers start late, go home early, have lots of vacations, and don't have to work in the summer time. We all know that. It's a good life; not too demanding; genteel; ideally suited to the upwardly mobile daughters of the lower middle classes or the occasional philanthropic predilections of the upper classes. But not a real job — not a *job* job! It lies somewhere between a volunteer scout leader and a missionary, with remuneration to match.

Images such as these are of obvious utility for administrators, politicians, and angry parents who want no one to defraud the children for whom they otherwise take little responsibility. And, of course, counter-stereotypes, of philistine administrators, provincial board members, or unscrupulous "union bosses," are powerful defenses. But, in any case, a school system in the hands of the partially competent and the partially employed will not do. We must have the best and the brightest. That, of course, implies that we do not and that (by virtue of some curious social mechanics) the failure of the public school to produce what we want rests solely on the teacher. We must, then, have a new policy for the American public school, one that attracts and, by appropriate awards, retains the keenest minds and the healthiest personalities for the nurturing of our young.

The optimistic notion that by creating and implementing a "new" personnel policy we can dramatically reverse the ebb-tide of mediocrity rests finally upon two very dangerous myths: First, as already noted, we do not now have, nor have we ever had, a single school system for which a single policy could be framed, even in the public sector. The elites have always maintained and patronized their own. Ethnic and religious minorities have been permitted to have their own. Respecting even the public "system," where is the system? We have fifty states, each with its own apparatus; some 15,-000 districts; a plethora of governmental and proprietary agencies; and a continuously unresolved dilemma between unity and diversity. There are no clear, universal, corporately derived goals. No ubiquitous principles of value undergirded by a common culture. Our hope for at least a procedural unity, through scientifically grounded educational theory, practice, and organization (in place of the older moral-philosophical consensus) so full of promise at the turn of the century, has exhausted itself.

Perhaps the leading contemporary contender for a definable policy structure is the growing forest of laws and regulations, especially those tied to financial aid, that are tending to replace the custom and consensus so characteristic of the Anglo-Saxon tradition. Historical analysis suggests, however, that even good legislators make bad school masters. Educational policy by law and financial coercion raises at least as many questions as it solves. Most disconcerting, perhaps, is its tendency to remove discussion from the broader social and professional context that would appear necessary for its fruitfulness. It also flies in the face of the tensions toward localism and decentralization that are also facts of our time. The memories and residual fears of immigrant and new native alike have persisted in our national psyche even against the technocratic liberalism of the turn of the century when we thought science *cum* efficiency would set everything right. Control of education and schooling we have thought too important and too dangerous to commit to the hands of either politicians or experts.

The second myth is that we have any effective framework within which even to consider common policy. The polarization of organized interests, buttressed by the stances and stereotypes so necessary for their perpetuation, has taken its toll. In days past — long past, of course — "higher education" had not only a stake but a productive role in public school policy. Questions about how to "improve the teaching force" would likely have been taken up under the benign and ostensibly non-political eyes of the nation's premier university presidents and with the aid of the professoriate, all of whom would have been listened to with polite respect. But that has all changed. The colleges and universities are no longer the seats of educational empire. There is no Charles William Eliot, no William Torrey Harris, no Nicholas Murray Butler — not even any "Committee of Ten" — to stand up and proclaim: Rome has spoken! In fact, one of the few stances common to all the competing interests in the school wars is precisely that "higher education" must be shorn of its pretensions, must lose its once vaunted power over school policy, and especially over preparation and certification of teachers. And the university, now itself happily balkanized along trade lines and enjoying its entrepreneurial life-style, seems to care little about the whole matter other than to blame "the schools" for what are often its own failures.

At this point, the reader serious enough to bother with an "introduction" rather than going straight to more useful content may well be inclined not only to stop reading here but to put the whole volume down unexamined. Is this not a counsel of despair? Could it be true that, in effect, there is nobody out there and hence nothing either to say or do? Actually, as a New England friend of mine once remarked about *Peyton Place*, "The trouble with the book is that it's a white-wash!" There is, in fact, even more that could be said, and little of it would cheer those of us concerned about schools and teachers. We have, for example, paid no attention to the social and cultural context, a context which every day renders educating and schooling more problematical than we like to think: e.g., the "thoughtless, normless, selfish, hedonistic individualism" that Michael Harrington has recently castigated; the preoccupation with self and sport and entertainment; the loss of community and the triumph of consumption; our chauvinistic arrogance on the world stage; etc., etc.

Neither this introduction nor this book is, however, intended as a counsel of despair. Far from it. There is a great deal we can think about and do that can make a difference. But, it will make a difference if and only if we are honest about the situation we are in. The purpose of these remarks is two-fold: To generate an appropriate humility and to induce a productive realism. The humility must come first. We — each one of us — must fear most of all the people with The Answer and the people who know What's Going on in the Schools! Education and schooling in America (as anywhere) are such complex, such variegated, such vast and pervasive phenomena that we can at best claim to study them continuously, not to "know" them once and for all.

We need to generate a productive realism because the task of guiding intelligently and responsibly some common educational strategy — whether in curriculum or methodology or, as in this case, the nature and structure of the teaching profession — is indeed difficult. (It involves, for example, the fundamental organization and administration of schooling as an institution, and to fail to take that into account would be to embark on a fool's journey.) The boundaries that now fracture the enterprise — an enterprise which requires wholeness in its very essence — and render it sterile, must at least be softened and permeated, if not entirely peeled away.

There is someone out there and there is much to do. The first thing is to think and talk over the boundaries: "Over" in two senses, in a fashion that transcends them but also in a fashion that candidly recognizes their presence and their effect upon ourselves and our schools. Academe may be the only place left to hold a conversation sufficiently comprehensive and sufficiently disciplined by truth as a goal to make an adequate discussion of school policy possible. If the university cannot any longer be the Imperial Court, can it at least be the point of communication? Stripped of its power, can the institution still render a crucial contribution, freed from at least the most egregious forms of self-serving and stance-taking? It is in the hope that the higher educational community can so serve, and bring about the possibility of policy discourse that will at least partially transcend trade lines and bridge special interests, that the College of Education of The Pennsylvania State University has commissioned these studies. They are not to terminate reflection but to initiate thoughtful investigation. Their aim is not to be exhaustive but to be provocative of deeper inquiry as the basis for considering policy, in whatever practical arena that process takes place in these difficult times.

Surely, there *is* something wrong with our public schools. There always is. There always has been. Educational discontent was abroad in our land before the flag — even before apple pie. It was, in fact, contemporaneous with the apple itself. Perhaps there always will be educational discontent, because (as I have already proposed) it is over schooling as a symbolic process, as much or more than anything else in our institutional life, that we anguish and quarrel and try once again to reform, in the face of those conflicts and changes with which time confronts any people trying to maintain free and responsible institutions. To form policy — indeed, to think at all — human beings need to talk. These studies were commissioned not to extinguish but to foster that flicker of dialogue that still persists.

Overview

The Limits and Potential of Performance-Based Pay as a Source of School Improvement

Willis D. Hawley

Introduction

Paying teachers some part of their salary on the basis of their performance seems to be an idea whose time has come. Several national commissions have endorsed merit pay. Seventy-five percent of those responding to a recent Gallup Poll favor basing teacher salaries on merit. Various forms of performance-based pay have been implemented in numerous school systems, about half the states have mandated such incentives or are actively considering them, and superintendents of schools overwhelmingly endorse "merit pay" (AASA, 1983). Of all the stakeholders in education, only teachers do not seem to favor performance-based rewards (although about one-third do) (Gallup, 1984a).

The momentum behind the merit pay movement is fueled by two basic assumptions: (1) the quality of teaching is the most important determinant of the quality of schools and (2) the quality of teaching is declining. The first of these assumptions is correct if we measure the quality of schools by their ability to influence student learning independently of the students' background and genetically based intellectual capacity (cf. Hawley and Rosenholtz, 1984). There is no direct evidence on the second assumption, though there is some evidence that the academic ability of teachers is declining (Schlechty and Vance, 1983).

Whatever one thinks about the comparative quality of teachers, it does seem sensible to argue that if the quality of teachers in our schools were higher, students would learn more. The issue is, then, will merit pay — which I hereafter refer to as performance-based pay, or PBP — improve the quality of teaching?[1]

My pursuit of an answer to this question proceeds in three stages. First, if the ultimate purpose of PBP is to increase the productivity of schools, it seems important to understand what makes schools effective and how PBP might influence those sources of productivity. The point of this analysis is to demonstrate that: (a) there are many things that can be done to improve schools; (b) PBP is but one potential source of improvement; and (c), even under the best of circumstances, PBP will not *in itself* bring about significant changes in educational productivity.

Second, I will outline a research-based theoretical framework for thinking about the relationships between incentives and human motivation. The available evidence on the primary sources of teacher motivation, viewed in the context of this analytical framework, suggests that while PBP could attract, motivate, and retain competent teachers, it is only one of several incentives available to schools systems and responds to only some of the needs educators have that might be satisfied by improved performance. This analysis also stresses the importance of the relation between the process by which PBP is administered and its probable influence.

Based on the analysis of sources of educational productivity and teacher motivation, the final section of this paper spells out the basic components of a model PBP system that is an integral part of a comprehensive approach to improving schools and teachers' performance. In other words, PBP should be seen as one of several interrelated reforms that will need to be pursued if the current energy available to bring about the change in the quality of our schools is to be fully exploited. However, even though PBP in itself is unlikely to bring about greater school effectiveness, the process of designing PBP systems presents opportunities to restructure the conditions of the teaching workplace which have considerable potential to increase the ability of schools to produce greater amounts of student learning.

In short, the argument of this paper is that PBP could make an important contribution to school quality but only if we see PBP as one element in a larger set of changes that we need to make in the way we organize the processes of teaching and learning. Moreover, the structures we will need to have an effective PBP system will have the greatest impact on the capcity and motivation of teachers than the extrinsic rewards PBP will provide.

The focus of this analysis is PBP for teachers. I think, however, that the basic argument applies to most educators and especially to school-level administrators.

What Makes Schools Effective?

Let me stipulate that the central purpose of schools is to produce student learning of those ideas, facts, and skills embodied in the formal curriculum. Schools have other purposes, of course, but no school would be judged effective, at least in public, if its students did not learn the things prescribed in the course of study. If schools produce learning, we may usefully liken them to other organizations concerned with production and say that their productivity will be determined, like other effective organizations, by four types of factors: (1) the quality of the raw materials; (2) the quality of the technology; (3) the quality of the craftmanship by which the technology is applied to the raw material; and (4) the time actually used in applying the technology. A somewhat more complete description of each of the first three of these factors is presented in Table I.

The productivity of schools, then, can be enhanced if (a) students come to school more able and willing to learn; (b) the tools of production — such as the learning resources and the instructional practices — are improved; (c) the abilities, motivation, and working conditions of educators in the school are enhanced; and (d) the time available for effective production is increased. While improvements in each of these sets of influences on students usually will result in more productivity even if there are no improvements in the others, the quality of craftmanship puts real limits on the return one can expect from investments in the other three areas. The reason for this is that teaching is a complex task that is not easily regulated and that necessarily involves considerable discretion and problem-solving skills. Thus, the best instructional practice can be rendered ineffective by an uncommitted or untrained teacher and the most primitive curriculum can come alive and be enriched by the excellent teacher. Similarly, student ambition can be quashed or enhanced depending on the way teachers interact with students. And if, as most critics and researchers who concern themselves with the process of schooling assert, time now allocated for instruction is seldom fully or well used, adding time for schooling is hardly the best way to improve schools. If a manufacturing plant is running at 80 percent capacity, managers do not open up on weekends.

The centrality of teaching quality to school effectiveness is attested to in study after study (Hawley and Rosenholtz, 1984). For example, even the effectiveness of computer-based drill and practice instruction has been found to be significantly greater when teachers are actively involved (Hawley and Rosenholtz, 1984, ch.4). Because differences in the quality of teaching account for substantial variance in the productivity of different schools, school improvement strategies focused on enhancing the quality and effectiveness of teachers seem a sensible priority. Thus, in trying to assess the potential benefits of PBP, it seems helpful to identify the probable effects of PBP on three general ways to increase teacher effectiveness.

First, we can improve the competence of teachers. The primary strategies for doing this are to (a) recruit able persons, (b) recruit teachers who share a commitment to high student achievement, (c) retain competent teachers, (d) monitor and evaluate teacher performance, and (e) provide opportunities for professional growth and development. As we will see in the next section, the attractions of teaching might be heightened by PBP if the size of the awards were substantial and the processes for administering PBP were fair and predictable. PBP will require school systems to develop ways of monitoring and evaluating teacher performance that will almost certainly be technically superior to most current methods. The key, however, to the contributions PBP can make to teacher competence is the capacity to use the information gathered on teacher performance to improve teachers' competence.

PBP is essentially a motivating device. It does not increase competence though it may induce teachers to try to attain more competence. The motivational effect of PBP will depend on clarity about the criteria of competence and, as we shall see, on the perceived attainability of levels of competence that would be rewarded. But few school systems have the capability to increase teacher competence significantly. Once on the job, teachers essentially learn to teach from each other and through informal experimentation (Hawley and Rosenholtz, 1984, Chs. 2-3). Thus, if PBP is to foster increased competence, it must be accomplished by a significant, systematic effort to provide in-service training that is tied to the PBP plan. Moreover, absent such opportunities for staff development, teachers are likely to feel that they cannot move from one level of performance to a more extrinsically rewarding one and, therefore, to feel tracked by, and hostile toward, the PBP plan.

A second general way to increase the effectiveness of teachers is to create conditions within schools that facilitate the exercise of the full competence that teachers have. Hawley and Rosenholtz (1984) reviewed hundreds of studies and concluded that, in order to foster effective teaching, school boards and administrators should take steps to: (1) minimize disruptions in instructional learning time; (2) reduce noninstructional burdens; (3) maintain student discipline; (4) facilitate interaction among teachers; (5) clearly define roles and responsibilities within the school; (6) structure the curriculum among grade levels; (7) foster effective linkages with parents and the community; and (8) provide feedback on teacher and student performance. The implementation of PBP is likely to have little effect on most of these conditions. However, the structure of the plan and the way it is administered could affect the levels of colleagiality and the nature of the feedback and support teachers receive from their supervisors and other administrators. I will return to these issues as I attempt to outline the components of an effective PBP systems in the concluding section of this paper.

The third general way to improve teacher performance is to motivate teachers to utilize fully their energy and ability. Most discussions of PBP usually focus on its motivational consequences and, likewise, the next section of the paper is devoted to this concern.

Before turning to an examination of teacher motivation, let me draw attention to two main points relating to the efficacy of PBP that follow from this discussion of the sources of educational productivity. First, while the effectiveness of teachers probably is the most important source of educational productivity, there are many ways to improve the contributions schools make to student learning. Moreover, attending to these other improvement strategies will significantly increase the contributions teachers can make. Conversely, failure to attend to some of these sources of educational productivity will place limits on teacher impact even if we are able to improve the competence, motivation and working conditions of teachers. Second, PBP is not the only way, and may not be the major way, to increase and facilitate the exercise of teacher competence. Indeed, some types of PBP systems are likely to reduce the collegial and supervisory support that research has shown to be related to teacher effectiveness.

The Effects of PBP on the Recruitment, Motivation and Retention of Highly Qualified Teachers

As we have seen, PBP's primary contributions to the capabilities of schools to improve student achievement will derive from its capacity (a) to motivate teachers to perform at the highest level of their competence; (b) to induce able teachers, who now seem to leave teaching more readily than less effective teachers to remain in the profession; and (c) to encourage persons of potentially high competence to enter teaching who would not otherwise have done so. Before turning to an analysis of each of these potential consequences of PBP, let me briefly outline a way of thinking about motivation and incentives that I believe puts the discussion of PBP's relative motivational value in context. Again, the central message this perspective conveys is that PBP needs to be seen as influencing and being influenced by other strategies for motivating and improving teacher performance so that we do not over-invest either our resources or our hopes in this proposal for school reform.

Putting the Motivation Value of PBP in Perspective

Perhaps the most widely accepted theory of motivation is that derived from the work of Vroom (1964) and Atkinson (1958). This theory holds that motivation is the highest product of the weight or salience individuals place on particular needs, the perceived relevance of the incentives available to meet these needs, and the probability the individuals assigns to the likelihood that he or she can attain the incentives.

Individuals, of course, have many needs and these vary in the extent to which they are potential motivators. These needs, which tend to be of different salience among workers and for individuals over time, can be grouped into nine categories:[2] (1) fear for physical well being; (2) security; (3) material rewards; (4) social acceptance, need for affiliation; (5) status or deference; (6) pride in self, self-esteem; (7) identification with group or organizational goals; (8) need for achievement; and (9) self-actualization.

Organizations have a range of incentives available with which they can respond to these needs, including: (1) mechanisms for monitoring performance and providing feedback; (2) pleasant working conditions; (3) pay and fringe benefits; (4) socialization to organizational ideologies; (5) nature of supervision; (6) control of status-difference (promotion, demotion and recognition); (7) job-enlargement; (8) professional or individual autonomy; (9) opportunities to shape organizational goals and procedures; (10) opportunities for social interaction; (11) peer-group evaluation; and (12) possibilities for dismissal.

At least three generalizations about the potential motivational value of PBP can be drawn from consideration of these lists of needs and incentives. First, PBP adds significantly to the resources school systems have to motivate workers. PBP obviously expands the range of monetary incentives available. In addition, the effective implementation of PBP should increase the mechanisms through which monitoring, feedback, and status can be provided. These incentives, in turn, are potentially relevant to a broader range of needs (e.g., status, self-esteem and achievement) than are conventional teacher pay plans that are typically tied to experience and formal education and that often "top out" even before teachers reach the mid-point of their careers.

A second conclusion is that school systems have many ways other than PBP to motivate and attract teachers and that many of them are underutilized. That is to say, with or without PBP, school systems have many incentives with which they can respond to teachers' work-related needs.

A third implication of the two lists is that PBP, *depending on how it is implemented*, could affect the nature of supervision, professional autonomy, peer-group interaction and other incentives so as to reduce their positive relationship to some needs such as security, social acceptance and group identity, and self-esteem. We will come back to this point below.

PBP and Teacher Motivation

Let us turn now to a discussion of the evidence on the relationship between money and teacher motivation. Alas, the evidence is scanty and is limited in its application to the issue of PBP because, so far as I can tell, all studies of the importance of money to teachers have been conducted in the context of conventional pay plans. Thus, it seems useful to integrate a consideration of the evidence from studies of teachers and schools with research on the motivational values of pay in other settings.

In a seminal review of 49 research studies on the relative importance employees give to pay as compared to other incentives (such as security, type of work, etc.), Lawler (1971) found that the average ranking pay received was third. The notion that other aspects of one's job are more important to most people than pay has been confirmed by other studies (cf. Herzburg, et al., 1957; Lawler, 1981). Similarly, studies of the importance teachers give to pay in describing the things that motivate them typically show pay to rank third or fourth (Rosenholtz and Smylie, 1984).

It is important to note that pay does not seem to compensate workers for unsatisfactory aspects of their jobs. In other words, if people seek a challenge in their job, being paid more does not make them value the challenge less (Gupton and Quinn, 1973). This means that the things about teaching which cause many teachers to leave the profession or to invest less energy in it are not likely to be neutralized by PBP. Not only do teachers not rank pay particularly high as a source of motivation, there is also recent evidence that teachers do not value upward mobility as much as they used to (Falk, et al., 1981; and Roberson, et al., 1983).

It is not surprising, of course, that teachers do not place a high value on pay, relatively speaking. It would be irrational for persons who give high priority to making money to enter a profession which historically has been low-paying. If teacher salaries or potential earnings were substantially higher, it might be that the type of person attracted to teaching would change and, therefore, the motivational value of pay would be greater. But we do not know this, and studies of other professions and jobs suggest that it is unlikely that PBP would significantly change the relative impact of monetary incentives of teacher behavior. The lessons one should draw from all this are not that teachers should not be paid more or that PBP will not be motivating. Rather, the point is that, unless the factors that most motivate teachers are attended to, PBP will probably have little long term effect on the average levels of teacher effort and effectiveness. What, then, are the things that do motivate teachers?

Both aspiring teachers and those on the job say that they want to become, or became, educators because they enjoy working with children and helping them learn. In general, they talk in altruistic terms about the contributions to others that they hope to make or feel they are making (Lortie, 1975; Wood, 1978; Roberson, et al., 1983; and Page and Page, 1982). As Rosenholtz and Smylie (1984:4) conclude in their extensive review of research on teacher motivation, "The primary reward they hope to derive [from their careers] is a sense of being instrumental to students' academic growth — a belief or sense of efficacy about their own ability to positively affect student performance. This sense of efficacy is highly related to teachers' perceptions of professional accomplishment..." Not surprisingly, teachers who do not believe in their ability to meet student needs are less effective than those with a strong sense of professional efficacy (Hawley and Rosenholtz, 1984: ch. 3). In short, the motivational value of PBP for those in the current teaching force and others like them is likely to be derived less from the increased earnings PBP can provide than from the characteristics of the PBP system and the way it contributes to other sources of teacher commitment.

Recruiting and Retaining More Effective Teachers

Would PBP induce more competent persons to enter the teaching profession? The answer to this question is probably yes, assuming that PBP would not result in holding down beginning and average salaries. But this conclusion rests on a rather shaky if seemingly reasonable foundation, the building blocks of which are as follows: (1) There is a relationship between teacher's verbal ability and student achievement (cf. Hawley and Rosenholtz, 1984: Ch. 3, for a brief review of this research). (2) There has been a decline in the average salary of both beginning and experienced teachers as compared to other professions. (3) This decline in relative salaries has paralleled a decline in the verbal ability of teacher candidates (Rosenholtz and Smylie, 1984) and a dramatic decrease in the overall numbers of college students aspiring to teach. (4) Persons who do not choose to teach often cite low salaries and low occupational status as their major reasons (Rosenholtz and Smylie, 1984). From these facts one might infer that the promise of higher earnings through PBP would induce persons to enter teaching who are likely to be more competent teachers than those who enter in the absence of PBP. But this conclusion is only an inference and it seems that the size of the effect would depend on candidates' perceptions that there was a high probability that (a) they would receive PBP that would result in a considerably higher income than would be probable under current pay schedules, and (b) that PBP would ultimately increase the social status of the teaching profession. For potential teachers to believe that PBP would bring them substantially higher earnings than are now possible in most school systems, the awards from PBP would have to be substantial, significant proportions of teachers would have to receive them, and the process by which rewards were allocated would have to seem fair and predictable.

Estimating the effects of PBP on the status of teaching as a profession is thus highly speculative. Sociologists have defined social status in different ways. Let me assume that the most relevant definition of status for our purposes is the subjective ranking of teaching by the public relative to other professions to which able college students might be attracted. One can examine such rankings (Blau and Duncan, 1978) and surmise that there are other relatively low-paying occupations that have much higher status than earnings would predict (such as the ministry and the college professoriate), and these professions seem to be differentiated from school teaching in the degree to which they are perceived to have access to knowledge or mysteries not accessible to most people.[3] One might infer from this that the status of teaching might be affected by PBP to the extent that the process of making awards embodied criteria and standards that could not readily be met by the average person or by persons without advanced academic training.

Some teacher educators have concluded that the status of teaching might be increased if students wanting to be teachers, like those pursuing careers in medicine and law, were required to pursue post-baccalaureate education before entry or if standards for admission to the profession were raised. But requiring a year or two of post-baccalaureate education for potential teachers would greatly increase the economic costs of entry to teaching and, unless something else happened to change the perceived benefits, the quality of teacher candidates would decline further (Hawley, 1984). PBP might be the required change in perceived benefits, but this seems unlikely. Moreover, if we turn the argument on its head and measure the status of a profession by the academic competence of the people entering it, we can see that California's requirement that all teachers must have five years of college has left teachers in that state close to the bottom of the distribution of average Scholastic Aptitude Test scores for persons pursuing thirty different occupations (Kerschner, 1983). Raising requirements for admission or graduation from teacher preparation programs, in itself, seems unlikely to raise the status of teaching in view of the fact that such requirements are already usually higher than those demanded of college graduates who earn more than teachers (Ishler, 1984). Moreover, large

Willis G. Hawley

numbers of experienced teachers do have master's degrees. In short, the relatively low status of teaching in the minds of persons who choose not to teach is probably rooted in factors other than the quantity of education required or admission and graduation requirements. The potential earnings of teachers, on the other hand, are a measure of the value society places on teaching and if PBP changed such earnings under the conditions set out above, the status of the profession could rise.

Given that teachers who plan to leave teaching and those who actually defect are more academically able, on the average, than teachers who want to stay in the profession (Rosenholtz and Smylie, 1984), would PBP help retain more effective teachers in the profession? The reasons teachers give for leaving or wanting to leave the profession do not focus on pay but rather on the absence of experiences that satisfy their need for the intrinsic professional rewards they believe should come from helping students achieve. Teachers do mention pay as a factor that contributes to their desire to pursue another career, but they emphasize the absence of conditions that would facilitate their ability to be effective. These conditions include: few opportunities for professional growth, lack of approval and support from principals and supervisors, and feelings that they have little evidence that they contribute to student learning (Rosenholtz and Smylie, 1984: 4-6).

Thus, taking into account the type of persons attracted to teaching, we would not expect the monetary rewards associated with PBP to affect attrition significantly. If, on the other hand, the process by which PBP is administered can increase teachers' sense of efficacy and, in general, improve the conditions which they see as undermining their effectiveness, PBP could contribute to the retention of competent teachers who care deeply about student achievement. It follows, of course, that a PBP plan that did not address teachers' needs for professional working conditions and relevant evidence of their effectiveness, could actually accelerate teacher attrition.

It may be, as suggested earlier, that the introduction of PBP would bring into teaching persons for whom monetary rewards and upward mobility are more important than they are for the present cadre. This, of course, would heighten the motivational influence of the PBP. But it seems doubtful that we would prefer a teaching corps that places relatively less weight on intrinsic rewards since teaching has a comparative advantage over most other professions in the degree to which such rewards can be delivered (Lowther, et al., 1984). It is, on the other hand, also at a disadvantage with respect to the profession's likely place in the hierarchy of average occupational incomes because of the massive numbers of teachers in the country and the dependence on local tax dollars for financial support. Moreover, one of the most significant contributors to student learning is the high expectations and hopes of their teachers. The trick, then, as I have asserted earlier, is to design a PBP systems that does not diminish the value teachers place on intrinsic rewards and the motivation they derive therefrom.

Designing a PBP System

Throughout this paper I have suggested the contributions PBP can make to increasing the productivity of schools depends on the characteristics of the PBP plan and how these fit with other school improvement strategies. What, then, should be the elements of a model plan?

The Purposes of a PBP Plan

Teachers and potential teacher candidates have a wide variety of needs that might be satisfied by their work experience. Ideally, a PBP plan should respond to as many motivators as possible and enhance, or at least not reduce, the rewards teachers get from teaching in the absence of PBP. The various needs of teachers that a PBP plan should address — which are, in effect, the design objectives of PBP — have been identified in the proceeding pages. They include: (1) intrinsic satisfaction derived from contributions made to student achievement; (2) self-esteem based on awareness of one's expertise; (3) recognition by peers and "relevant others" of professional competence; (4) some opportunities for self-direction; (5) positive social interactions with peers and supervisors; (6) protection from arbitrary use of authority that might threaten job security or possibilities for advancement; (7) opportunities for professional growth and development; and (8) economic benefits. These eight types of needs represent potential consequences of work that appear to be valued by effective teachers. What principles for designing a PBP system would maximize these outcomes?

The Design of a Model PBP System

There are a number of principles or guidelines for structuring a PBP plan that seem likely to increase the positive influence of PBP on educational productivity if they are implemented in ways that are responsive to local conditions and circumstances:

1. The size of the economic rewards for high performance should be significant.
2. The attainment of performance-based incentives should require continuing demonstration of high performance.
3. Rewards should not be competitive.
4. The probability of receiving PBP should not be constrained by predetermined quotas.
5. The criteria against which performance is measured, and the goals they manifest, should be clear.
6. The measures and processes used to assess performance should be perceived as fair and predictable.
7. Evaluation, monitoring, and feedback should be frequent.

Willis G. Hawley

8. Summative and formative evaluation processes should embody the same criteria but should be administered independently.

9. In-service training or staff-development programs should be an integral part of the PBP system and should have as their goals the improvement of teachers' likelihood of earning PBP.

10. Differences in rewards should lead, at least in some cases, to differences in roles and responsibilities.

11. Teachers should have a role in the design and assessment of the PBP plan.

Let me briefly elaborate on the rationale for each of these principles.

Principle 1. The size of the economic rewards for high performance should be significant. The small monetary rewards that could be derived from superior performance under many merit pay plans is one of the most common criticisms of these plans (Porwoll, 1979). Small awards provide limited incentives to undertake the risks and to expend the energy involved in achieving new levels of competence. But how large an award needs to be to motivate cannot be determined from any evidence I could find. Since the PBP systems emerging in different states are very different in terms of the size of the award, the opportunities to give this principle more content may soon exist.

Principle 2. The attainment of PBP should require continuing demonstration of high performance. The most influential theorist of motivation is probably Abraham Maslow. While many of Maslow's original ideas have since been modified or shown to be wrong, the notion that a need that is met ceases to motivate or, at least, is superseded by other needs, continues to be seen as basically correct. As this applies to PBP, it means that once a teacher has acquired the money and status that can be derived from a given increase in pay, this incentive diminishes in its importance as a motivator and, therefore, the cost-effectiveness of PBP may decline as the system matures. Further, even if quotas on awards are not established, resources for PBP will always be limited. And, if persons who receive PBP do not have much chance of losing it once they receive it, access by others to PBP will be constrained. These potential problems of PBP can be addressed by treating PBP as a bonus for a specified period so that the award does not become part of the winner's base salary and must be re-earned.

Principle 3. Rewards should not be competitive. A basic element of motivation theory is that the incentives must be seen as attainable. Awards that are based on comparisons among individuals or that are limited in number (a point we turn to below) will be assumed by many workers, especially those who seek the most improvement, to be beyond their reach. Moreover, competitive awards will discourage peer interaction and social approval. Rosenholtz and Smylie (1984) have succinctly summarized relevant research on this point:

There is evidence that competitive rewards function to close communication and sharing among those who work together, bias a person's perception and comprehension of the viewpoints and positions of other individuals, and destroy trust among group members. In competitive settings, persons are generally less tolerant if individual differences and encouragement among peers is substantially reduced. Competition diminishes the problem-solving effectiveness of groups and may lead individuals to deliberately frustrate their counterparts' efforts to succeed.

This does not mean that teachers should not "compete" against set criteria. The distinction here is akin to the difference between the golfer's effort to beat par, a standard set by agreed-upon conventions, and match play in which a golfer competes directly with another individual. In the match play situation, winning is defined by the best score among the competitors even if performance is not very good. One does not find competitors in these situations working to better each other's strokes or strategy. If the rules of the game, however, set the standards of achievement within reasonable reach (the analogy to golf may break down here) and the attainment of the standard by some players does not diminish the opportunities for others to reach the goal, it is in everyone's interest for the players to exchange advice and encouragement.

Principle 4. The probability of receiving PBP should not be constrained by predetermined quotas. As just noted, for an incentive to motivate, it must be seen as attainable. Quota systems that limit performance awards to a specified number or proportion force those who would earn the awards for the first time to replace previous winners and this may affect perceptions of feasibility. Quotas may also discourage cooperation among teachers. As Thompson and Dalton (1970: 156) have argued, closed reward systems focus attention on competitive aspects of the work situation and a high proportion of workers will probably come to believe that their prospects of receiving an award are remote no matter how hard they try to improve their performance. Another likely consequence of "closed reward systems" is that they may force meaningless distinctions to be made in the performance of winners and near winners, thus undermining the credibility of the evaluation system.

Principle 5. The criteria against which performance is measured and the goals they manifest should be clear. This principle seems obvious enough, but it is not easy to implement. Schools typically have multiple and diffuse goals. These goals may vary from school to school and from district to district. Thus, district-wide or state-wide systems for assessing performance may not fit school or district priorities. Even within schools, the goals being pursued by different educators and the ways they could best achieve them may vary (e.g., special educators, vocational specialists, and science teachers). This complexity has forced PBP designers away from outcome goals and toward generic process criteria. There are good reasons for doing this, but the relationship between the values and processes embodied in the evaluation system necessary to implement PBP may be attenuated. Moreover, emphasizing process criteria in the assessment of performance may lead to the displacement of student achievement goals as the primary definition of organizational effectiveness (Merton, 1957). The solution to these problems seems to relate to the continued reassessment, redefinition, and specification of the goals and criteria. This will result, however, in a tension between the desirability of localizing and contextualizing decision criteria on the one hand and the desire to centralize and standardize on the other so as to permit comparisons, avoid subjectivity, and invoke accountability.

Principle 6. The measures and processes used to assess performance should be seen as fair and predictable. The most common concern of teachers who have experienced PBP is that the plan was administered unfairly (Porwoll, 1979). No doubt, many of the evaluation systems used have been primitive and the way they were applied was subjective. Moreover, fair or not, teachers — like other people — who do not receive PBP are likely to seek explanations outside their own performance. This human propensity is the inevitable outcome of implementing an evaluation system since most workers, especially professionals, have higher estimates of their abilities than do their supervisors (Meyer, 1975).

There is no way to satisfy everyone that the measures of teacher performance and the way they are administered are fair and predictable. Some guidelines the implications of which seem likely to increase the perceived legitimacy and reliability of performance evaluation are: (1) The behavior assessed should include all of the behavior the system seeks to influence. As "they" say, what gets measured, gets done. (2) Multiple ways of assessing the same phenomena help to deal with worries about the validity of measures and the potential frailties of evaluators. (3) The measures of the behavior or outcome being assessed should cover the period for which the rewards are being made. Past performance and future promise should be discounted entirely. (4) Several data points within the period being assessed are better than one or two measurements. (5) Evaluators should be allowed some discretion in the weight they assign to different measures when the various sources of information collected are aggregated. There are risks that such discretion will be seen as a source of arbitrariness, but imperfect measures, which is all we have, do not deserve excessive respect. (6) Measures of teacher performance should focus on teaching processes rather than teaching outcomes.

This last point is the subject of considerable controversy. Many legislators and citizens seem to want to define teachers' competence by their ability to increase student test scores. Student gain scores have several limitations as measures of teacher competence (cf. also Soar and Soar, 1984). The fit between the curriculum and the standardized test is seldom good. Student gain scores are affected by a number of factors — previous teachers, home environment, peer values, etc. — over which teachers have no control and there is no reliable algorithm we can formulate to adjust for these factors statistically. Focusing on student gain scores will not only cause teachers to teach to the test, which will inevitably narrow and dilute the substance of what is taught, but it will encourage an emphasis on test-taking itself as a high order skill. For example, how will we evaluate teachers who cause their students to reflect and to think or to develop an appreciation for the uses of theory? Finally, knowing that teacher A "produces" higher gain scores than teacher B does not tell us anything about the possible strengths and weaknesses of the two teachers so that we have a way to improve teacher B's performance.

Enough knowledge is now available on effective teaching to develop process criteria for evaluating teacher performance and several states and localities have done this or are doing it. The validity of these measures can and should be assessed against student gain scores by looking at a sample of teachers and classrooms independently of the evaluation of specific teachers.

Principle 7. Evaluation, monitoring, and feedback should be frequent. I noted earlier the importance teachers attribute to having confidence that they can help students learn and otherwise develop. Such confidence is difficult for teachers to acquire in the absence of relevant information that what they do makes a difference. In their review of research on teacher motivation, Rosenholtz and Smylie (1984) concluded that the frequency with which teachers are evaluated and feedback is provided is correlated with teachers' confidence in their supervisor's evaluation, teachers' satisfaction with their work, and student achievement. Not all of the evaluation and feedback should, however, be part of the PBP plan. Indeed, most of it should be separate from the formal summative evaluation necessary to implement PBP. At the same time, it should contribute to teachers' competence with respect to those practices, along with others, that are evaluated for purposes of allocating bonus awards.

Principle 8. Summative and formative evaluation processes should embody the same criteria but should be administered independently. One of the sources of failure in some of the merit pay experiments has been tension that existed between teachers and principals over evaluations. Similarly, performance appraisal by other teachers with whom the teacher must work on a regular basis has often been a source of conflict and competition among teachers (Porwoll, 1979). Yet, one of the potential benefits of PBP is that it provides opportunities for feedback on performance that can motivate and give direction to efforts to improve further professional skills. Many observers believe that those who evaluate performance for purposes of making decisions about monetary rewards, advancement, or retention cannot also provide support for professional growth. The logic here is that the employee whose work is being judged in order to award incentives will not disclose her or his weaknesses and will resent negative evaluations. Moreover, the supervisor, under these circumstances, may avoid more negative ratings and yet be concerned whether a supportive relationship with an employee in need of help will jeopardize objectivity. That may cause other employees, who may need less help, to think that the supervisor

Willis G. Hawley

is playing favorites. Implementing this principle would require that subjective evaluations for purposes of allocating PBP be done by trained observers and judges who do not work regularly with the teacher involved. Principals could, of course, be given the evaluators' information but their job would be to foster improvement and to hold teachers accountable for that improvement.

Principle 9. In-service training or staff development programs should be an integral part of the PBP system and should have as their goal the improvement of teachers' likelihood of earning PBP. Providing teachers with information that they are falling short of performance goals without providing them support to reach those goals invites teacher alienation and frustration. Unfortunately, most school systems invest little in in-service training and what they do invest usually is not spent well. PBP could provide the impetus for improving in-service training. The evaluation system necessary to implement PBP should provide evidence on teacher needs and motivate teachers to seek improvement. Further, the PBP system should identify teachers who can serve as models and peer tutors, thus enriching the resources that can be employed in a school's or a district's professional development efforts.

Hawley and Rosenholtz (1984) reviewed the research on effective staff development efforts and concluded that they: (a) focus on needs identified by learners; (b) are both practical and theoretical; (c) take place, as much as possible, in work settings; (d) often involve administrators; (e) follow up training with collegiality exchanges; (f) provide on-going assistance for the development of specific knowledge or skills; and (g) evaluate the consequences of particular training strategies and modify them accordingly.

It might be noted that paying teachers to learn rather than paying them for what they learn (which is presumably what PBP would do), may be unproductive. McLaughlin and March (1978) found that teachers who received pay for in-service training were less likely to change in the ways called for in the training than those who were not.

Principle 10. Differences in rewards should lead, at least in some cases, to differences in roles and responsibilities. One of the most common findings of studies of PBP in private industry is that it can lead to social pressure on high achievers because their high performance is seen as increasing the expectations management has of others. Thus, high performers may be ostracized if they continue to out-perform others. Such socially imposed constraints on performance will occur whether PBP exists or not, but, because PBP results in a visible and formal reward system, this problem will be exacerbated. One way of addressing this possible consequence of PBP is to create career ladders that distinguish teachers by rank and create different roles for each rank. It is not clear whether differentiation of responsibilities and functions is essential to the success of career ladders. Colleges and universities do not create different roles for persons of different rank and very great differences in pay are found across professional ranks. In any case, career ladders may reduce some of the dissatisfaction teachers have had with merit pay. Moreover, opportunity for advancement up the career ladder is an incentive school systems have not previously had available. As Lortie (1975) points out, teaching traditionally has offered little opportunity for upward mobility and this may create a concern for one's present condition rather than for one's future development. Most teachers apparently see this absence of opportunity to change their duties and to be promoted as a major source of job dissatisfaction (Lowther, Gill and Coppard, 1984).

Principle 11. Teachers should have a role in the design and assessment of the PBP plan. As with any innovation, PBP is likely to be most effective if those most affected by it understand it and believe that it will benefit them. Thus, the probabilities that PBP will find acceptance among teachers will be increased if teachers have an opportunity to help design and redesign the system.

Conclusion

While increasing the quality of teaching in schools is the general strategy for educational reform that has the most promise to produce more student learning, there are many other ways to improve schools, some of which will help teachers succeed. There are a number of ways to increase the quality of teaching and the economic incentives provided by PBP is but one of these. It follows, then, that PBP, *in itself*, is a limited strategy for school improvement even if one could put aside the fact that PBP has enjoyed little success in the school districts that have tried it.

In order to implement PBP successfully, however, it would be necessary to put in place a number of other mechanisms that could increase the competence and motivation of teachers while creating conditions that would facilitate effective teaching. These conditions, when coupled with the added economic and advancement incentives that PBP provides school administrators, significantly enhance the prospects for improving the educational productivity of schools. Gaining approval for, and implementing, such a comprehensive approach to educational reform is, of course, no small matter. But if PBP is not an integral part of a larger approach to systemic change, its consequences could be political conflict, the undermining of the supportive and cooperative climate that is found in successful schools, and the loss of self-esteem by teachers, among other possible troubles.

While it has been very difficult to implement effective PBP programs and to achieve comprehensive change in schools, the prospects for doing both of these may never have been better. Many current reform proposals are multidimensional; researchers and practitioners have probably never worked so well together; the body of knowledge that can be employed to give direction to change efforts is more robust than ever; and the attention being given to education by politicians and community leaders is very high. Perhaps the most significant aspect of the current context for instituting

Willis G. Hawley

PBP is that the initiative is coming from increasingly professional and ambitious state governments, often at the instigation of state governors. This situation is unprecedented. State-mandated plans and state financial support will make local boards and administrators less vulnerable than they have been to pressures from opponents of PBP. States, in turn, are increasingly self-conscious about their status vis-a-vis other states so that the successful implementation of PBP in one state probably will reinforce others so long as PBP continues to enjoy popular support. Ultimately, however, the institutionalization of PBP will depend on whether most teachers believe that it, and the structures that support it, enhance the contributions they make to the students they serve.

NOTES

1. The term "merit pay" means different things to different people and in many contemporary discussions it is used to mean any form of financial reward that is tied to higher levels of teacher or student performance. This general meaning is fine for our purpose, but, because "merit pay" carries a lot of baggage with it, I prefer to use the term performance-based pay, or PBP, in lieu of merit pay.

2. Different researchers have arrived at different ways of classifying the various needs-incentives listed on this and the next page. My approach has been to draw from a number of studies in compiling this list. For overviews of this literature, see Katz and Kahn, 1978, and Hersey and Blanchard, 1982.

3. It seems reasonable to believe, in this regard, that the relatively low status of teaching, which seems to have dropped in recent years (Gallup, 1984:15), is at least partially related to the fact that the average person entering teaching appears to have less academic aptitude than the average person going to college.

REFERENCES

American Association of School Administrators. (1983). *Superintendents Respond to Merit Pay*. Washington, D.C. AASA.

Atkinson, J.W. (1958). "Towards Experimental Analysis of Human Motivation in Terms of Motives, Expectancies, and Incentives." In J.W. Atkinson (Ed.) *Motives in Fantasy, Action, and Society*. Princeton, NJ: Van Nostrand.

Azumi, J.E., & Madhere, S. (1983). "Professionalism, Power, and Performance: The Relationships Between Administrative Control, Teacher Conformity, and Student Achievement." Paper presented at the Annual Meeting of the American Educational Research Association, Montreal.

Bishop, J.M. (1977). "Organizational Influences on the Work Orientations of Elementary Teachers." *Sociology of Work and Occupation*, 4(2), 171-208.

Blau, P. & Duncan, O.D. (1978). *American Occupational Structure*. New York: The Free Press.

Bogard, C.M. (1983). "The Process of Deciding Not to Become a Teacher." Paper presented at the Annual Meeting of the American Educational Research Association, Montreal.

Calhoun, F.S., & Protheroe, N.J. (1983). *Merit Pay for Teachers: Status and Descriptions*. Arlington, VA: Educational Research Service.

Chapman, D. (1983a). "Career Satisfaction of Teachers." *Educational Research Quarterly*, 7, 40-50.

Chapman, D. (1983b). "A Model of the Influences on Teacher Retention." *Journal of Teacher Education*, 34, 43-49.

Chapman, D., & Hutcheson, S.M. (1982). "Attrition from Teaching Careers: Discriminant Analysis." *American Educational Research Journal*, 19, 93-105.

Coates, T.J. & Thoresen, C.E. (1976). "Teacher Anxiety: A Review with Recommendation." *Review of Educational Research*, 46, 159-184.

DeVries, D.L.; Muse, D. & Wells, E.H. (1971). *The Effects on Students of Working in Cooperative Groups: An Exploratory Study* (Report No. 120). Baltimore: Johns Hopkins University, Center for the Social Organization of Schools.

Frataccia, E.V. & Hennington, I. (1982). "Satisfaction of Hygiene and Motivation Needs of Teachers Who Resigned From Teaching." Paper presented at the Annual Meeting of the Southwest Educational Research Association, Austin, Texas.

Gallup, G.H. (1984a). "The 16th Annual Gallup Poll of the Public's Attitude Toward the Public Schools." *Phi Delta Kappan*, 66(1), 5-19.

Gallup, G.H. (1984b). "The Gallup Poll of Teachers' Attitudes Toward the Public Schools." *Phi Delta Kappan*, 66(2), 97-107.

Glidewell, J.C., Tucker, S., Todt, M., & Cox, S. (1983). "Professional Support Systems: The Teaching Profession." In A. Madler, J.D. Fisher, & B.M. DePaulo (eds.), *Applied Research in Help-Seeking and Reactions to Aid*. New York: Academic Press.

Gupta, N., & Quinn, R.P. (1973). "The Mirage of Trade-Offs Among Job Facets." In R.P. Quinn & T.W. Mangione (Eds.) *The 1969-1970 Survey of Working Conditions: Chronicles of an Unfinished Enterprise*. Ann Arbor: Institute for Social Research, University of Michigan.

Hawley, W.D. (1984). "Should We Abolish Undergraduate Teacher Education: A Critical Analysis of an Increasingly Popular Idea." Nashville, TN: Peabody College, Vanderbilt University.

Hawley, W.D., & Rosenholtz, S.J. (1984). "Educational Strategies That Increase Student Academic Achievement." *The Peabody Journal of Education*, forthcoming.

Hersey, P., & Blanchard, K. (1982). *Management of Organizational Behavior: Utilizing Human Resources*. 4th ed. Englewood Cliffs, NJ: Prentice Hall.

Ishler, R.E. (1984). "Requirement for Admission and Graduation from Teacher Education." *Phi Delta Kappan*, 66, 121-122.

Katz, D., & Kahn R.L. (1978). *The Social Psychology of Organizations*. 2nd ed. New York: John Wiley.

Kerschner, C.T. (1983). *Flood Times and Aging Swimmers: An Exploration Into the Supply and Demand for Teachers*. Claremont, CA: Claremont Graduate School.

Lawler, E.F. (1971). *Pay and Organizational Effectiveness: A Psychological View*. New York: McGraw-Hill.

Lawler, E.F. (1981). *Pay and Organization Development*. Reading, MA: Addison-Wesley Publishing Co.

Litt, M.D., & Turk, D.C. (1983). "Stress, Dissatisfaction, and Intention to Leave Teaching in Experienced Public School Teachers." Paper presented at the Annual Meeting of the American Educational Research Association, Montreal.

Lortie, D.C. (1975). *School Teacher: A Sociological Study*. Chicago: University of Chicago Press.

Lowther, M.A., Gill, S.J., & Coppard, L. (1984). "Worklife Issues of Teachers and Other Professionals." Paper presented at the American Education Research Association, New Orleans.

McFaul, S.A., & Cooper, J.M. (1983). "Peer Clinical Supervision in an Urban Elementary School." *Journal of Teacher Education*, 34(5), 34-38.

McLaughlin, M.W., & Marsh, D.D. (1978). "Staff Development and School Change." *Teachers College Record*, 80(1), 69-94.

Merton, R. (1957). *Social Theory and Social Structure*, Rev. ed. Glenview, IL: The Free Press.

Meyer, H.H. (1975). "The Pay for Performance Dilemma," *Organizational Dynamics*, 3(3), 39-50.

Morris, M.B. (1982). *The Public School as Workplace: The Principal as a Key Element in Teacher Satisfaction: A Study of Schooling in the United States* (Technical Report Series, No. 32). Dayton, OH: Institute for Development of Educational Activities.

Page, F.M., Jr., & Page, J.A. (1982). "Perceptions of Teaching That May Be Influencing Current Shortage of Teachers." *College Student Journal*, 16, 308-311.

Pavalko, R.M. (1970). "Recruitment to Teaching: Patterns of Selection and Retention." *Sociology of Education*, 43, 340-353.

Porwoll, P.J. (1979). *Merit Pay for Teachers*, Arlington, VA: Educational Research Service.

Purcell, T.D., & Seifert, B.B. (1982). "A Tri-State Survey of Student Teachers." *College Student Journal*, 16, 27-29.

Roberson, S.D., Keith, T.Z., & Page, E.B. (1983). "Now Who Aspires to Teach?" *Educational Researcher*, 12(6), 13-1.

Rosenholtz, S.J., & Smylie, M.A. (1984). "Teacher Compensation and Career Ladders: Policy Implications from Research." *Elementary School Journal*, 85(2), 1-18.

Sarason, S. (1982). *The Culture of the School and the Problem of Change*, 2nd ed. Boston: Allyn & Bacon.

Schlechty, P.C., & Vance, V.S. (1981). "Do Academically Able Teachers Leave Education? The North Carolina Case." *Phi Delta Kappan*, 63, 106-112.

Schlechty, P.C., & Vance, V.S. (1983). "Recruitment, Selection and Retention: The Shape of the Teaching Force." *Elementary School Journal*, 83, 469-487.

Soar, R.S., & Soar, R.M. (1984). "Teacher Merit Pay: Can Research Help?" *Journal of Human Behavior and Learning*, 1(1), 3-13.

Thompson, P.H., & Dalton, G.W. (1970). "Performance Appraisal: Managers Beware." *Harvard Business Review*, 48, 149-157.

Vance, V.S., & Schlechty, P.C. (1982). "The Distribution of Academic Ability in the Teaching Force: Policy Implications." *Phi Delta Kappan*, 64, 22-27.

Vroom, V.H. (1964). *Work and Motivation*, New York: John Wiley.

Weaver, W.T. (1981). "Demography, Quality, and Decline: The Challenge for Schools of Education for the 1980's." In *Policy for the Education of Educators: Issues and Implications*. Washington, DC: American Association of Colleges for Teacher Education.

Wood, K.E. (1978). "What Motivates Students to Teach?" *Journal of Teacher Education*, 29, 48-50.

TABLE I

SOURCES OF EDUCATIONAL PRODUCTIVITY —
A RESEARCH BASED MODEL

CHARACTERISTICS AND QUALITY OF RAW MATERIAL/STUDENTS

1. COGNITIVE CAPABILITIES
2. ACQUIRED KNOWLEDGE
3. MOTIVATION
4. OUT OF SCHOOL RESOURCES FOR LEARNING
5. OUT OF SCHOOL CONSTRAINTS ON LEARNING

THE TECHNOLOGY FOR PRODUCING LEARNING

1. INSTRUCTIONAL STRATEGIES
2. ORGANIZATIONAL ARRANGEMENTS (CLASS SIZE,
   SIZE OF SCHOOL, STRUCTURE OF CLASS, ETC.)
3. CURRICULUM
4. LEARNING RESOURCES (TEXTS, MATERIALS,
   TECHNOLOGY, ETC.)

CRAFTSMANSHIP

1. ABILITY AND COMPETENCE
2. WORKING CONDITIONS THAT FACILITATE GOOD TEACHING
3. MOTIVATION

TIME AVAILABLE FOR LEARNING

Retrospective

Old Wine, Old Bottles?:
Merit Pay and Organized Teachers. .*

Wayne J. Urban

I

The subject of merit pay for teachers has recently come to the fore in the public discussions of American education. One spark for this movement was provided by President Reagan's National Commission on Excellence in Education and its report, *A Nation At Risk*.[1] In that report, after substantial critical discussion of American schooling, the Commission makes a number of recommendations grouped into categories such as Content of Schooling, Standards and Expectations, the Time to be devoted to various subjects, Teaching, and Leadership and Fiscal Support.

Under the Teaching category, we find seven recommendations, including the following stipulations relating to merit pay:

> Salaries for the teaching profession should be increased and should be professionally competitive, market-sensitive, and performance-based. Salary, promotion, tenure, and retention decisions should be tied to an effective evaluation system that includes peer review so that superior teachers can be rewarded, average ones encouraged, and poor ones either improved or terminated.[2]

This suggestion has provoked a number of initiatives and reactions at the local, state, and national levels. The topic that interests us here is the reaction of teacher organizations to merit pay proposals from the National Excellence Commission and other national, state, and local bodies. The fact that this reaction has not been uniformly negative is surprising to anyone familiar with the history of teacher organizations and their position on the merit pay issue. Before accounting for the contemporary reaction, and its difference from the past, a look at merit pay proposals and organized teacher reaction to them in the past is in order.

II

Merit pay plans have been a controversial part of the American educational picture at least from the earliest part of the twentieth century. An integral part of the controversy, when teacher organizations have

---

* A slightly altered version of this paper has been published in Great Britain, in Martin Lawn (Ed.), **Politics of Teacher Unionism**. London: Croom Helm, 1985. Used by permission.

existed in places where merit pay has been proposed, is the implacable opposition of the organizations to the merit pay plans.

As early as 1903, Chicago's organized elementary teachers, through their Chicago Teachers Federation, fought the imposition of a merit pay plan which involved examinations and supervisors' ratings of experienced teachers. This merit plan was introduced shortly after teachers had been granted a salary scale with regular increments for each year of service. The fact that the scale had yet to be fully funded indicated to teachers that merit ratings would provide a rationale for not funding the salary scale. In 1915, Atlanta's organized teachers fought an attempt by the school board to substitute a merit system of pay for the existing salary scale. Though the Atlanta Public School Teachers Association was initially unsuccessful in opposing merit pay, the results of the first year under the merit system, a net reduction in the total system payroll of $15,000, confirmed the organization's worst fears about the intention of the board, namely that it wished to punish some teachers and reduce the total payroll. This sparked the teachers to renewed and finally successful agitation against the merit system. The early twentieth century experience of merit rating and salaries based on the ratings was not limited to Atlanta and Chicago. Minneapolis, St. Paul, Cleveland, and several other American cities saw battles between superintendents and teachers over merit rating plans and other administrative reforms which served to consolidate the superintendents' executive powers and bureaucratic control over the schools.[3]

These early battles over the merit rating and merit pay issues found teacher organizations, which had just recently won or were currently engaging in battles to establish regular salary scales, bitterly fighting the merit pay principle as a throwback to the earlier system of teachers being rewarded on the basis of the local board's undocumented opinion of their worth. Merit pay proposals continued to spring up from time to time in the 1920s in various localities, as did organized teacher opposition to them. By and large, teacher organizations successfully fended-off merit pay, though they often did not eliminate the actual rating of teachers by superiors. The rating process proved to be one of a number of steps which provoked a tension between teachers and principals that had not been present previously. Teachers and their organizations were not happy with this situation but consoled themselves with the understanding that the defeat of merit pay plans preserved the seniority principle and the salary scale which institutionalized it. Teacher organizations, like most occupational organizations, have been vigorous protectors of seniority rights since that time.

In the 1930s, the schools in almost every American locality were beset by a financial crisis precipitated by the Great Depression. In this climate, merit pay receded from the forefront as an issue, replaced by the struggle by all teachers and administrators to maintain existing levels of school support, or at least minimize the budget cuts which were often proposed and implemented. World War II brought still another set of circumstances to the schools which forced the merit pay issue into the background. The schools concentrated on helping to wage the war effort. They struggled to find faculty to staff the classrooms abandoned by men called to serve in the armed forces and women who left the schools for the higher paying factory jobs which often opened up to them because of the shortage of able bodied men to do this kind of work. Shortly after the war's end, however, the merit pay principle once again surfaced as an issue of controversy.

Several factors contributed to the rise of merit pay as a topic of controversy in the post-World War II period. A great deal of movement out of teaching during the war meant a concern for stability in teaching once the war was over. This stability was thought likely to be accomplished through higher salaries. The realization that the war and post-war years were producing a baby boom which would soon overtake the elementary schools also was cause for concern that salaries would be raised enough to attract the number of teachers which would be needed to staff the schools. Merit pay was to be a way to raise some salaries without having to raise all salaries. Neither of these factors, however, was the primary reason behind the movement for merit pay. Merit pay was proposed, it seems, mainly because teachers in most American big cities and many smaller cities and rural areas were being paid on the basis of a "single salary scale." What the single salary scale provided was equal pay for equal work for all teachers. Prior to enactment of the single salary scale, men teachers were often paid on a different scale and received more than women, elementary teachers were often paid less than secondary teachers, and black teachers were sometimes paid less than white teachers. With the enactment of the single salary scale, however, all teachers, whatever their sex, level taught, or race, were paid according to their place on *the* salary scale. One's place was determined on the basis of number of years taught and amount of higher education (college and university study) completed. Teacher organizations had worked hard in the early 1940s and immediate post-war years to institutionalize the single salary scale and, like the teachers three and four decades earlier who fought merit pay as an attack on the principle of a salary scale, teachers and their organizations now saw merit pay as an attack on the recently won single salary scale.

One of the first of the post-war attempts to establish merit pay was undertaken in the state of New York in 1947. In that year, in response to a push from the New York State Teachers' Association and groups of New York's school administrators, the legislature adopted a new set of state salary minimums for teachers as well as specified yearly increments. These increases were substantial, raising the state minimum from $1000 per year to $2000 per year, but they were not uniformly felt in localities throughout the state, since many communities already paid well above the minimum by supplementing the state moneys with locally appropriated funds. Nevertheless, the legislature felt that it was making a significant increase in its financial commitment to the schools and, not wanting to make a simple, across-the-board commitment, specified that some of the proposed increments would be granted on the basis of the merit principle rather than on the basis of seniority. The legislature empowered the State Commissioner of Education to set up a committee to decide how merit would be determined.

The committee recommended that merit be based on evaluation of performance by superiors as well as other factors such as service in outside of school organizations like the Boy Scouts, Girl Scouts, Rotary, and Kiwanis. Its recommendations proved to be quite controversial, particularly among the state's organized teachers.[4]

At the National Education Association convention in June of 1947, New York's teachers were instrumental in getting a report on teachers' salaries approved that reflected the point of view of most of the organized teachers. Among the provisions of the salary resolution was one that spoke specifically to the subject of merit pay.

> *Second*, early in our discussion the group considered and rejected so-called merit-rating schemes as related to salary schedules. These rating schemes, now commonly advocated by tax fighting groups, and others with special interests, are recognized throughout our profession as being incomplete and inadequate measures of teaching performance. Yet such schemes are being urged in many states, even to the point of state legislative enactments. We, in the profession know how destructive to morale so-called merit ratings can be and how easily these devices lead to favoritism and violation of professional ethics.[5]

In 1948, New York's teachers were again active at the NEA convention in spearheading opposition to merit pay. One New York teacher proposed a resolution on merit pay that after a number of preliminary clauses stated: "Be it resolved: That salary differentials be based only on objective evidence of professional preparation and successful experience; and that subjective merit rating for salary purposes be rejected as invalid, unreliable, and detrimental to professional morale."[6] In subsequent discussion of that resolution, another New York teacher who had been called in to serve on the state committee to determine criteria for merit described meetings of teachers, held by the committee throughout the state, where "at every one . . . the opinion of the teachers was unanimous against this law . . ."[7] He went on to say that the law was used to avoid paying the top salaries on the scale to all teachers who qualified, since only a certain percent of teachers were to be paid the increment at the top step of the scale, and that it used such irrelevant criteria to determine merit as participation in the Boy Scouts. Other teachers from Ohio, Indiana, Michigan, Washington, and Massachusetts added their voices to those of their New York colleagues against the merit system.

The merit issue continued to be discussed at NEA conventions for the next several years and, in 1951, the organization went on record reaffirming its traditional support of the single salary scale and opposition to merit pay.[8] By this time, New York's teachers had successfully opposed merit pay to the point that the governor and legislature amended the merit pay provision, removing the percentage limits for those who could receive merit pay, and applying the merit principle to salary increments only in the last year of a non-tenured teacher's probationary period and in the twelfth year

Wayne J. Urban

of service. These provisions signalled the effective end of the merit pay fight in New York state. However, the issue would continue to be debated in the educational literature throughout the 1950s and into the 1960s. In 1952, for example, the *Harvard Educational Review* devoted an entire issue to the teachers' salary problem. In this issue, the NEA had a chance to air at length its views on the topic. In an article on teachers' salary schedules, two members of the Research Division of the NEA began with a reiteration of the Association's commitment to the principle of equal pay for equal work and its implementation through the single salary scale. With regard to the single salary scale, the authors commented that it represented "the best thinking of the profession" to that point in time, that it gave credit "for experience under the assumptions that quality of work increases with professional maturity," and that it allowed teaching to stand as "a career, with the higher rewards for those who devote their lives to the profession."[9] Moving on to discuss the "merit principle," the authors noted that merit rating was borrowed from the business world and was usually advocated by businessmen, most of whom erroneously assume "that teaching has many of the same characteristics as the mass production lines of industry," and believe "in the objectivity and reliability of current rating techniques." Some business advocates of merit pay were not just misguided, however, according to the authors. They "are motivated by a general conviction that through merit rating linked with salary schedules the total cost of schools can be reduced."[10]

The authors concluded that most "teachers object to the application of existing merit rating schedules to salary schedules" and that the NEA had long been on record against merit rating. Reflecting the fact that the NEA had administrator as well as teacher members, the article did defend the practice of evaluating teachers, but again pointed out that any teacher evaluated as competent should make normal progress on the salary schedule. After discussing a number of other aspects of teachers' salaries, the authors ended their discussion with a lengthy quotation from an official NEA document on "Professional Salaries" which contained the following explicit repudiation of merit pay: in salary matters, "Equity of treatment to classroom teachers of like qualifications and experience" is a must.[11]

Despite the success of teachers in stopping merit pay in New York state and in several other places, merit pay schemes continued to pop up in several states and local school districts throughout the 1950s and 1960s. The educational journals also continued to run articles debating the merits of the issue and keeping track of the latest places to implement and/or give up their merit pay schemes. Few, if any, authors doubted the fact that most teachers opposed merit pay plans. For example, the *Journal of Teacher Education* devoted its June, 1957 issue to the topic of "Merit Salary Schedules for Teachers." In this issue, again, the NEA Research Division was responsible for an article on the topic, but this time the opposition of teachers to merit pay, though mentioned, was not referred to as favorably. The tack of this article was to describe the various attempts to implement merit pay, to define carefully what did and did not constitute genuine merit pay proposals, and to indicate the great difficulty in arriving at a fair merit pay plan.[12] Despite this apparent softening in the NEA Research Division's position, none of the other articles, though some favored merit pay, argued that teachers supported merit pay plans.

The minutes of the NEA convention for that same year, 1957, indicate that though some association staff might seek a more moderate position on the merit pay issue than flatfooted opposition, the Department of Classroom Teachers, the sub-unit of the association most attuned to the concerns of working teachers, was not interested in moderation on this issue. In a discussion of a resolution on merit pay, a former president of the Department of Classroom Teachers noted that the Department, in its 1956 and 1957 meetings as well as in a special conference called on the topic during the previous year, had consistently opposed merit pay plans because teachers considered the merit principle to be "an objectionable thing" which has "invariably resulted in failure" wherever it has been tried, and has "harmed the students and the schools and teachers." The entire debate on the issue of merit pay during that year revealed that some elements of the NEA no longer felt that simple opposition to merit pay was a sufficient position for the association. Speaking of the NEA's public relations image and efforts, these elements tried to make sure that the association not appear as simply an opponent of merit pay. Thus, the resolution which was passed contained two paragraphs, one of which opposed merit rating or what the resolution called "subjective rating" and a second which called for continued efforts to "discover means of objective evaluation of teaching performance." Thus, one could have concluded that the NEA position was in opposition to existing merit pay plans, all of which involved "subjective" rating of teachers by their principals and other administrators, but that the NEA might not be in opposition to a merit plan that would use some kind of "objective" rating scheme to arrive at salary recommendations.[13]

The NEA's major rival for the organizational allegiance of teachers was the American Federation of Teachers. A part of the larger labor movement through its affiliation with the American Federation of Labor, the AFT did not have to make as many turns and twists on merit pay and any other issues as did the NEA, which strived to maintain its administrator members. The AFT membership was limited to classroom teachers and thus it was freer to advocate a strictly pro-teacher position on merit pay and other issues. Of course, because of its single minded advocacy of teacher interests and its affiliation with the labor movement, the AFT did not have a ready access to educational journals for its opinions and positions as did its less militant rival. In 1961, however, the AFT did break into the professional discussion of the merit pay issue.

As part of a five article series on merit pay which appeared in the educational journal *Phi Delta Kappan*, Carl Megel, president of the AFT, discussed the AFT position in an article entitled "Merit Rating is Unsound." Megel noted that merit rating tended to appear in times of high living costs and to be used as a way to pay high salaries to some but not all teachers who deserved them. He stressed that the AFT had been opposed to merit rating for over thirty years and that it had seen merit pay plans fail in city after city. While merit pay had some allure in an ideal world, Megel contended that "it is the impossibility of fairly judging and rating one teacher above another on a dollar and cents basis which makes the merit system unworkable." He contended that the only way to pay teachers fairly was "by the use of an adequate single salary schedule based upon training and experience." He then proceeded to list the foibles of merit rating including the following points: merit rating rewards conformity, puts a premium on acquiescence in teachers, fosters competition rather than cooperation among teachers, strikes at the job security of teachers, cannot improve the quality of education, will not relieve the teachers shortage, and does not reward superior work. The AFT alternative, according to Megel, was "a sound, satisfactory salary schedule" which will both "interest competent, capable young men and women in choosing teaching" and "permit the experienced teachers to perform their services in an atmosphere of dignity and personal satisfaction."[14]

III

The 1960s were a decade punctuated by a good deal of controversy in various aspects of American life, and education proved to be no exception. The most notable activity among organized teachers in this decade was their frequent recourse to strikes to win various concessions from local education authorities. Most of these strikes were undertaken by AFT local organizations in the largest cities of the country, particularly in New York City. Merit pay was not a key issue in these strikes or in much of the educational literature in this decade. Given that in strike situations and in the early collective bargaining negotiations that often followed strikes teachers took the initiative in making proposals to school boards, this is hardly surprising. By the end of the decade, however, the controversies surrounding merit pay or merit rating were to be resurrected, though this time under a new name, differentiated staffing.

Differentiated staffing proposed to separate teachers into several roles and or positions, and pay the occupants of the different positions at different rates. An early article in favor of differentiated staffing attempted to distinguish it from merit pay plans that had failed, but the authors tellingly noted that what differentiated staffing shared with merit pay was the repudiation of the single salary scale. "So long as we have the single salary schedule," argued the authors, no one will get the highest amounts which should go to the highly specialized teachers who would advance to the highest ranks of the profession.[15] While differentiated staffing plans varied considerably from district to district, they usually involved some expansion of steps in a teaching career on a ladder similar to that found in the university faculty rankings of Assistant, Associate, and full Professor. For example, one California school district differentiated its teaching staff into the positions of Associate Teacher, Staff Teacher, Senior Teacher, and Master Teacher. Of course, since teachers advanced through the ranks, not automatically through seniority and education, but rather through some process by which their work was judged as satisfactory and worthy of promotion, many teachers and teacher organizations were suspicious of these plans as merit pay in disguise. The arguments of advocates did little to allay this suspicion. The article illustrating the four tier plan discussed above, for example, noted that it was but one of several plans and remarked that what all plans had in common were the elements of "job responsibilities, functions, and rewards (typically monetary)."[16]

Differentiated staffing was advocated by administrators and other educators because it did offer a way to pay some teachers handsome salaries. But, since these salaries were not to be granted on a seniority basis in terms of one's place on a single salary scale, advocates pointed out that differentiated staffing need not result in greatly inflated total salary costs for school systems.[17] Since differentiated staffing hit at the single salary scale and was often advocated in journals such as that of the (then male) educational honorary fraternity, *Phi Delta Kappa*, women teachers had serious reason to question whether or not differentiated staffing was simply a way to re-establish sexual differences in pay among the teaching force which had been bridged by the single salary scale.

Teacher organizations, as already indicated, were not persuaded by the new attack on the single salary scale. The NEA first considered a resolution on differentiated staffing in 1969. The resolution came from a part of the NEA which was concerned with teacher education and personnel standards. It carefully avoided taking a firm position for or against differentiated staffing, preferring instead to prescribe the criteria which should be followed if a plan were to be acceptable, the most notable of which was that "any design for differentiating staffing . . . must meaningfully involve classroom teachers and the local associations from the initial stages of development through implementation and evaluation." One teacher opponent of the resolution argued that it was too generous to the concept of differentiated staffing which was, in reality, "just a code name for merit salary pay." By 1972, the Association had come a way toward the position of the delegate who had flatly opposed differentiated staffing in 1969. The 1972 resolution, while not specifically opposing differentiated staffing, made clear that any plan needed to adhere "to the Association's principles for professional salaries," namely the single salary scale, and that the NEA "strongly opposes adoption of unilaterally imposed differentiated staffing plans and will assist any local affiliate in its opposition to the same."[18]

In the late 1970s and early 1980s, the merit principle would resurface in American educational discourse, this time in a version which reflected some of the changing conditions in which American schools and teachers now found themselves. Because of a decline in the number of school age children, combined with a general funding crisis that affected all public institutions because of a decline in the American economy, American schools found themselves in the 1970s and early 1980s in a position for which they were ill-prepared, a situation where they had to contemplate how to "lay off" or remove teachers for whom there was no longer sufficient work or funds to pay them. In this context, teacher organizations again resorted to their time honored principle of seniority and argued that teachers should be laid off, if there were to be any layoffs, on a last hired, first fired basis.

One illustration of this phenomenon was provided in the city schools of Atlanta, Georgia, in the early 1980s. In May of 1981, the city school board passed a Reduction in Force or RIF policy which called for teachers to be laid off on the basis of a complicated point system which purported to be based in large part on an evaluation of their performance. Both of the city's teachers associations, one affiliated with the American Federation of Teachers and the other with the National Education Association, reacted vigorously to this attack on seniority as a basis for layoffs. The president of the AFT local addressed the board while it was contemplating the proposed performance-based RIF policy and spoke in behalf of a seniority based RIF.

AFT contracts elsewhere traditionally provide for layoff by seniority. You have [had] proven the quality and dedication of your most senior employees. The use of seniority as a means of determining who will be RIFed . . . protects the employee from abuses often advocated by school systems which would prefer to replace a $20,000 employee with a less senior $12,000 one.[19]

Despite the organized teacher opposition, the board passed the performance-based RIF procedure and the teacher groups responded with an even more vigorous attack on performance as a basis and in defense of seniority. In August, 1981, the local AFT president paraphrased comments by Albert Shanker, national president of the American Federation of Teacher, which attacked performance-based alternatives to the seniority principle. After noting several weaknesses in performance-based schemes, the Atlanta Federation of Teachers president quoted her national leader "Seniority, like democracy, is certainly not a perfect system. But also, like democracy, it's better than any other yet invented."[20]

Through continual lobbying and political action, Atlanta's teachers were finally able to get the performance-based layoff system lifted in favor of a return to the existing seniority system. One of the sources that both Atlanta's unionists and Albert Shanker relied on was the work of an economist of education at Yale University, Richard Murnane. In several studies of educational productivity, Murnane concluded that given a number of factors currently operative in American public schools, including the existing technological characteristics of education and evaluation and the commitment of the school to education for all children, "seniority-based employment contracts may be more effective in promoting public education than performance-based contracts."[21]

Another researcher who studied performance- or merit-based layoff procedures in four suburban Massachusetts school systems, Susan Moore Johnson, failed to endorse ringingly these procedures, even though she indicated that she entered into the study as an advocate of performance-based reductions over seniority-reductions. Johnson found that, while all four school systems claimed to have some combination of performance and seniority in their criteria for layoffs, in two of the systems, the procedure for laying off in practice followed strict seniority. In the two which did utilize performance evaluations as part of the layoff procedure, the results were not uniformly positive. In fact, in the one district which most strictly followed standard evaluation and rating procedures in layoffs, the results included, in the words of one school principal, that "he had never seen morale as bad" as it was, because of the ill will created by the performance evaluations and layoff procedures. According to Johnson, the system-wide evaluation procedures which were required to implement a merit-based layoff procedure were shown to "alter the role of the principal, undermine staff morale, and threaten the autonomy of the teacher, principal, and local school." She described the assumptions underlying performance-based evaluation, namely that "teacher effectiveness can be defined, observed, and measured," as unwarranted by the existing research literature on the topic. She concluded her article by noting that the effect of performance-based layoffs on the total school climate, teacher-principal, and teacher-student interactions, was likely negative: "In an institution that, at its best, promotes acceptance and inclusion, performance-based layoffs introduce competition and exclusion."[22] A fair reading of this article, not authored by a friend of teacher organizations and their opposition to merit based procedures, indicates that there is significant agreement between the views of the author and the arguments that teacher organizations have made against merit based personnel policies throughout this century.

IV

Having looked at merit pay plans in the early twentieth century and in the 1940s, at differentiated staffing which utilized some performance evaluations in 1950s and 1960s, and at merit-related layoffs in the 1970s and early 1980s, it seems clear that teacher organizations, as well as many of the teachers whom they represent, have consistently opposed these measures. Also, the research evidence introduced in the discussion of the latest merit-based measures, performance-based layoff procedures, indicates that there is ample reason to sympathize with the suspicions of organized teachers about the implementation of the merit principle in personnel procedures. Of course, our purpose here has not been to judge the adequacy of the procedures, but to get a perspective on the teacher organizations' opposition to them and the reasons for this opposition. Still, it seems in order at least to suggest that suspicions of the merit principle by organized teachers reflect legitimate suspicions of the enterprise. What remains in this essay now is to discuss the very latest invocation of the merit pay idea in American education, that of President Reagan's National Commission of Excellence in Education, and the organized teacher reaction to it which, at first glance, may reflect a softening of organized teacher opposition to merit.

Before making specific the two main teacher organizations' reactions to the President's educational initiative, it must be noted that the discussions of merit pay are almost all taking place at the central or national level of American educational discourse, while the actions and plans for implementing merit pay or any other educational proposals will take place at the state and/or local district level. This situation reminds us of a fundamental anomaly in American education in the late twentieth century; while policies are made at the state and local levels, public opinion on education and most other issues, under the influence of the centralizing power of the national media, is shaped at the national level. Thus we have a conservative, Republican president, committed to a diminution of the national effort in educational funding and control, also successfully setting a rhetorical agenda for educational reform at the national level and making merit pay a prime item on that agenda. It is this situation that accounts, at least in part, for the changes in tone of the organized teacher reaction to merit pay that appear to be taking place.

Both national organizations, the NEA and the AFT, considered and passed lengthy resolutions on educational reform at their respective national conventions which took place in July of 1983. The two organizations are now more alike in their orientation and policies than they have been at any time previously. In the early 1970s, the NEA cast off its stance of being open to all educators and became an increasingly teacher-oriented union, alike in most ways to the AFT. Yet, the two organizations are now, more than ever, locked in combat with each other for the dues money of prospective members and local affiliates. Thus, it is not surprising that they may attempt to differentiate themselves from each other on merit pay or any other issue, in an attempt to appeal to unaffiliated teachers and teachers who belong to the other organization.

The NEA, meeting in 1983 a few days before the AFT, passed a statement on educational excellence, drawing the title of the statement from the title of the President's commission's report. This statement, according to newspaper reports, includes a position on merit pay that is quite similar to the statements and reactions that have characterized organized teacher opinion throughout most of the twentieth century. It notes that the NEA, "is categorically opposed to any plan, whether designated a merit pay plan, a master teacher plan, or by some other name, that bases compensation of teachers on favoritism, subjective evaluation . . . or other arbitrary standard." The new Executive Director of the NEA, Don Cameron, was quoted as attributing the motivation behind the President's advocacy of merit pay to the fact that "Ronald Reagan is attempting to distract the nation's attention from his abominally poor education record by pulling a merit pay rabbit out of his hat."[23]

At its own convention, the AFT also passed a lengthy statement on educational reform which was a bit more ambiguous on the issue of merit pay. According to the union's newspaper, "The statement did not express support for any merit pay proposals, saying that most of those proposed in the past have not worked." However, "since the public is discussing merit pay and wants a response from teachers, the AFT offered one." The paper goes on to indicate that the AFT, while recognizing that merit pay is not union policy, understands that certain conditions may make appropriate the negotiation of merit pay clauses or policies by state or local affiliates. It then went on to list seven qualifications before any merit pay should be approved, including higher pay for all teachers, evaluation procedures that prevent subjectivity and local school political pressure from being applied, all teachers being eligible to be considered for extra pay, no sanctions against teachers who do not receive merit increases, and teacher approval of the plans through collective bargaining or some other suitable process.[24]

The difference in emphasis in these two statements caused some newspaper reporters, and President Reagan (who was invited to and did address the AFT convention), to contrast the AFT's position with the more rigid opposition to merit pay from the NEA. Fueling the notion of difference between the two organizations on the issue was the opposition of the NEA's state affiliate, the Tennessee Education Association, to a master teacher (differentiated staffing) plan proposed by that state's governor. The AFT, in its own publications, also stressed the flexibility of its own views and contrasted them with the rigid NEA position.[25] Close scrutiny of the situation, however, leads one to conclude that the differences in the positions of the two organizations are not as large as one would think. The reasons that the NEA's Tennessee affiliate opposed the governor's master teacher plan, according to NEA reports, included the facts that the plan contained a limitation on the number of teachers who could receive the promotion the the higher paid ranks and that the governor proposed the plan without consulting with the state education association.[26] Both of these seem to be violations of the AFT's conditions under which it could endorse a merit pay plan. It therefore seems likely that if the state organization in Tennessee had been an AFT affiliate, that national union would also have opposed the governor's plan.

At a panel on merit pay and master teacher plans at the August 1983 meeting of the Education Commission of the States, Tennessee's governor discussed the issues with AFT President Albert Shanker and NEA Executive Director Don Cameron. According to reports of this discussion, the NEA leader softened his group's opposition to master teacher plans, stating that it was the Tennessee plan his group's affiliate opposed, not the concept of master teacher itself. A reading of one set of excerpts from this panel discussion leads to the conclusion that the differences between the two union leaders on the issue are minimal. Both seemed to court the governor by indicating the conditions under which they would be inclined to accept a master teacher plan.[27] In another apparent softening of its flatfooted opposition to current master teacher plans, the NEA's president partici-pated in a coalition of national education organizations which drafted a report favoring many current reforms proposed for American education, including a plan for "Establishment of a career ladder with different roles for beginning teachers, experiences teachers, and master teachers." The NEA president pointed out, however, that the group did not endorse merit pay, that history shows that merit pay does not work, and that it did endorse the career ladder plans as more palatable to teachers because they allow all teachers who meet the criteria to advance.[28]

Thus it seems that the differences between the two organizations on the issues are overdrawn. The common thread linking the two groups' stances on the issues of merit pay and master teachers is that they both realize that, rhetorically, a conservative national administration has managed to focus attention on the merit pay issue and to distract attention from many other real educational issues. The groups must, in their own minds, meet the rhetorical advantage of the President and other conservatives by not simply restating their traditional opposition to merit pay in whatever is its current version. They thus must state conditions under which they might endorse merit pay or master teacher schemes. None of these sets of conditions has yet to be met and it seems likely that they will not be met. If a plan contains enough guarantees and protections for the rank and file members of the teachers that the unions serve, it is unlikely to serve the purposes that caused it to be offered in the first place.

To believe that a teachers' union, whose first job is to protect the interests of its members, would participate in a pay plan which would give some of its members a considerable financial advantage over most of its other members seems to me to contradict the very reason for being of the union. The bulk of this essay has been devoted to showing how opposition to merit pay in many versions has characterized teacher organizations in this century. It is political disadvantage that now pushes these organizations to avoid flatfooted opposition to current master teacher plans. To expect them to go further and support the plans, thereby reversing their traditional orientation to protection of their members, is unrealistic. Further, much evidence and argument, only a small portion of which has been cited in this essay, indicates that merit pay in the versions we have known it in America in this century is a flawed concept that does not and will not work. Why would we expect teacher organizations to abandon their members for an idea whose "merit" has yet to be proven?

NOTES

1. The National Commission on Excellence in Education, *A Nation at Risk* (Washington: U.S. Government Printing Office, 1983).

2. Ibid., p. 30.

3. Wayne J. Urban, *Why Teachers Organized* (Detroit: Wayne State University Press, 1982).

4. J. Cayce Morrison, "History of New York State's Approach to the Problem of Relating Teachers' Salaries to the Quality of Teacher Service," *Harvard Educational Review*, Vol. 22, (Spring, 1952), pp. 124-31.

5. *Journal of Addresses and Proceedings* of the National Education Association, Vol. 85, 1947, p. 61; hereafter cited as NEA *Proceedings*.

6. NEA *Proceedings*, Vol. 86, 1948, p. 195.

7. Ibid., p. 197.

8. NEA *Proceedings*, Vol. 89, 1951, p. 160.

9. Frank W. Hubbard and Hazel Davis, "The Constructions of Salary Schedules for Teachers," *Harvard Educational Review*, Vol. 22 (Spring, 1952), pp. 83-96; quotations on p. 86.

10. Ibid., p. 86.

11. Ibid., pp. 87, 95.

12. Hazel Davis, "Facts and Issues in Merit Salary Schedules," *Journal of Teacher Education*, Vol. 8 (June, 1957), pp. 127-35.

13. NEA *Proceedings*, Vol. 95, 1957, pp. 216, 214.

14. Carl J. Megel, "Merit Rating is Unsound," *Phi Delta Kappan*, Vol. 42 (January, 1961), pp. 154-56.

15. M. John Rand and Ferwick English, "Towards a Differentiated Teaching Staff," *Phi Delta Kappan*, Vol. 49 (January, 1968), pp. 264-68; quotations from p. 264.

16. James L. Oleveio, "The Meaning and Application of Differentiated Staffing in Teaching," *Phi Delta Kappan*, Vol. 52 (September, 1970), pp. 36-40; quotation from p. 36.

17. Carl W. Swanson, "The Costs of Differentiated Staffing," *Phi Delta Kappan*, Vol. 54 (January, 1973), pp. 344-48.

18. NEA *Proceedings*, Vol. 107 (1969), pp. 280, 580, and Vol. 110 (1972).

19. Remarks of Mary Lou Romaine, President, Atlanta Federation of Teachers, to the Atlanta Board of Education, May 4, 1981, (Document in possession of author).

20. Romaine to the Atlanta Board, August 3, 1981, (Document in possession of author).

21. Richard J. Murnane, "Seniority Rules and Educational Productivity: Understanding the Consequences of a Mandate for Equality," *American Journal of Education*, Vol. 90, November, 1981, pp. 14-30; quotation on p. 14.

22. Susan Moore Johnson, "Performance-Based Staff Layoffs in the Public Schools: Implementation and Outcomes," *Harvard Educational Review*, Vol. 50 (May, 1980), pp. 214-33; quotations on pp. 225, 232-33, 233.

23. "Merit Pay Stiffly Opposed by NEA Convention," *Atlanta Journal-Constitution* (July 4, 1983).

24. *The American Teacher*, Vol. 68 (September, 1983).

25. Ibid. and Atlanta Teachers' Federation *Voice of the Union* (August, 1983). Both have headlines indicating AFT "leads the way" on education reform.

26. "Interview with Don Cameron," *Education Week* (June 8, 1983) and Tennessee Education Association's *TEA News* (July 15, 1983).

27. *Education Week* (August 17, 1983).

28. *Education Week* (October 26, 1983).

Questions—Political, Economic, and Professional

The Politics of Teacher Incentive Plans

Deborah Inman

Introduction

The renewed interest in merit pay and other teacher incentive plans is a direct result of the politics of the times and can be specifically traced to Governor Lamar Alexander's initiatives in Tennessee and the subsequent release of the President's National Commission on Excellence in Education report, *A Nation at Risk: The Imperative for Educational Reform*. The conclusions reached in Tennessee and the findings of the President's Commission report, along with other national studies, have generated a momentum for quality education unlike any experienced in many years.

One of the underlying problems associated with the poor quality of public education is the low salary level of school teachers. As a result, many of the best teachers leave the classroom in an effort to upgrade their standard of living through other and more lucrative employment. This departure of many of the more competent teachers is one explanation for the lower standards of quality in our public schools. Merit pay was advanced by the Reagan administration as a solution to the teacher competency problem on the grounds that such a plan would not only retain the best teachers but would also attract the most capable individuals to the public schools. As a result, great interest in merit pay and other teacher incentive plans has been generated among school districts and across entire state systems. The hope prevails that such plans will create an environment of opportunity that will attract and keep the most capable individuals as teachers in the public schools.

Numerous variations of merit pay and other teacher incentive plans have appeared, which has led to some confusion regarding the relationship between these plans. The Merit Pay Task Force Report of the 98th Congress, 1st Session defined merit pay and career ladder programs as:

Merit Pay is a system that rewards exemplary teaching by either a bonus or an increased annual salary.

The **career ladder system** creates levels of teachers from apprentice teacher through several intermediate steps to the highest level of master teacher. Different salaries and responsibilities are associated with each step. Examples of a career ladder are apprentice teacher, professional teacher, senior teacher, master teacher. (Report No. 98, 1983, p. 4-5)

The purpose of this paper is to examine the role of politics in the implementation of teacher incentive plans. More specifically, it is to emphasize the role of politics in such plans by (a) generally reviewing some local plans: (2) describing the development of the two state-wide master teacher career ladder plans; and (3) presenting the findings of a survey which was administered to local and state administrators regarding the politics of teacher incentive plans.

The Role of Politics

Any discussion of the role of politics must be somewhat nebulous. Due to the hierarchy of bureaucracies, politics is often simply the process of individuals doing their jobs in a fashion that will ensure their retention of employment. Politics has been defined by Lasswell (1936) as "who gets what, when and how" and by Mosher, Hastings and Wagoner (1976) as "the authoritative allocation of social values . . . Since resources are seldom or never adequate to satisfy the claims made upon them, the imbalance between demands and resources underlies the conflicts that constitute the seedbed of politics." Both of these definitions are particularly applicable to the politics of teacher incentive pay plans since they emphasize both power and values. Although education leaders of the past preferred to keep politics out of the public schools, it has become evident over the past thirty years that all major decisions on educational policy (especially those involving funding) must be made by political process.

Teacher incentive plans have been influenced by politics at the national, state, and local levels. The renewed interest in merit pay and other teacher incentive plans was initially spurred by the aforementioned efforts of Governor Lamar Alexander of Tennessee. The publicity of *A Nation at Risk* added fuel to the flames and sparked various alternatives to teacher incentive plans nationwide. The condition of the economy, the policy of the news media, and the negative attitudes toward the public schools contribute heavily to the support for or against teacher incentive plans. Presently, there are two state-wide master teacher plans (Florida and Tennessee), one mentor teacher program (California), and several district-wide merit-pay/teacher-incentive plans. The political processes of state-wide and district-wide teacher incentive plans are, of course, different. The political system at the district level is not nearly so complex as that at the state level.

The Politics of District-wide
Teacher Incentive Pay Plans

The major decision-makers at the local level include, of course, the superintendent and the board of education. Both the superintendent and the school board are influenced by the teachers, principals, students, parents, teacher unions and associations, the business community, the chamber of

Deborah Inman

commerce, citizens as taxpayers, and the news media. The role of each of these groups determines its attitude toward teacher incentive pay plans. It is not surprising that the constituencies of these groups vary in their support for such plans from district to district due to demographic differences.

In Round Valley School District, the California Teachers Association (an affiliate of NEA) has been cooperative with the administrators in the implementation of the program. The merit pay plan was strongly influenced by the teachers, who helped to create their own programs. The school board's involvement in the merit program is also quite strong due, in part, to the small size of the district. The school board members are part of the merit evaluation committee; they draw up the annual guidelines for teacher's proposals; and then they negotiate (through their participation on the evaluation committee) with individual teachers' discussing possible objectives and appropriate methods of evaluation. The school board provides $2800 per teacher in the budget each year for potential merit pay earnings. The plan is covered by the teachers' association's three-year contract. Unlike some other local plans, the evaluation committee consists of the school's principal, a teacher selected by the union, and two members of the school board. This conveys the shared political strength of the union and the school board in the implementation of the plan in Round Valley School District. Because the plan is a bargained agreement with the association, the political influence of the union is prominent.

The politics of the merit pay plan in the Catalina Foothills District of Arizona were quite different from the Round Valley program. To begin with, the teachers' association (an affiliate of NEA) did not participate in the formulation of the plan. The plan focuses only on individual incentives, and the superintendent makes the final decisions of award based on recommendations from the principals. This suggests that the teachers' association is not politically very strong. Since the principals make recommendations to the superintendent who makes the final decision, the political influence of the superintendent is obviously rather strong, and the relative union influence is diminished.

In the Houston Independent School District, the politics of the Second Mile Incentive Pay Plan were unique to that system. Although Texas does not permit collective bargaining, the Houston Independent School teachers have had limited representation from the National Education Association (NEA), the American Federation of Teachers (AFT) and a State association. The teacher organizations opposed the plan and the teachers expressed mixed reactions. The Houston school board has supported the plan and has been further encouraged by the community. The principal, instructional supervisor, or assistant superintendent conduct the teacher evaluation. Because there is no collective bargaining law, implementation of the plan was simplified considerably.

Another local plan in Texas, Bryan Independent School District[1], solicited and used input from business, PTA members, administrators, and teachers in its development. Although teachers are not unionized (due to Texas law), the Bryan school teachers, like the Houston school teachers, are members of several professional organizations and were therefore influenced by them. The school board supports the program and determines the amount of money available each year for merit bonuses. The principal, assistant principal, department head, and the curriculum leader from the central office conduct the teacher evaluation and the principal makes nominations for merit awards. The evaluation process in both the Bryan and Houston plans exemplifies one of the most controversial issues regarding merit pay — the evaluation of teachers by administrators only.

The merit pay plan in Lebanon (Connecticut) Public Schools was established for a three year term. The principal made recommendations for merit pay to the superintendent and the school board. The implementation of the plan was introduced by the teachers and the community. However, there was a change in union leadership and these new officials did not support the plan approved by their predecessors. As a result, teachers were not allowed to participate formally in the development of the plan. This led to teacher dissatisfaction regarding the evaluation process and dissension among the teachers. The plan was not renewed when the three-year contract came to an end. It is evident that the political influence of the union was quite strong since the change in the organization's leadership had such a significant impact on the plan.

The politics of the Penn Manor (Pennsylvania) School District merit pay plan were somewhat different from those previously discussed. This plan was developed by the assistant superintendent, the elementary school coordinator, the middle school principal and the high school principal. They did not solicit teacher participation for fear it would cause delay in reaching consensus for a plan. The Teacher's Association did not participate in the development of the plan, and the plan was not pilot tested. The Board of Education approved the plan as presented by these four administrators without seeking input from others concerned. The reaction of the plan appears to be mixed. School officials perceive teacher attitudes to be better than expected. There is disagreement regarding the impact on teacher morale; union officials believe morale has suffered while school principals believe morale has actually risen. But then, it would be politically questionable for the union officials to agree that the plan was a success when neither the association nor the teachers has any input. The political strength of the Board of Education is evidenced by their immediate approval of the plan.

The merit pay plan in Seiling (Oklahoma) was also developed solely by administrators. Although the teachers are members of an NEA affiliate, the association has not formally participated in the development or implementation of the plan. Unlike most other plans, merit pay is determined by student achievement. Teachers have mixed feelings about the plan due to their concerns regarding the weakness of the testing instrument to measure student achievement.

The outcome of local teacher incentive pay plans is due, in large part, to the strengths of the various influential groups. Districts with strong unions are obviously going to have plans that incorporate teachers' inputs, whereas districts with weak unions will incorporate the inputs of other more influential groups (administration, community, etc.). Obviously, the implementation of merit pay and other teacher incentive plans is much less complex in non-unionized districts than in unionized systems.

The Politics of State-wide Teacher Incentive Pay Plans

At present, two states, Florida and Tennessee, have enacted laws for state-wide master teacher programs. California has a Mentor Teacher Program, but because it is considerably different from the Florida and Tennessee plans for the purpose of this paper it will not be addressed. Much of the opposition to teacher incentive plans is caused by the confusion associated with traditional teacher merit pay schemes. This is due largely to the numerous discussions on merit pay and the various commissions on merit pay. Neither the Florida[2] nor the Tennessee plan is a merit pay plan. Rather, both are master teacher career ladder programs.

The Tennessee Master Teacher Program was the culmination of a special session of the legislature called by Governor Alexander to consider education reform that would make Tennessee education a model for the nation. Governor Alexander described the plan as ". . . an incentive pay system that will make teaching a fully professional career, draw our best young people into it, challenge our best teachers to do even better, and inspire excellence in our classrooms by rewarding excellence in our teachers." (1983, p. 722) The combined efforts of the Governor and the Commissioner of Education, Robert McElrath, were politically important in gaining support for the plan. It was the responsibility of the state department of education to establish a workable incentive pay system with appropriate evaluations that both the teachers and the taxpayers would perceive as fair. As a result, the state department of education policy analysts negotiated between the legislature, the teacher associations, and the Governor.

Specifically, the master teacher plan had been endorsed by the Tennessee School Boards Association, the Tennessee Organization of School Superintendents, the Principals Study Council, the Supervisors Study Council, the Tennessee Municipal League, the Tennessee Taxpayers Association, and the Tennessee Manufacturers Association. The Tennessee Education Association, however, was opposed to the plan. As the Governor said, "Just about everyone is for it . . . the only original opposition comes from the one group you would expect to be leading the charge for it — the teachers union." (1983, p. 722) Although the American Federation of Teachers was supportive of the plan, because it had a membership of only 1000 teachers, it was too small to be influential. The Tennessee Education Association (an affiliate of NEA), on the other hand, with its membership of 37,000 had considerable influence in its opposition to the plan. A visit from Albert

Shanker, President of the American Federation of Teachers, was instrumental in gaining cooperation from the teacher associations. Shanker told the teachers that the only way they would receive a raise would be with some type of merit pay plan, since the legislature had made the decision to hold back salary increases until the master teacher plan was enacted.

Obviously, the teacher organizations in Tennessee are significant political forces since their opposition to the plan created grave concern counteracting the overwhelming support from the other influencing groups. Although the AFT had a significantly smaller membership in Tennessee than the NEA, through the efforts of Shanker, support was generated from the teachers for the master teacher plan as a *quid pro quo* for salary increases. The NEA, realizing that teachers would prefer membership in an organization that was seemingly more concerned about the vital issues (salary raises), decided to support the Governor. It is important to note at this point, that nationwide the AFT has used merit pay and career ladder plans to attract teachers from the NEA. Had the union competition between the AFT and the NEA not existed, the reactions to the master teacher plan would have been quite different.

The political composition of the Tennessee legislature is predominantly Democratic, while the Governor is a Republican; yet the Tennessee Master Teacher Plan had bipartisan support. Two Democrats and four Republicans were the primary sponsors of the bill. Due to heavy lobbying by the Tennessee Education Association, the master teacher proposal was initially delayed in the Senate, and the Senate voted in April 1983 to defer action on the bill until February 1984 in an effort to incorporate suggestions or establish compromises with the teacher associations. In the meantime, political forces were also reacting to the financing of the plan. Governor Alexander requested a one cent sales tax increase to pay for the master teacher plan. The Governor was not immediately supported on this issue by the Democratic legislature, which wanted to broaden the tax base and leave the rate at the same level. Compromises were eventually made, the sales tax was enacted, and the master teacher plan was approved.

While Governor Alexander was certainly instrumental in implementing the Tennessee Master Teacher Program, he declines credit for it, stating that most of it is based on recommendations from the legislature's Comprehensive Education Study. He attributes the program to a coalition of interests from business, taxpayers, boards of education, educators, parents, students, and especially the classroom teachers, which surfaced in the legislature's study. The political implications here are quite clear and obviously important. By crediting these other groups for the plan, the Governor encouraged broader public support since it implied that the people actually requested the program. The Tennessee struggle is a well documented example of the political process as part and parcel of educational policy.

The Florida master teacher program is similar to Tennessee's in that both programs were initiated by their respective governors. Florida's Governor Robert Graham formed a committee composed of educators and business leaders to study educational reform. According to Graham, "The political message of this group was simple: 'education means business,' both today and in the future, and a richer economy for all of us. The pay off is a better quality of life." (1983, p. 42)

The political influence of the business community was demonstrated in Florida during the legislative sessions in which the master teacher plan was enacted. The business community indicated that it would not support additional expenditures for education unless teachers' pay was based on performance. Incentive pay plans were, therefore, specifically endorsed by the business community. However, the support of the business community was not reflective of all concerned groups. In fact, the Governor indicated it was indeed an arduous task to convince the AFT and the NEA that he was serious about the master teacher plan. Although both unions opposed the master teacher plan, they eventually realized that "merit pay is a national movement that is central to educational reform . . . and merit pay can be fairly administered if the teachers participate in formulating the merit pay programs." (1983, p. 44) It should be noted that the concepts of master teacher (career ladder) and merit pay were continuously confused in legislative committee discussions. Today it is doubtful that more than a handful of Florida legislators could distinguish the two.

The Governor's staff prepared the master teacher plan that was presented to the legislature in May 1983. In June 1983, it adopted the Florida Meritorious Pay Plan, which included the Master Teacher Plan and a vague local merit pay system that was subsequently repealed by the 1984 legislature. The legislature established the Quality Instruction Incentive Programs (QIIP) Council to provide specifics on the two plans and to recommend implementing regulations to the State Board of Education. Thirteen meetings and $173,000 later, the Council was unable to make such recommendations to the State Board. Ultimately, in June 1984, the QIIP Council was dissolved by the legislature because of its inability to deal with the politics of the incentive pay issue. When it became apparent that political strife and poor leadership would prevent action by the QIIP Council, the Governor's Office and the State Department of Education staff stepped in and drafted State Board of Education rules to implement the state master teacher plan. Both teacher unions were involved in negotiations with the Governor's Office over the nuances of the rules, which were ultimately submitted to the State Board. Although both unions maintained throughout that the rank and file teacher was opposed to merit pay, when the deadline arrived for consideration, the Department of Education received applications from twenty-eight thousand teachers who wanted to become associate master teachers under the career ladder plan.

The State Board continued to modify rules and in April, 1984, waived the criterion for eligibility which required that teachers must pass an appropriate subject matter portion of the NTE. In June 1984, a 172-page bill which revised the Florida Meritorious Plan and modified the master teacher plan was passed by the legislature. Currently, the Governor's Office and the State Department of Education are devising tests to be used in lieu of the in-field Master's Degree as one criterion for eligibility for Associate Master status. These tests are, by law, to be completed and implemented by February 1985.

According to Graham, "The struggle over merit pay was not the biggest single political battlefield. The greatest effort went into the fight to obtain resources." (1983, p. 45) Here the Governor had to veto a "stand-pat, no-new-taxes budget for education" in June 1983 and to bring the legislature back into special session to squeeze out another $230 million for teacher salaries.

The politics of state-wide teacher incentive pay plans are, as may be expected, much more complex than district level programs. The major actors in educational decision-making at the state level include the governor, the state board of education, the governor's education policy coordinator, and the state legislature. The actual decisions made are impacted by many influential groups. The major external forces regarding state-wide teacher incentive pay plans are: labor and teacher unions, the news media, parent associations, school board organizations and administrators organizations, associations of industry, chambers of commerce, and citizens as taxpayers. It is the role of each of these groups within the environment that determines their perspective toward state-wide teacher incentive pay plans. In addition to these external forces, internal conflict among state department personnel who advise the governor can subtly influence the outcome of teacher incentive plans.

Inter-State Politics

Although Florida was the first state to actually enact a master teacher law, it is important to recall that Tennessee did much of the groundwork in developing the master teacher program. Florida built on the Tennessee plan and adapted it to Florida. While Tennessee was trying to work out compromises with the Tennessee Education Association, Florida's Governor took his plan directly to the legislature, and with the help of the business community and strong support by key members of the Florida House, the plan was passed. The state AFT affiliate ultimately vigorously opposed the program and maintained that the potential for a good plan in Florida was bypassed when the Governor decided not to wait and iron out all the details. The Governor was charged with rushing headlong into the plan simply to be "first" among the states.

Despite the fact that the Governor's Office has documentation indicating that both unions had the opportunity for early and continuous involvement in the Florida plan, both organizations today claim they were closed out when the master teacher plan was being developed.

The experiences of both Florida and Tennessee suggest two important levels of political activity — the healthy competition among states and the competition for power and authority between the unions and the state government. There are, of course, several possible interpretations for the actual outcome. First, the Florida's teacher unions were politically weaker than the Tennessee teacher organizations, and, because the legislature was strongly influenced by big business, the Governor's job was much easier. Another potential consideration is the difference in the governors' powers in their respective settings. Governor Graham thought it was politically important to implement a state-wide teacher incentive program and to accommodate the interests of the business community and the taxpayers, while Governor Alexander believed it was more important to have a workable plan agreed to by teachers. But then Governor Alexander had a greater obstacle to overcome since he was a Republican Governor with a Democratic legislature and without teacher acquiescence his pay plan may never have been enacted.

To emphasize the role of inter-state politics, an incident was relayed by one of the education analysts in the Florida Department of Education that on the day Florida announced approval of the Florida Meritorious Teacher plan, Governor Alexander, who was building a sandcastle with his son while on vacation at a beach, stood up, kicked the sandcastle (destroying it), and said, "But I wanted to be the first!" Whether this anecdote is true is not the issue. The mere fact that it was told conveys the interstate competition which developed among some states and appeared to drive the states to greater achievements.

This apparent competitiveness among young and aggressive governors of the South to exceed the others in improving education probably establishes a new benchmark in education and political involvement. Ironically, this appears to be good politics because Alexander, Graham, Hunt (North Carolina) and Winter (Mississippi) have been very popular governors.

A Model for the Politics of Teacher Incentive Plans

Teacher incentive plans may be viewed from five perspectives that are derived from interactions of unions, teachers and the public. This can be illustrated by a concentric model (see Figure 1) in which the inner-most circle (a) represents the local/state union leadership consisting of individuals trying to retain their jobs and their personal power and prestige. The next circle (b) represents the concerns and influences of the national union leadership. Of utmost concern is their interest in the continuous growth of their organizations and their fear of arbitrary administration and the subsequent changes in delegation of power — the removal of some of their decision-making authority to local levels. In other words, the most logical explanation as to why teacher organization leadership is so distraught over merit pay is the union leaderships' concern over the way that merit pay would influence the power of the union and cause divisiveness in the ranks. The union is, therefore, hard pressed to come up with reasons to support

FIGURE 1

CONCENTRIC MODEL

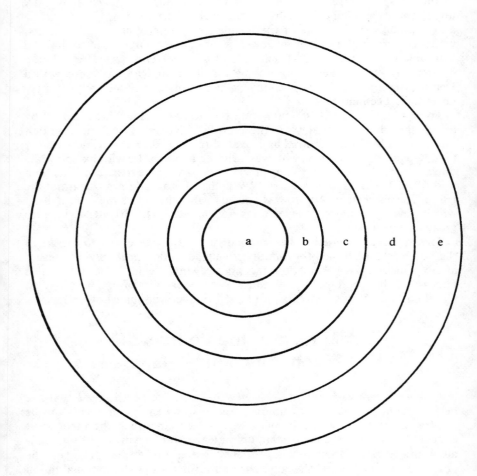

a = local/state union leadership
b = national union leadership
c = teacher constituency
d = student interest
e = public interest

Deborah Inman

merit pay, since such a plan would categorize funds that unions have no power or say over. The self-interest of unions as organizations may determine their position on education policy, which may not be in the best interest of the teacher. For example, some state unions now support abrogation of tenure laws because it strengthens teachers' dependency on the union. The same principal applies to merit pay — while it might be good for the teachers, it is not necessarily good for the union. From the perspective of the union organization, merit pay is just not good for business. Further, unions want the school administrators to have *ministerial* functions only. The administration of teacher incentive plans invades union prerogatives and expands the role of administrators. Under such plans school administrators are suddenly vested with much greater discretionary authority in dealing with teacher evaluations and pay. Unions are concerned, and in some cases rightfully so, about arbitrary and capricious actions of the part of administrators.

The succeeding circle (c) represents the teacher constituency which can be broken down into two groups: the rank and file perspective and the teacher organization leadership. The rank and file perspective is composed of two types of teachers. First, are the teachers who are aspiring to get ahead. They appreciate the challenge and do not mind working and being evaluated for it. The other group consists of those unsure and incompetent teachers who fear the unknown and, therefore, want to keep the system exactly as it is.

The next circle (d) represents the students who are concerned about their classroom and school environment, which may be altered if teacher dissension should result from various teacher incentive plans. Also of interest to the student is the impact of good teachers as opposed to inadequate teachers on achievement. The last circle (e) represents the public interest. The public has become increasingly concerned about incompetent teachers and the expenditure of dollars for teachers who are not doing their job. The question of accountability is rampant in the public sector and this is rapidly becoming an era of accountability and testing. Much of the support for merit pay and other teacher incentive plans is related to the premise that they employ measures for testing teachers.

Each of these circles represents competing interests that manifest themselves in different degrees of political pressure. These specific interests result in new coalitions as different pressure are brought to bear. Obviously, the composition and strengths of these influencial groups have a direct relationship to the implementation of teacher incentive plans, since governors, legislatures, and school boards are supposed to oversee these interests and be responsive to the legitimate claims of each.

The Outlook for Teacher Incentive Pay Plans

The nationwide attention generated by the Tennessee and Florida master teacher plans has raised considerable interest regarding the politics of such plans. In an effort to determine whether local and state administrators believe merit pay and other teacher incentive plans might be feasible, a survey was conducted among nine local school districts with successful merit pay/teacher incentive programs and among eighteen states. The survey of local administrators was limited to school districts with successful programs in an effort to identify implementation problems and determine the feasibility of overcoming them. The selection of the states to be included in the survey was random except for the three states with state-wide teacher incentive programs, California, Florida and Tennessee.

General Feasibility of Merit Pay and Other Teacher Incentive Plans.

There was unanimous agreement among the local administrators that merit pay and other teacher incentive plans are indeed feasible. The most cited supporting statements were: (1) It is the only way to gain public support for higher salaries for all teachers; and (2) Administrators, teachers, parents and students already know who the best teachers are, so why can't we pay them more? After all, equal pay for unequals perpetuates inequality. Although all local respondents agreed that these programs are feasible, 33 percent had qualifying statements such as: (1) Given reasonable criteria for distribution of funds and a reasonable means of implementing the criteria, merit pay and other incentive plans are feasible. (2) They are feasible, but not without problems brought about by those with determined convictions that it will not work. (3) If you define teachers as managers, incentive plans will work, but if you define teachers as workers, then incentive plans will not work. These responses suggest that even though merit pay and other teacher incentive plans are difficult, at best, to implement, when all is said and done, local administrators are pleased with their plans and believe that, in general, merit pay and other teacher incentive plans are feasible.

The majority (75 percent) of the state administrators also agreed that merit pay and other teacher incentive plans are feasible. Politically, they believed the point has been passed where the public will support paying all teachers at the same rate regardless of the quality of work. These programs provide educators a substantial reason to improve and a reward system for those who are successful. Education for too long has operated unto itself, and it can be compared to other American enterprises — e.g., business, where recognition depends on productivity. There were, of course, some qualifying statements such as: (1) If an agreed-upon, fair, and quality performance assessment plan is developed, and if enough time is spent on evaluation, then it is feasible. (2) They are especially feasible when specific, measurable outcomes are identified. (3) If administrators and others involved in teacher evaluation have the time, training, and skill to do it well, it will succeed. The remaining 25 percent of the state administrators responded adamantly that merit pay and other teacher incentive plans are not feasible. The most cited arguments against all such plans were: (1) Lack of agreement on how merit should be defined and who should select the meritorious; (2) lack of control over background influences, both of which seem to have a stronger impact on levels of student achievement than does teaching; (3) the imprecise and artistic nature of teaching; and (4) their impracticality (on a state-wide basis) in a large, diverse state in which collective bargaining has been accepted practice for many years.

State-wide versus School-wide or District-wide Plans.

The majority (67 percent) of the local administrators did not believe that state-wide plans would be a better alternative to school-wide and district-wide plans. In fact, they were adamantly opposed to the concept of a state-wide plan. The other responses were mixed, suggesting that the state should give support and direction, but the actual plan should be adapted to the district. If was believed that, although state-wide plans have merit, district-wide plans allow more diversity and can be designed to address needs at the district level. It was also emphasized that the teachers might feel more ownership of locally developed plans, which could contribute to the success of the plan. Only one respondent supported state-funded plans over individual locally funded plans. The most common arguments by those adamantly opposed to state-wide plans were: (1) Most state-wide plans create operational and paper-work burdens that tax the small district's manpower. (2) State-wide plans are so unwieldy at this point that they are not cost-effective. (3) Plans should never be imposed on teachers or handed down from a central office or from a state agency. In essence, it was agreed that we are on the cutting edge of ignorance in this business. What the state should do is provide incentives for many small pilot projects and carefully evaluate them. Pilot plans should be implemented in districts in order to discover the things that will work and eliminate the things that will not work. The negative responses to state-wide plans are not surprising, considering controversy over the shift of control and responsibility from the local level to the state level during the past several years.

The majority (63 percent) of the state administrators, on the other hand, believed that state-wide plans would be a better alternative to school-wide and district-wide plans. Most of these respondents recommended that state plans be broad enough to allow some district flexibility. The remaining 37 percent of the state administrators did not believe that state-wide plans were a better alternative to local level programs. Of these, all but one respondent supported locally conceived and supported plans at either the school or district level. This respondent felt that no single plan would work effectively in a large state. It was recommended that a plan to improve teaching should combine the best elements of: (a) a meaningful minimum salary; (b) a career ladder; (c) adequate working conditions; (d) incentives, bonuses, or other rewards for teaching in areas with high teacher needs; (e) reduction in salary disparities between high- and low-wealth areas; and (f) a market-sensitive teacher salary schedule.

Political Feasibility of Merit Pay and Other Teacher Incentive Plans.

There was unanimous support from the local administrators regarding the political feasibility of merit pay and other teacher incentive plans. In fact, most respondents indicated that teacher incentive plans are not only feasible, but are a political necessity, since parents, patrons, and other taxpayers are demanding greater productivity. The majority (88 percent) of the state administrators also supported the political feasibility of merit pay and other teacher incentive plans. However, it was stressed that sometimes political feasibility must be put aside in favor of bipartisan efforts to affect change in areas of great need — there is much evidence of diverse political factions joining forces to reform the educational system. It is interesting to note that some believed merit pay and other teacher incentive plans are more politically feasible than they are feasible in actuality, and that, although incentive plans are politically feasible, they are politically distasteful. It was also suggested that teacher incentive plans are certainly politically feasible in states with politically weak teachers' associations. The remaining 12 percent of the state administrators did not believe teacher incentive plans were politically feasible. They were opposed to the idea that the political use of incentive plans should determine their usefulness. They also believed that without sufficient funds to pay teachers adequately, improvement based on limited funds awarded to selected teachers tends to decrease staff morale.

Impact of Merit Pay and Other Teacher Incentive Plans.

Regarding the positive potential limitations that such proposals may have for reshaping the teaching profession and improving the quality of our schools, the responses were varied among both the local and state administrators. The results indicate: (1) Without some radical restructuring, schools are certain to get worse and therefore doing something is better than doing nothing. (2) The catchword of the past decade has been "accountability." Plans must be formulated to improve the profession. Evidence of such improvement should be publicized and supported.

The positive potentials of merit pay and other teacher incentive plans were thought to include: (1) Keeping master teachers in the classroom by recognizing them and paying them more; (2) providing incentives for continuing to do a good job or to improve; (3) possibly influencing weak teachers to leave the profession (those marginal cases not weak enough to justify formal non-renewal); (4) attracting and retaining those high quality people who want to teach but who also want a profession with rewards for competence; (5) emphasizing quality and rewarding it; and (6) motivating staff members.

The limitations of such plans were thought to be: (1) Slightly increased costs of true merit plans; (2) lack of agreement on who is meritorious; (3) limitations due to the ability of evaluators, for whom training programs would have to be established; (4) lack of time for administrators to make an adequate number of classroom observations; and (5) limitations by the amount of local funds available.

Deborah Inman

Summary

The present-day political situation has generated renewed interest in merit pay and other teacher incentive plans. The negative attitude towards the public schools resulting in this era of accountability and testing has sparked various alternatives to teacher incentive plans. The actual decisions made by the major actors in education at both the local and state levels regarding such plans are impacted by many influential groups. The political strength of each of these influencing forces plays a significant role in the implementation efforts for teacher incentive plans.

These plans may be viewed from five perspectives as illustrated by the Concentric Model: (1) local/state union leadership, (2) national union leadership, (3) teacher constituency, (4) student interest, and (5) public interest. Politics is at the core of each of these perspectives. This was particularly evident in the review of the local and state teacher incentive plans. The local/state union leadership responded to these programs based on how they would affect their job and their personal prestige and power. The response of the national union leadership was determined by how the plan might affect the organization. This was particularly evident in the case of the President of the AFT, who played an instrumental role in the effort to gain further adherence to the Tennessee program. The response to local and state plans by the teacher constituency was again based on how they as teachers would retain their jobs and how the union leadership would retain its authority. Naturally, the concern regarding the quality of education being provided to the students, as well as the dissatisfaction of the public with expenditure of their tax dollars for inadequate teachers, applied political pressures that resulted in various types of teacher incentive plans.

Overall, the findings of the survey support the review of the local and state plans, suggesting that, while the implementation of merit pay and other teacher incentive plans may be difficult at best, they are not insurmountable. It is evident that we must attract and retain a quality staff or educational excellence will become an impossibility. Teacher incentive plans have potential to attract bright individuals and to help retain those who would likely leave the profession to seek more lucrative salaries in the business world. It is also quite likely that the politics of the times will continue to set the direction of teacher incentive plans at least as long as the competition to excell in improvng education prevails among young and aggressive governors.

Notes

1. Much of the following information regarding Bryan Independent School District; Lebanon Public Schools; Penn Manor School District; and Seiling, Oklahoma, Public Schools was obtained from *Issues in Teacher Incentive Plans* by Harry Hatry and John Greiner (Urban Institute Press, 1984).
2. Florida in 1984, enacted, additionally, a merit school plan wherein teachers can qualify for extra pay if their schools are meritorious.

References

Bossone, Richard, and Irwin Polishook (eds) *School Reform and Related Issues* (Proceedings: Fifth Conference of The University Urban Schools National Task Force, Graduate School and University Center of the City University of New York, 1983), pp. 42-45.

Hatry, Harry, and John Greiner, *Issues in Teacher Incentive Plans*, (Urban Institute Press, Washington, D.C., 1984).

Lasswell, Harold, *Politics: Who Gets What, When and How?* (New York: McGraw-Hill Book Company, 1936).

"Merit Pay Task Force Report of the 98th Congress," Report No. 98, 1983, pp. 4-5.

Mosher, Edith K., Ann Hastings and Jennings L. Wagoner, Jr., *Pursuing Equal Educational Opportunity: School Politics and the New Activists* (New York: ERIC Clearinghouse on Urban Education, 1979), p. 1.

Parish, John, "Excellence In Education: Tennessee's 'Master' Plan," *Phi Delta Kappan*, (June 1983) pp. 722-726.

The Rhetoric and Reality of Merit Pay: Why Are They Different?

Richard J. Murnane*

I. INTRODUCTION

With considerable reluctance I agreed to write a paper explaining the economics of merit pay. It may be useful in understanding why the concept of merit pay poses a thorny set of issues to explore the reasons for my reluctance.

Many introductory economics texts make extensive use of examples labelled "The economics of . . . " to motivate interest in economic theory. These examples work best when the application of relatively simple principles provides significant insight into messy policy problems. The economics of the farm problem and the economics of rent control provide two such examples. Although a detailed analysis of either of these policy problems reveals that the issues are more complicated than the textbook example implies, it is nonetheless true that application of relatively simple economic principles aids in predicting the consequences of particular policies. The reason this is the case is that it is possible to define relatively clearly the incentives provided by the policies and to predict how economic agents (producers and consumers) respond to these incentives. In my view the economics of merit pay is not a good candidate for a textbook example because it is not easy to identify the incentives that merit pay really provides *or* to predict how economic agents (teachers, administrators) will respond to these incentives. Let me explain.

In examining pay for teachers the relevant section of the introductory economics text deals with compensation for workers. The principle outlined in most texts is that workers in competitive industries are paid their marginal products — that is, what their employment adds to the value of the output of the firm. The logic underlying this principle is that firms

* The research on which this paper is based was supported by the Institute for Finance and Governance, School of Education, Stanford University. I would like to thank David Cohen, Patrick Murnane and Edward Pauly for helpful comments on earlier drafts.

paying workers more than their marginal products will be forced out of business. The reason is that these firms will be forced to charge higher prices than their competitors, and consumers will choose to buy the products of the firms with lower prices. Firms that pay workers less than their marginal products will not be able to keep a stable work force. The reason is that workers will leave to take jobs at firms that are willing to pay marginal products.

The marginal product principle is relevant to discussions of employment contracts for teachers in that it focuses attention on the *behavioral responses* of economics agents. It is the actions of consumers, workers, and firms that lead to the conclusion that firms in competitive industries pay workers their marginal products. Similarly, it is the behavioral responses of teachers, and administrators — and perhaps students and taxpayers as well — that determine the relative efficiency of alternative types of employment contracts for teachers.

But can we predict the behavioral responses to alternative types of contracts? Implicit in the rhetoric supporting merit pay for teachers is the presumption that we can. Take for example, President Reagan's words:

> We spend more money per child for education than any other country in the world — we just aren't getting out money's worth. . . . Teachers should be paid and promoted on the basis of their merit . . . Hard-earned tax dollars should encourage the best. They have no business rewarding incompetence and mediocrity. (*Washington Post*, May 22, 1983, as quoted in Bacharach et al., 1984).

These words seem to suggest that merit pay for teachers will elicit behavioral responses that will result in the country getting more of its money's worth from public education. The logic might be that since the textbooks claim that firms in competitive industries pay workers differentially according to their contribution to output, public schools would operate more efficiently if they would do the same.

Let us for a moment accept this logic and decide to implement a system in which teachers would be paid their "marginal products." This decision immediately raises the questions: (1) How is marginal product to be assessed? (2) Who is to do the assessing? When we return to the introductory economics text in search of answers to these questions, we find no help. The typical treatment of employee compensation levels is abstract, devoid of institutional content, and unconcerned with issues of measurement. Why are these issues not discussed? Is it because they are not of primary importance? If so, then perhaps we can proceed in designing merit pay plans by using the same methods to measure teachers' contributions that have been used in the past — for after all, merit pay is a very old idea. Turning to the history of merit pay plans in the U.S. over the last seventy years reveals a disturbing pattern, however: merit pay has not lasted very long in most districts in which it has been tried. Moreover, the geographic and temporal distribution of the evidence indicates that the brevity of most merit pay life histories cannot be explained by the power of teachers' unions.

These histories pose a puzzle. If merit pay is an efficient type of employment contract for public school teachers, why have merit pay plans in most districts died after a few years? The introductory economics texts offer no solution to this puzzle. This is the source of my reluctance to write a paper on the economics of merit pay. My task would have been much easier if I had been asked to explain the economics of the farm problem, for this is an issue where the insights from introductory economic theory are consistent with the historical trends.

II. Insights from the Literature on Efficient Employment Contracts

A. Definitions

Fortunately, there is an economics literature — albeit one that has had little impact to date on the teaching of introductory economics — that is helpful in thinking about merit pay for teachers. This literature is a part of a growing body of work dealing with organizational forms. The value of this literature stems from its explicit consideration of factors that influence the efficiency of alternative types of employment contracts. One factor is the cost involved in determining the marginal products of individual workers. A second factor is the potential for workers who are imperfectly monitored to engage in "opportunistic behavior" — that is, activities that are personally rewarding but dysfunctional for the employing organization.

From the outset it is important to recognize that this literature does not provide an answer to the question: What is the optimal type of contract for teachers? In fact, I hope that after reading this essay, the reader will agree that, given the vast variety of working conditions among the 15,000 school districts in the U.S., this is a silly question. What this literature does provide is an analytical framework and a set of terms that are helpful in understanding why merit pay plans have typically not lasted in U.S. school districts, and why particular exceptional plans do survive.

B. Three Types of Contracts

The insights from the economics literature on employment contracts can perhaps be best summarized by describing conditions under which three polar types of contracts are efficient.

Consider, first, employment contracts in which the compensation of the individual worker is based on a measure of the worker's output. The simplest of such contracts is the piece-rate contract. Such a contract is efficient — that is, it promotes the productivity of the employing organization — if the contribution of the individual worker to the firm can be measured accurately at relatively low cost. Commercial laundries' contracts with workers who iron shirts provide an example (cf. Alchian and

Demsetz, 1972). A single worker does the ironing of any given shirt, so the problem of joint products is not present. Counting the number of shirts ironed is not expensive, and the quality is controlled by consumer complaints. Output (number of shirts ironed) provides a good measure of the worker's marginal product because there are no significant factors other than the worker's effort and skill that affect output. Consequently, the worker can be quite sure that greater effort will result in higher measured output. Even the problem of multiple outputs (ironing dresses as well as shirts) can be dealt with by adjusting the piece rates so that workers are indifferent among alternative tasks.

Thus, the piece-rate contract is an efficient way to compensate workers ironing clothes because, with relatively low monitoring cost, workers are provided with incentives to behave in a manner that promotes the goals of the employer — that is, to iron clothes as rapidly as possible, subject to a minimum quality constraint. In effect, the clothes ironing example fits quite well the textbook example of workers paid their marginal products.

A second type of employment contract specifies that compensation depends on supervisors' assessments of observed actions of individual workers. This type of contract is common in situations in which employees work in groups and the marginal product of individual workers cannot be determined directly, but their contribution to output can be relatively accurately assessed by their effort level and by the extent to which they adhere to actions known to be related to productivity. An example would be workers employed to unload a truck (Alchian and Demsetz, 1972). Since several laborers work as a team unloading a truck, the output of an individual worker cannot be measured at low cost. However, since the actions required to empty the truck are well understood and easily observable, the performance of individual workers can be assessed by observing their actions. These assessments can then be used to determine compensation levels.

The requirements for this type of contract to be efficient are two. First, the relationship between worker actions and desired output must be clear-cut and agreed upon by supervisors and worker. This is necessary for workers to face the proper incentives — namely, that actions such as working rapidly will be rewarded and actions such as taking a nap will be penalized. The second condition is that the cost of monitoring must be low relative to the productivity gains associated with using this type of contract instead of a contract that involves less monitoring of worker actions.

A third type of employment contract specifies that compensation be determined by internal labor market rules. While the details of these rules vary widely, a common element is that workers doing the same job with the same amount of experience are paid the same wage. This type of contract is efficient in work situations characterized by the following two conditions: (1) As a result of on-the-job experience, individual workers acquire specialized knowledge, the use of which has a significant impact on the performance of the firm. (2) It is very costly for supervisors to assess accurately the performance of individual workers, including their use of the specialized knowledge. In industries in which the nature of the work is characterized by these conditions, workers have the potential to engage in opportunistic behavior that enhances supervisors' estimates of their productivity, but does not contribute to the firms' productivity. In these situations, it is important to minimize the incentives for workers to engage in such behavior. A contractual system in which compensation is attached to the job and to experience levels, and not to assessments of performance reduces incentives to engage in such opportunistic behavior.

An often cited example of a situation in which there is potential for opportunistic behavior is the operation of machine tools (Thurow, 1976). Experienced workers acquire knowledge of the idiosyncrasies of particular machine tools. Efficient operation indicates that new workers acquire this knowledge as rapidly as possible. However, since the information is not codified, it can be transmitted to new workers quickly only if experienced workers provide informal on-the-job training. If compensation and job security depend on supervisors' assessments of the performance of individual workers, experienced workers have the incentive to conceal such knowledge.

In summary, the first two types of employment contracts discussed above can be viewed as performance-based contracts. The difference between the two stems from the way the performance of individual workers is assessed. In the first case, worker performance is judged by assessed output; in the second, performance is judged by evaluations of individual worker's actions. The efficiency of each of these types of contracts depends on the characteristics of the production process in which workers are engaged. When the characteristics of a production process do not satisfy the conditions for either of the two types of performance-based contracts to be efficient, then employment contracts that tie compensation to job descriptions and seniority tend to be used. If performance-based employment contracts were used for workers engaged in these types of production processes, workers would have incentives to engage in behaviors dysfunctional to the firm, and the cost of monitoring workers to prevent such opportunistic behavior would be high — higher than the loss in productivity resulting from the lack of incentives for supervisor performance implicit in this type of contract.

Economists differ in their assessments of the extent to which each of the three types of contracts is used in private industry. However, in recent years an increasing body of evidence suggests that workers employed in a variety of private sector jobs experience compensation profiles over time that do not match productivity profiles (Wise, 1975; Medoff and Abraham, 1981). This new evidence calls into question the validity of the introductory textbook principle that workers in competitive industries are paid their marginal products and highlights the importance of investigating the factors that influence the efficiency of alternative employment contracts.

III. The Production Process in Education: An Explanation for the Failure of Most Merit Pay Plans

A. Definitions

Merit pay for teachers can be viewed as a performance-based employment contract in which performance is assessed either by measuring increases in students' skills over a school year (the output of a year of teaching) or by monitoring teacher actions. Either of these types of employment contracts would be efficient if it enabled school districts to attract and retain talented teachers and provide them with incentives to use their time and skills in a manner that promotes the learning of all students. This section discusses whether the production process in education meets the conditions required for either of the two types of performance based contracts to be efficient.

B. Ironing Clothes Is Not a Good Metaphor for Teaching

The weekly salary of a worker ironing clothes on a piece rate basis is calculated by multiplying the number of each type of clothing ironed times the piece rate for that type of clothing and then adding the products. This type of contract not only provides incentives for employees to work rapidly. It also provides incentives for workers to be selective concerning what types of clothing they iron. For example, if cotton shirts take longer to iron than polyester shirts do, but the piece rate for each type of shirt is the same, then workers will try to avoid ironing cotton shirts. Similarly, if it takes three times as long to iron a dress as a shirt, workers will avoid ironing dresses unless the rate is at least three times the rate for shirts.

In the case of clothes, the firm can adjust piece rates to make workers indifferent between the types of clothing they iron. These rate adjustments will then be reflected in the prices charged to customers. If, for example, customers are unwilling to pay, three times as much to have a dress ironed as a shirt, then the laundry won't get much dress business. In other words, the market provides feedback concerning the acceptable structure of piece rates.

Basing teacher's salaries on their output (student skill gains) requires a calculation similar to that done by the laundry manager. The skill gain of each teacher's students in each skill area must be measured. Then the gains must be aggregated to a single number, to permit comparison of each teacher's aggregate performance either with that of other teachers or against a predetermined standard. This aggregation implicitly places a value (analogous to a piece rate) on each child's gain in each skill area. As was the case with the ironing employees, the structure of the rates provides incentives for teachers to allocate time and effort in particular ways. For example, if the achievement gains of all children in reading are weighted equally (as is implicitly assumed in calculating the average gain of students in a class), then the teacher has incentives to minimize time spent working with children whose skill levels are slow to increase. Similarly, if student achievement gains in history are given less weight than gains in math, but take just as much of the teachers time to foster, the teacher has an incentive to minimize time spent teaching history.

As was the case with the laundry, the incentives for teachers to allocate their time to particular students or subjects can be altered by changing the "piece rates." But what are the appropriate rates? How much do we value the achievement gains of slow achievers relative to those of rapid learners? How much do we value gains in reading skills relative to gains in math skills, or relative to increases in children's artistic skills? These issues do surface obliquely in debates about the level of resources to be devoted to compensatory education, or talented and gifted programs. But because such issues are divisive, discussion of them tends to be avoided. Implicit in this avoidance is a mandate to public school teachers to help all children to develop to the fullest extent of their abilities. Such a mandate, however, is inconsistent with the incentives built into any contract that compensates teachers on the basis of their students' skill gains. Would teachers working under such a contract honor their mandate and neglect the incentives embedded in their employment contract, or respond to the incentives? We have almost no direct evidence on this question. However, it seems naive to assume that such a contract would induce teachers to work harder — which presumably is an important reason for introducing performance-based contracts — without also inducing them to pay attention to the opportunities to reallocate their teaching time. It may be the case that the conflict (between professional norms and compensation-maximizing time allocations) that such contracts introduce may reduce teachers' morale sufficiently to be judged as dysfunctional from the point of view of the school system. This would help to explain the short life histories of most merit pay plans, and their unpopularity even among talented teachers perceived to gain the most financially from such plans (Jackson, 1968).

A second difference between ironing clothes and teaching students concerns risk. Workers ironing clothes can be quite sure that greater effort will produce more ironed clothes and consequently greater compensation because there are no factors other than worker skill and effort level that significantly affect the number of clothes ironed. Teachers, on the other hand, cannot be sure that greater effort will produce measurable increases in student skill levels because so many factors, including the continually changing influences of peers and family, influence achievement. A consequence of this is that output-based performance contracts will provide teachers with strong incentives to work harder only if the salary premiums for student skill gains are very large, perhaps much larger than the merit pay performance bonuses used in most districts.

C. Unloading a Truck Is Not a Good Metaphor for Teaching

The compensation of workers employed to unload a truck depends on supervisors' assessments of their productivity, as judged by observing their actions on the job. The contract form is efficient because supervisors can monitor the actions of a large number of workers at relatively low cost *and* because there is widespread agreement among both supervisors and workers concerning which actions are productive. For example, everyone could agree that workers who routinely unload two cartons at a time are more productive than employees working at the same pace who unload one carton at a time. As a result, supervisors can give employees clear signals concerning what actions will be rewarded and employees can agree that these actions are in fact productive.

This type of employment contract creates incentives for workers to engage in behaviors that supervisors will view as productive. Thus, it is reasonable for employees to ask: Are there actions I can take that are easier than unloading two cartons at a time, but will be judged by supervisors to be just as productive? In the case of unloading a truck, the nature of the production process provides little potential for such opportunistic behavior.

The nature of the production process in teaching is quite different. As is the case with all jobs, some teachers are more effective than others in helping children to acquire cognitive skills. There also is evidence that supervisors' evaluations of teachers are positively related to other indicators of their performance such as students' test score gains, although the correlations are in the range of 0.3, not 1.0 (Murnane, 1984). One important respect in which teaching is different from unloading a truck is that supervisors' assessments of teachers are not based on behaviors that everyone would agree are clearly related to performance. In fact, the vast majority of the evidence suggests that teaching cannot be viewed as an activity in which there are clearly defined behaviors that consistently result in high performance. In other words, there is no analog to carrying two cartons on every trip.

A compelling reason why there are no blueprints for effective teaching is that the effectiveness of particular instructional techniques depends critically on the characteristics of the children in the class, on the skills and personality of the teachers, and on the nature of the interaction of students and teacher. The critical characteristics of students and teachers that influence the effectiveness of particular instructional techniques may be very subtle and, consequently, cannot be documented through even detailed research. Teachers find effective techniques through a process of trial and error and adaptation. In other words, effective teaching is characterized by a careful search process rather than by rote application of well-specified techniques.

If supervisors cannot base their evaluations of teachers' performance on the extent to which productive blueprints are followed, what do they base their evaluations on? Although the answer surely varies among supervisors, sources of information include parental comments, noise level in the classroom, and a variety of other relatively diffuse indicators.

Why does it matter that evaluators of teachers must judge performance on the basis of a variety of diffuse indicators rather than on the extent to which teacher actions conform to blueprints known to be productive in enhancing student learning? There are two reasons. First, recall that this type of employment contract creates incentives for workers to ask what actions they can take to enhance supervisors' assessments of their productivity. The nature of the teaching process creates numerous opportunities for teachers to engage in behaviors that are opportunistic in the sense that they enhance supervisors' assessments, but actually are dysfunctional when viewed against the public schools' goal of helping all children to learn to the extent of their ability. These opportunities are especially numerous for experienced teachers familiar with children's family backgrounds. Examples of such opportunistic behavior include: devoting disproportionate attention to children whose parents are known to be assertive in expressing their opinion concerning how their children are treated in school; neglecting children whose parents are unlikely to complain; avoiding sharing curricular materials and ideas with colleagues.

Would teachers working under this type of employment contract engage in such opportunistic behavior? We have little direct evidence. However, it is important to remember that one of the presumed advantages of this type of contract is that it provides employees with financial incentives to alter their behavior. Is it plausible to assume that teachers would respond by working harder, but not by taking advantage of less taxing opportunities to appear productive? It is possible that the short lives of most merit pay plans can be explained by the presence of opportunistic behavior. Another explanation is that the conflict between professional norms and the incentives provided by the contract lowered morale and reduced teacher performance to the point where this type of contract was declared dysfunctional.

A second reason that the lack of blueprints for good performance influences the efficiency of this type of contract concerns supervisors' responses to the question: What do I do to get a better performance rating? The supervisor of the truck unloaders can say: "Carry two boxes at a time," and the worker will acknowledge that his action is something he can do and will appreciate that it will in fact increase productivity. More often than not, supervisors of teachers can only respond in one of two problematic ways.

Supervisors can suggest that teachers take action to, for example, reduce the noise level in the classroom. Some teachers are not sure what actions will produce this result. Uncertainty may reduce the incentive for behavioral changes. Most experienced teachers do know how to reduce the noise level. However, they may feel that this can be done only be eliminating practices that they believe enhance learning, such as encouraging students to help each other. In this case the conflict between the supervisor's and the teacher's definitions of a good learning environment may reduce incentives for teachers to alter their behavior.

Another way that a supervisor can respond is to suggest that the teacher make neater lesson plans or engage in more community activities. The problem here is that these actions may not be related to the teacher's performance. If the teacher does respond to the suggestion, the evaluator faces a dilemma: whether to raise the performance rating, and hence the teacher's compensation, even though the teacher's performance may not have improved, or not to raise the rating, and hence eliminate the incentive for behavioral changes. Thus, the imprecise nature of the production process in teaching and the high cost of monitoring closely enough to prevent opportunistic behavior makes this type of employment contract inefficient for employing teachers.

D. The Default Option: Contracts that Base Compensation on the Job Description and Seniority

The nature of the production process in teaching makes both types of performance-based contracts inefficient. Thus, we are left with the third type of employment contract, which bases compensation on job description and seniority. Analysts have always been uncomfortable with this type of contract because its attractiveness does not stem from the incentives it provides for superior performance — in fact, the archetypical contract in this category provides no financial incentives for superior performance. Instead, its value comes from reducing the incentives for workers to engage in behaviors that are dysfunctional to the productivity of the employing organization. This negative defense frequently leads to the question: Can't we do better in providing positive incentives for workers? In fact, there is a large variety of contracts that fall into the general class of contracts with strong internal labor market components. Some of these do offer modest incentives for workers to respond in ways that enhance the productivity of the employing organization. In fact, some of these contracts even include language about merit pay. As we show in the next section, however, the types of merit pay plans that survive are quite different from the type of strong performance-based compensation plan implicit in President Reagan's proposal.

IV. Changes In Teachers' Contracts

Although the nature of the education process renders inefficient strong performance-based compensation schemes for teachers, two reasons make it worthwhile to consider the potential benefits of changes in teachers' contracts. First, as the quotation from President Reagan suggests, there is considerable political pressure at this time for changes that will increase the link between the perceived performance of teachers and their compensation. While some of this pressure may be political scapegoating, responding positively may be more productive in terms of protecting the quality of education provided to American children than simply resisting this pressure. Second, while much of the rhetoric suggests that there are only two alternative ways to compensate teachers (uniform salary scales that base compensation on seniority and degrees, and strong performance-based contracts akin to piece-rates), there is in fact a wide range of contractual practices used in the 15,000 school districts in the United States. For example, some districts pay teachers for unused sick days; some compensate teachers for taking courses; some pay teachers for running extracurricular activities. There even are a number of districts that for many years have used compensation systems that they call merit pay. David K. Cohen and I are studying how merit pay works in a number of these districts.

B. Our Research Strategy

Our research strategy has two parts. First, we are reviewing the vast literature on merit pay programs. Second, we have conducted case studies of five districts whose contracts with teachers include elements of pay for performance. Although these contracts vary enormously, for ease of exposition I will refer to all of them as merit pay. (All five districts responded to a recent national survey by indicating that they had merit pay.) All five of the districts have had some form of merit pay for at least five years; all five include compensation bonuses of at least $600 per year.

Each of our case studies included open-ended interviews with central office administrators, school principals, and teachers. The goals of these interviews were to learn how merit pay worked in each district, how practitioners regarded particular aspects of the plan under which they worked, and what experiences they reported as responses to the incentives provided by their plan.

V. Rhetoric and Reality

A. Incentives for Whom to Do What?

Implicit in the rhetoric advocating merit pay is the presumption that it will provide strong incentives for *teachers* to improve their *classroom performance*. The reality of merit pay, as my colleagues and I observed it in five districts, is considerably more complicated. There are incentives for teachers to change their behavior. Some teachers indicated that they did respond to the incentives; others stated that they did not. Many of the reported responses were unpredicted. Moreover, in many cases it was unclear to what extent the responses facilitated or hindered the goal of improving the education provided to children.

The rhetoric supporting merit pay makes little mention of incentives for *administrators*. Yet, our interviews suggested that merit pay creates at least as strong incentives (or pressures) for administrators to change their behavior as it does for teachers. Again, the responses to these pressures varied, and often it was not clear how the responses affected educational quality.

The rhetoric supporting merit pay does not consider behavioral responses by *taxpayers*. Yet our interviews suggested that many teachers and administrators felt that one of the most important benefits of merit pay was that it made taxpayers more willing to support educational expenditures.

These comments included:

> [Merit pay] does give the school board and the community the feeling that they've got some control over the staff; that there is an evaluation process here and the process can be used in a way which will reward the good and punish the wicked, so to speak.

From another administrator:

> It has meant a lot of money for a lot of teachers that would otherwise not have been provided, knowing the Board of Education.

From a teacher in a different school district:

> I would describe [merit pay] as an attempt on the part of the school board and administration to have some type of device to justify paying teachers extra money. The people out there who are paying taxes want to make sure that in the area of teacher pay, those who are doing the real work are the ones who get the rewards, above and beyond the standard.

Even on the issue of taxpayer attitudes, however, teachers were not in agreement. Many practitioners commented that they did not think most taxpayers were aware that their districts had merit pay.

B. The Problems are More than Details

The *American School Board Journal* (Rist, 1983) recently reported that a majority of public school teachers who responded to a survey indicated that they were in favor of merit pay. How can this be reconciled with the history of failure of most merit pay plans? Part of the answer may lie in the perception that the past problems resulted from improper design and the belief that artfully designed merit pay plans can be powerful levers promoting high quality education.

C. Common Characteristics of the Districts

To retain the proper perspective, it is important to remember that the five districts we examined are exceptions to the pattern of the many districts that have tried and discarded merit pay. As such, it is interesting to note that these five districts have certain common characteristics. While our research strategy does not permit us to conclude that these characteristics are necessary to the maintenance of merit pay, the comments of practitioners in these districts concerning these characteristics are informative.

First, all five have salary schedules (to which merit pay is added) that are above average for their geographical area. The importance of this is suggested by one teacher's comment: ". . . If you're a parent . . . and you have a number of children, some of your children are going to be taught by teachers that are not on the top of the merit scale. So I think for these situations you want a qualified, well-paid teacher."

Second, the teachers in all five districts agreed, in general, that the conditions under which they worked were good. While some grumbled about particular aspects of their jobs, the general sense in all of the districts was that the community valued teachers and was willing to support them. An indication of the level of support is suggested by one administrator's summary of the resources supporting classroom teachers in a middle school attended by 900 students: two full time special education teachers, three and one half remedial reading teachers; one full time Title I math teacher.

Third, all of the districts had a history of basically amicable working relationships between teachers and building administrators. As one teacher characterized the relations: "I think that as a staff we take a very active part in working with administrators. We have what we call administrative training. As soon as they get too pompous, we let them know. . . . If our administrators were . . . more aloof from us than they are, I don't think the teachers would accept a system like this."

In summary, none of the districts represented a case in which merit pay was introduced to solve a problem of poor teacher performance or high teacher turnover. Instead, in these five districts merit pay was introduced in settings in which teachers felt supported and administrators felt that the teaching staff, as a group, was of exceptional quality.

D. Common Characteristics of Merit Pay Plans that Last

Our cases studies and our reading of the literature on merit pay suggest that programs that last have certain common characteristics. First, the plans are voluntary: no teacher is compelled to participate in the merit pay plan; any teacher is free to refuse the extra work that applying for merit pay entails, and to receive a salary as specified by the appropriate step on the uniform salary scale. Second, merit pay was not thrust upon resistant teachers; teacher representatives were actively involved in the design of the plan. Third, the plans evolved over time, both in the way regulations were interpreted, and in the design of the regulations. These three characteristics of plans that have endured make the plans quite different from the vision of merit pay implicit in much of the rhetoric advocating its use.

VI. Design Options and Practitioner Responses

A. Design Issues

While there are some common elements among programs that last, even more striking is the diversity among these programs. This diversity is reflected in the different ways districts resolved a number of issues that must be addressed in the design of an operational merit pay plan. These design issues include: (1) To what extent do activities outside the classroom play a role in determining a teacher's eligibility for merit pay? (2) To what extent is the teacher responsible for documenting that he or she has satisfied the criteria for receiving merit pay? (3) To what extent does the school principal's evaluation of a teacher's performance influence whether a

---

teacher receives merit pay?

The next sections explore arguments related to each of these design issues from the perspective of the behavioral responses that each option evokes. It is important to recall that the presumed benefits of performance-based contracts are that they elicit responses that promote the employing organization's productivity. The dangers lie in the possible incentives for opportunistic behavior. Each section describes potential benefits and dangers related to each design option, and then reports comments of teachers and administrators concerning the particular design option.

B. Activities Outside the Classroom

The role of outside-the-classroom activities in determining eligibility for merit pay varied significantly among the five districts. Moreover, the range of relevant activities also varied, including in one or more districts: committee work at the school and school district level, community service activities, professional advancement (as demonstrated, for example, by taking courses), and leadership in the profession (as exhibited, for example, by publishing articles in education journals).

One advantage of giving significant weight to outside activities is that teachers who want to satisfy the criteria for merit know what is required and the relevant behaviors are things that all teachers can do. Such clear cut incentives are important in motivating behavioral responses. It is interesting that heavy weight attached to outside activities in a merit pay plan creates incentives that are very similar to those present in districts that do not describe their contracts as including merit pay but which pay teachers for engaging in a range of outside activities as prescribed by a uniform contract. In effect, such contract clauses, whether they are called merit pay or not, provide extra pay for extra work. This fact was evident to a teacher in one of our merit pay districts who commented on the plan in her district: "This isn't merit pay. This is called how do we get someone to do the yearbook."

A critical question involved in the decision about the weight to be given outside activities is the extent to which they contribute to the quality of classroom teaching and student learning. This is a difficult question because the answer implicitly assumes knowledge about how the teacher would spend his or her time if not pursuing these outside activities. If the time would be spent preparing lesson plans, one might argue that pursuit of many of the outside activities detracts from teaching quality. This was the perception of one teacher who commented: "I wouldn't want my child in the class of a [top rated] teacher given the requirements for attaining that status." On the other hand, if the time would be spent on a second job totally unrelated to teaching such as house painting, then one might argue that a reallocation of time from house painting to many of the rewarded outside activities would improve a teacher's effectiveness in the classroom.

One final issue concerns the extent to which merit pay for pursuit of outside-the-classroom activities provides stronger incentives for some teachers than for others. One principal commented that many teachers found it difficult to demonstrate community leadership in their school district because they could not afford to live in the district. Another commented that one of his best teachers lived 70 miles away and consequently played no role in the district. Should these circumstances disqualify a teacher from the top merit categories?

C. Teacher Responsible for Documenting Fulfillment of Merit Pay Criteria

One advantage of making the teacher responsible for documenting that he or she has fulfilled the merit pay criteria is that it may make the teacher feel he or she is in control of the process. If the teacher wants to do the work of documenting, he or she can have the additional compensation that merit pay entails. As one teacher commented: "How can anyone really gripe about it when any one of us could do it if we so desired?"

The questions about the wisdom of requiring heavy documentation (or producing "evidence," as it is called in some districts) are similar to those concerning the role of outside activities. First, does the process of documenting promote good teaching? The reactions of teachers included:

I felt I learned a lot from it. There were several changes that I made from doing it; you know I'm not even sure the money was the biggest benefit. It definitely picked my ego up getting it . . . and I think the administration at my school maybe appreciated me more . . . we're over here and we teach different things and I think . . . they didn't really realize all the things that we do.

. . . it was difficult to get together all the substantiation of your work and put it on paper, put it in a folder and hand it in. But the thing which I found positive was the fact that when you sat down with administrators . . . I wish I had done this long ago because I have heard some of the best things I have ever heard about me from the beginning of time, and I wish I had known these things all along.

It helped me evaluate myself. It is an excellent self-evaluation tool, I believe . . . I saw where I was weak in some areas . . . and I saw some areas where I had maybe given too much time. I think it helped me realize where I was in the profession.

Other comments from teachers, in a different vein, included:

When I finished this last time, I had a volume no less than three inches thick of evidences, arguments, materials. . . . I found having to prepare all those areas that I didn't see as germane to classroom instruction as unbelievably tedious and time-consuming and I really question . . . the value of all that.

People started going around taking pictures, and making bulletin boards that they had never done before. It was just so obvious, and handing in books, I mean books, 150 to 200 pages of all the wonderful things they did in the classroom and in my mind . . . any dope could go to the library and write up a bunch of good lesson plans; that didn't take much . . . [It's] the baloney factor.

> It's not just a couple of afternoons of sitting down, it's a whole year. It's right up there with doing a doctorate. A teacher here last year got it [merit pay] but she put together a notebook, a binder notebook, that thick [indicating several inches with her hands] full of documentation from parents and photographs of things she had done. I felt like there was more attention spent in the classroom on [documentation for merit pay] than on the kids. In that respect I think it's a terrible program because they do make you pat yourself on the back to such an extent that you are not being the excellent teacher that you're trying to prove yourself to be. . . . You're supposed to be a great teacher but you don't have time to teach because you have to get all your stuff together and if you have any kind of family life at home . . . you know there's enough extra hours in teaching without adding. This teacher last year, she spent ungodly amounts of time on it.

And the reactions of one principal:

> . . . the focus is on gathering the evidence and not really evaluating how good the evidence was. It just seemed to be an activity that led to satisfying the Superintendent's office and the School Board but not satisfying the real reason why we are here, that is, to improve the teaching act. I am not really sure that it did a lot more than pile on a whole lot of work and take our attention away from other things.

A second issue concerning the documentation requirements is whether the practice favors teachers with certain attributes (good writing skills) and certain demographic characteristics (few family responsibilities) and whether this pattern promotes the school district's productivity. The differential impact on teachers is suggested by remarks made in districts with a documentation requirement.

One principal remarked:

> A problem I see in working with this for six years is that the people that can write and organize, your English and Social Studies teachers, the people with a writing background who have done a dissertation, have an advantage over those that do not write. A number of . . . people here . . . that were not successful were people in science and math — their brevity [was a problem].

A teacher commented:

> One year I did try and I started it out and it was just too much paperwork. They expect just tons and tons of things. . . . I have a family of my own and it's just too cumbersome for me to try to get that into it. I feel the judge should be the principal.

Richard J. Murnane

D. The Role of the School Principal's Evaluation

One advantage of the school principal's playing a central role in determining teachers' merit ratings is that it facilitates giving great weight to teachers' classroom performances, something that many teachers who disliked an emphasis on outside activities advocated. A second advantage is that it may reduce the burden on teachers to document their accomplishments and consequently make merit pay more acceptable to teachers who resent spending time documenting or are reluctant to "blow their own horn" — a term used by many teachers in describing the documentation requirement. A third advantage to principals' evaluations coupled with post-evaluation conferences is that it creates a forum in which principals may give the positive feedback that excellent teachers deserve, but often do not get. As one teacher described the post-evaluation conference:

I heard things that I had never heard before . . . from administrators, who are busy I suppose, and do not have time to say these kinds of things either when they see it happen, or when they hear about it they just don't say anything; they go their own way and so do teachers. So when a meeting of the minds finally comes, they say this is great; this is terrific. So you say well I did something right back a year and a half ago.

Of course, not all post-evaluation conferences work that way. As one teacher, who received the maximum merit pay bonus commented:

Then you have a post observation conference in which he shows you what he wrote up and then you have a chance to say whether you like it or you don't like it. You sign it; he signs it, and that drops into your file. We collect these over the years. I don't know for what reason.

One problem with using principals' evaluations to determine merit pay qualification is that it transforms the principal's role from coach to referee. Several administrators stated that they liked to use the evaluation to encourage teachers, to compliment them on what they do well, and perhaps gently, but only gently, to suggest areas for improvement. Many principals stated that these gentle suggestions worked best in the context of a positive overall evaluation. Implicit in their emphasis on "gentleness" appeared to be the perception that angry or hurt teachers could engage in opportunistic behavior.

The use of evaluations to determine merit pay eligibility changes the rating from a tool to encourage better teaching to a status report concerning how good the teaching has been. Many principals resist that change. The result is grade inflation. As one principal explained:

I . . . know that if I did not give everybody a high rating they feel that they're a failure; that I do not appreciate their work. Then I've got an employee who forever is angry until I give that employee the top rating.

In the words of another administrator:

> If I give you an honest evaluation . . . that is lower, substantially lower than what you expected, that is going to destroy you. Now when you walk out of this office you are going to be angry with me, with the system, with the kids, with the institution. You are going to walk back to the class and say well screw these people . . . I've given my time, and so forth, and they don't appreciate me, they don't appreciate what I am doing . . . This, in fact, a colleague of mine told me happened to him with a very good teacher. When the teacher who expected to be put in the top category was put in the second category, there was, he felt, a palpable change in her behavior. She was still a good teacher, but she wasn't as eager, . . . as enthusiastic as she was before. So you've got that problem. If you want to keep that person alive, you can't give too low a rating.

Different principals respond in different degrees to the grade inflation pressure. This creates yet another problem, different grading standards across schools. One district dealt with this problem by making the monetary differences between the top merit ratings relatively small and implicitly allowing principals to give all of their good teachers one of the top ratings. The net effect of this procedure is to make merit pay something quite close to an across the board salary increase for all experienced teachers in the district. (This response may not be perverse since, along with the salary increases, came extensive classroom observation by, and interaction with, the principal — which may be important stimuli to productivity.)

Another strategy for dealing with the problem of different standards across evaluators is to force evaluators to use a detailed instrument, with the overall merit pay rating being the sum of the ratings of the individual items. In fact, much discussion about merit pay concerns the design of the evaluation instrument. One difficulty this practice creates is that administrators feel they know who their best teachers are, but they cannot defend their judgments by pointing to clearly defined actions that the best teachers undertake and other teachers do not. As one administrator put it:

> It is like a chimera; now you see it, you think you can grab it, but it's an illusion of some kind. I know who the good teachers are. They're so and so, so and so, and so and so. Why are they good teachers? Well, I don't know; they are just good teachers; but I know who they are . . .

One way in which administrators reacted to the imprecise linkage between particular teaching practices and overall teaching effectiveness — imprecision that is well documented in the research literature on teaching — is to make the decision about where a teacher belongs on the merit pay scale before using the instrument to evaluate the teacher's performance. In the words of one administrator:

What happens more often than not with this process as I have participated in it and observed it is that, teacher A comes up for merit evaluation. You're going to be the evaluator, so . . . inside your mind, a voice says, Teacher A belongs in category two, or category three. This is before the process even starts, mind you. And then you go through the process and Wow, the numbers come out with teacher A in category two or category three. . . . There is that tendency to make the judgment at the outset as a holistic judgment.

Several teachers also commented that they felt that the evaluation instrument was used more to justify the merit pay rating than to determine it. As one teacher recounted:

One classic case in point was the person who had taken eighteen hours of graduate courses over the course of two years and that item happened to be down towards the end of the rating system — professional growth. And I have forgotten whether the person was graded a 2 or a 3 on professional growth. And when questioned as to why with that amount of course work in that period of time, how you would justify a 2 or 3, the person was told that is what was expected of them and what else did they do? Another point would have put them into another category and therefore the point was not going to be given.

These comments raise questions about the extent to which better instrument design can solve the problem of different grading practices.

Another solution to the problem of differential grading standards that several principals mentioned is having several principals do each evaluation. Often these same principals would go on to comment on how difficult they found it to complete the evaluations of teachers in their own schools, and how they resisted spending time out of their buildings for any reason. These comments point to the high cost of monitoring — to use the expression from the efficient contracts literature.

B. The Problems are More than Details

The *American School Board Journal* (Rist, 1983) recently reported that a majority of public school teachers who responded to a survey indicated that they were in favor of merit pay. How can this be reconciled with the history of failure of most merit pay plans? Part of the answer may lie in the perception that the past problems resulted from improper design and the belief that artfully designed merit pay plans can be powerful levers promoting high quality education.

One of the striking features of many of our interviews is that the practitioners in districts with ongoing merit pay plans shared many of these perceptions. Comments like, "Merit pay is a good idea, but not the way we do it" were common. When asked what they would do differently, practitioners often had suggestions for changes. However, listing these changes would spark respondents' memories of experiences that suggested why these changes would be problematic. For example, one administrator disliked the practice under which teachers receiving merit pay could wave evaluations after six years and continue to receive extra compensation. Later in the interview he recounted a distressing experience stemming from lowering a teacher's rating — an experience that led him to decide never to lower a teacher's rating again. Another principal suggested that principals work as a group in evaluating teachers. Later in the interview he complained about the difficulty he had each year in finding time to complete the evaluations of teachers in his building.

It seems that many Americans find it difficult to challenge the principle that under a truly efficient employment contract, every teacher would be paid what he or she is worth — just as most introductory economics texts assert that such a phenomenon takes place in competitive industries. The lesson of this paper is that this idea, particularly when embodied in rhetoric advocating merit pay, is itself dysfunctional because it diverts attention from the significance of the educational process.

There is a great variety in the contracts under which school districts compensate teachers. There also is potential for many districts to make changes in their employment contracts that will modestly enhance educational quality. But discussions of changes in teachers' contracts should be made in light of the knowledge that the education process is different from ironing shirts or unloading trucks and these differences matter in designing employment contracts for teachers.

REFERENCES

Alchian, A., and H. Demsetz. "Production, Information Costs, and Economic Organization." *American Economic Review* 62 (1972): 777-95.

Bacharach, S.B., D.B. Lipsky, and J.B. Shedd. *Paying for Better Teaching*: Merit Pay and its *Alternatives*. Ithaca, NY: Organization Analysis and Practice, Inc., 1984.

Jackson, P.W. *Life in Classrooms*. New York: Holt, Rinehart & Winston, 1968.

Medoff, J.L. and K.G. Abraham. "Are Those Paid More Really More Productive?" *Journal of Human Resources* 16 (1981): 186-216.

Murnane, Richard J. "Selection and Survival in the Teacher Labor Market," *Review of Economics and Statistics* forthcoming, 1984.

Rist, M.C. "Our Nationwide poll: Most teachers endorse the merit pay concept." *The American School Board Journal*, September 1983: 23-27.

Thurow, L. *Generating Inequality*: Mechanisms of Distribution in the U.S. Economy. New York: Basic Books, 1976.

Wise, D.A. "Academic Achievement and Job Performance." *American Economic Review* 65 (June 1975): 350-66.

Does Virtue Merit Pay? Reflections on the Better-Teachers-Deserve-More-Money Argument

Philip W. Jackson

> *There are callings so noble that one cannot follow them for money without proving oneself unworthy of following them. Such is that of the man of war; such is that of the teacher.*
>
> —Jean Jacques Rousseau, *Emile*

The argument on behalf of merit pay for teachers entails three major premises. The first claims that some teachers are better than others, the second insists that those who are better can be identified with reasonable accuracy, and the third concludes that those so identified should receive a higher salary than do their teaching colleagues who fail to make the grade. *Superior* teachers, who *can* be identified, *should* receive more pay. That, in a nutshell, is the argument.

There is a lot more to it than that, of course, especially when it comes to putting the idea to work. Before any such plan can be made a reality many additional questions must be answered, such as how great the pay differential should be between average and superior teachers, how resistance to the plan might be overcome, how to safeguard the system against abuses, and so forth. Nonetheless, the three premises that have been named comprise the skeleton, so to speak, of all such proposals. Should any one of them be logically indefensible or empirically unworkable or morally reprehensible the argument for merit pay would collapse at the start. Indeed, if these three rudimentary notions suffer any defects or weaknesses whatsoever the force of the overall argument will be correspondingly diminished.

Now, as we know, the notion of merit pay for teachers, though intuitively appealing to all who favor the rewarding of merit in general, is actually quite controversial. In fact, judging from all that has been written about it lately in both the popular press and elsewhere, the idea seems to have fully as many detractors as supporters. To understand why this is so we need but examine a little more closely the bare bones of the argument, those being the trio of premises already identified. What we find when we do is not that any one of them is absolutely untenable on logical, empirical, or moral grounds.

Instead, we discover complexities of a kind conducive to argument and debate. In the remarks to follow I shall discuss some of the more troublesome of those complexities. Following that, I shall comment, albeit briefly, on the entire range of rewards associated with teaching, of which salary is but one. The latter observation, incidentally, seems to be overlooked by some of the most enthusiastic proponents of merit pay plans, who characteristically speak as though money were the only reason for doing anything. Nor is it attended to sufficiently by many who oppose those plans. They too, it seems to me, fail to consider as fully as they might the total riches that could and should be the prize of a career in teaching.

My own position with respect to the matters about to be discussed might be described as that of a disinterested bystander. Whether merit pay becomes an accepted practice nationwide or remains an isolated regional or local phenomenon as in the past matters little to me. I have no axe to grind one way or the other.

But the advantage of avowed neutrality can sometimes backfire, as no less keen a critic than the famed William James once pointed out. He warned that "if you want an absolute duffer in an investigation, you must, after all, take the man who has no interest whatever in its results: he is the warranted incapable, the positive fool" (found in *The Will To Believe and Other Essays in Popular Philosophy*, 1912). James" warning forces from me a confession. I admit at the start to a bias in the direction of believing that the worth of the central idea, the merit of merit pay, one might say, is being oversold these days in some quarters by those who see the practice as some sort of panacea for the several ailments said to be plaguing today's public schools. I wish I could share the optimism of those who hold such a belief, but I cannot, for reasons soon to become evident. Also, though lacking a personal stake in the success or failure of merit pay proposals, I do care very much about the status of teachers and of teaching in our society. I would like to see both improve. That too, I trust, will soon become evident.

Before turning to the main body of my remarks a couple of comments about underlying assumptions are in order. Most discussions of merit pay usually concentrate on how the idea might be applied to the salaries of public school teachers, both elementary and secondary. That will be my focus as well. There is obviously nothing to prevent the same arguments and the same procedures from being applied, *mutatis mutandis*, to teachers other than those who work in our public schools. However, the latter comprise the largest and most readily identifiable category of teachers in the land. Moreover, it is they and the services they provide that everyone seems to be worried about these days. Consequently, whenever reference is made to teachers and teaching in the remarks to follow it is intended to refer chiefly if not exclusively to the people and the practices employed in our public schools.

My use of the term "merit pay" also requires a few words of explanation. The nub of the idea, as the term itself implies, requires basing a portion of a teacher's salary on merit alone. Moreover, it further requires that not all teachers within the same school or system be treated alike in this regard.

Thus, for a merit pay system to be accurately titled, it must eventuate in the judgment that not all teachers are of equal merit.

These two requirements clearly allow for other determinants of salary to operate at the same time, as indeed they typically do, whether or not criteria of merit are employed. Years of service and academic qualifications are standard determinants of teachers' salaries throughout the nation. And so they likely will continue to be, even should merit plans become more popular than they are today. But this minor complication must not be allowed to obscure the fact that the contribution of merit, *per se*, must be distinguishable in a genuine merit pay plan.

All other things considered, the latter must not be confused with arrangements whereby salary increments are attached to the assignment of additional administrative and supervisory responsibilities above and beyond the teacher's regular classroom duties. Thus, a plan to identify superior teachers and then elevate them to a higher level of occupational status — such as making them "instructional leaders" at a particular grade level, let's say, while raising their salaries in the process — is not a pure form of merit pay as I shall be using the term. Such plans may make use of the idea of pedagogical merit in determining promotion to an altered assignment, but the fact that the latter carries with it new and additional duties and responsibilities is what makes it something other than a pure form of merit pay. The latter might be called "merit promotion" plans or something like that but I shall not worry about what to call them for they are of no concern to me at present.

In sum, the focus throughout the remainder of this essay is exclusively the better-pay-for-better-teachers argument. More money for superior teaching with no strings attached. That's merit pay as the term will be used here.

I

The first of the three premises to be inspected, the one claiming that some teachers are better than others is so obviously true that it hardly bears further comment. Teaching is a kind of performance, a form of human action, and what is true of all performances, as we all well know, is that they can be executed with greater or lesser skill and artistry. Thus, it makes just as much sense to talk about good teachers and poor teachers, better ones and worse ones, as it does to speak of good and poor tennis players or lawyers or auto mechanics or any other category of skilled performer.

Furthermore, the personal experiences of most of us merely confirm what logic and common sense assert. We've all had some teachers whom we have judged to be better or worse than others and, while acknowledging that we could possibly have been mistaken now and again about such matters, it would take an awful lot to convince most of us that we have been consistently wrong.

So all three sources that we usually turn to when in doubt — reason, commonsense, experience — yield the same conclusion: some teachers are definitely better than others. Few propositions seem truer than that. What more is there to say?

Quite a bit, it turns out, at least there is if we want to move beyond the obvious. For as soon as we take a step in the direction of trying to find out what good teaching entails at a conceptual level, leaving aside for the time being the tricky business of identifying live teachers who match what we believe good teachers to be like, we quickly become entangled in a web of complexity from which there seems no escape.

Of course there are good and poor teachers, better and worse ones, everyone agrees on that. What they fail to agree upon, however, is what is meant by "good" or "poor," "better" or "worse," as those terms apply to teaching.

How significant is this disagreement? What does it portend for the prospect of developing merit pay proposals capable of winning wide support within both the teaching profession and the public at large? Turning to what has been written on the subject, we discover two schools of thought — one optimistic, the other pessimistic.

The optimistic point of view, held by most advocates of merit pay, acknowledges that not everyone might agree on a conceptual definition of good teaching. However, it plays down the significance of that fact by observing that the amount of disagreement is by no means absolute and, in fact, is far less than some people believe it to be. From this perspective there are hallmarks of good teaching that nearly everyone, presumably, could agree upon.

Among the first things named in any effort to identify universal criteria of teaching effectiveness is usually some measure of how much and how well students learn. Good teachers, or better as opposed to worse ones, so the argument goes, surely must be those whose students learn the most and who do so with the greatest speed and efficiency. To many people the logic of that premise is irrefutable. From there it naturally follows that the proper way to identify teachers of merit is to seek evidence of how much and how well students learned under the tutelage of this teacher or that. Before-and-after testing of one kind or another is the obvious way to go from there.

An alternative approach available to those seeking to play down the controversy that the notion of good teaching generates is to concede the complexity of the phenomenon but to insist on it being analysable all the same. In this view good teaching is acknowledged to be multi-dimensional, a fact that might help to explain some of the disagreement over its definition. However, the elements making up this composite picture of good teaching can ultimately be agreed upon and additively combined in a way that will yield a singular judgment of a teacher's worth. For example, a set of such elements might include classroom management, lesson planning, oral exposition, and so forth. From such premises grow rating scales and observational devices designed to do justice to what is acknowledged to be the complex nature of the teaching process.

A third argument, still on the optimistic side, says that even if the concept

Philip W. Jackson

of good teaching defies precise definition of the kind that might make up a checklist, let's say, the act of deciding who is the best can be carried out all the same. This is so because good teachers are readily recognizable by their fellow teachers (and presumably by other trained judges as well) even if the latter cannot state precisely the criteria on which their judgments are made. In this view the assessment of pedagogical quality is a more discursive affair, a matter calling for clinical judgment rather than quantitative measurement or rating scales. From this presupposition there follow any number of schemes calling upon the evaluation of teachers by their peers and by other supervisory personnel as well.

Here then are the three most dominant points of view comprising the optimistic reply to the question of whether good teaching can be defined in the abstract or recognized when it is come upon. All make some degree of sense, quite obviously, or they wouldn't be put forward as often as they are. Moreover, there is no reason why any of them must be chosen to the exclusion of the others. Student gains in learning, composite ratings of teaching competence, clinical judgments of teaching ability — each is rationally defensible, at least superficially, and there is nothing to prevent all three from being used at once, should anyone choose to do so.

On the despairing side of the question of what constitutes good teaching there are also discernible differences in the grounds for pessimism and in what that has to say about the nature of teaching in general and about merit pay proposals in particular. One line of argument, which might be called a "contextual" point of view, emphasizes the idiosyncratic nature of the relationship between the teacher and pupil or between the teacher and the material being taught. It points out that some teachers apparently are good for some students but not for others, suited to the teaching of this subject or grade level, but not that one. Thus, it is near impossible, so the argument goes, to talk about the good teacher in general. Instead, what must be done is to identify many different kinds of good teaching, each dependent on some aspect of the setting in which it occurs.

Another line of argument sees the differences among definitions of good teaching as reflecting incommensurable views of what teaching is all about. In this view there is no hope of ever coming to agreement about what good teachers are like for the simple reason that the disputants operate within different universes of discourse. As a result, they talk past each other rather than joining a common dispute. Their arguments never really become engaged.

The example of this kind of odds-on disputation that comes most readily to mind is epitomized in the difference between those who believe that teaching is fundamentally devoted to the transmission of knowledge and those who insist that the main business of teachers is to modify the psychological well-being of those being served. This division calls to mind the well-known dichotomy of the tough-minded and the tender-minded, made famous by William James. From the tough-minded point of view, teaching is or should be a no-nonsense activity of transmitting information and skills to the youth of our nation. From the tender-minded point of view, the task is more akin to that of saving souls.

Confronted with such a dramatic difference in the interpretation of what teaching is all about, we are tempted to ask whether one of these views is right and the other wrong. But the more fundamental question is whether the two views can be compared at all. Do they co-exist in a universe of discourse that makes them commensurable? Pessimists, which is to say those who despair over the possibility of a single definition of good teaching, say no. Optimists say yes.

What then shall we make of these divergent perspectives on what good teaching is all about and how it might be defined? Might it be possible ultimately to agree on a single definition, as the optimists say it is, or will we be forever divided on such matters, as the pessimists declare? Do we know enough at present to answer such a question or will we have to wait until further investigations are undertaken and further philosophizing is done?

Personally, I am on the side of waiting for a time, which seems like the safe thing to do, yet my sympathies lie with those whose outlook is pessimistic. They do so for several reasons, not the least of which is an inherent distrust of an engineering mentality applied to human affairs. Let someone but sound cocksure of what good teaching is all about and my natural inclination is to believe them wrong.

Why should this be? It is so, I suspect, because there truly is no such thing as good teaching in an absolute sense, at least none that will stand uncontested by everyone else. Not even poor old Socrates, who epitomized the ideal teacher for centuries, makes the grade. The world's admiration of his pedagogical talents remains as high as ever, I suppose. But think about it for a minute. How many high school principals in America today would hire that grand old Greek if he came shuffling in, bug-eyed and barefooted, looking for work in the Social Studies Department? "Darned few" is the answer I would give.

And the point is not that we would now object to what might have been overlooked before: his low standard of cleanliness, let's say, or his fondness for young boys. Rather it is that our understanding of what teaching is all about has undergone such a profound change over the centuries that we would barely recognize Socrates as a teacher today if he should suddenly show up in our midst. The same would be true of countless other teachers of ages past, even those of a generation or two away. They too would no longer be looked upon as what we think of today as a "genuine" teacher.

So what shall we conclude about the question of whether or not good teaching can be conceptually defined? What the facts of the matter say to me is that the goal of arriving at a single definition upon which everyone will agree is not worth striving for. There are just too many different kinds of teaching and too many competing conceptions of what teaching is all about. Moreover, our notions of what constitutes good teaching obviously undergo historical change as well, which means that whatever is agreed upon as the sign of a good teacher today may be significantly altered over the years, not simply because of new teaching methods and materials

Philip W. Jackson

awaiting future discovery but also because of unpredictable shifts in related domains of thought and culture.

That leaves us with the question of how to proceed with the merit pay argument in the face of there being not one but several definitions of good teaching. We first must note that the sheer existence of multiple standards of pedagogical worth does not do in the argument completely. There are all kinds of ways of sidestepping the issue, any one of which would allow the proponents of merit pay to proceed to the next stage of actually identifying teachers who meet the standards of excellence that have been set.

For example, it might be argued that even though there are a host of criteria useful in identifying good teachers, a small number of them, the latter easily identifiable, can be shown to be more central than others on either empirical or ideological grounds. Thus, though most people would probably agree that good teachers commonly have pleasing personalities, let's say, most would also acknowledge that a truer test of how well a teacher has done or might do his or her job would be evidence of some kind having to do with what his or her students have learned. Proceeding in this way it may be possible to establish an ordering of potential criteria with a small enough number standing out near the top to allow the advocates of a merit pay proposal to move on to the stage of implementing their plan.

Whether such maneuvering will actually work is a matter yet to be established. What we already know, however, is that the argument for this or that set of criteria has to be made. It is by no means self-evident.

II

Let's suppose for the time being that some kind of tentative agreement on what constitutes good teaching has indeed been reached. Now it is time to go out and look for teachers who actually match that standard. This brings us to our second premise, the one contending that good teachers can be identified with reasonable accuracy. What difficulties, if any, stand in the way of establishing the truth of that assertion?

The issues here would seem to be chiefly empirical, as opposed to conceptual. What is called for is a demonstration of some kind. We need be shown that good teachers (according to criteria agreed upon) can indeed be identified and reliably so.

There are of course a host of technical questions to be answered before any such demonstration can take place, as all evaluators hardly need be told. We need decide in advance the margins of error that will be tolerated and what kinds of error will be considered most serious. For example, would it be worse to overlook a teacher who is truly good than to mistakenly elevate an average teacher to the rank of superior? What assumptions, if any, need be made about the ultimate distribution of teaching quality? In other words, how many good teachers is it reasonable to anticipate finding and how do we arrive at that estimate?

Does Virtue Merit Pay?

The difficulty with many of these questions is that their answers are not to be found by either empirical investigation or logical deduction. Instead, they are arrived at through the use of conventions, rules and other forms of argumentation whose authority is contestable in ways that empirical and logical judgments are not. This is not to call them arbitrary, by any means, but the fact that they could be other than they are does mean that they are vulnerable to criticism in ways that could be threatening to any or all merit pay proposals.

The reason for calling attention to these potential weakspots on the technical side of merit pay plans is because the latter stand to be challenged by teachers themselves. This is so because teachers as a group are naturally wary about any kind of evaluation of their performance. They are so for several very good reasons, none of which appears to be fully understood and respected by those proponents of merit pay proposals with whose arguments I am acquainted.

What first needs understanding is that the concerns many teachers have about being evaluated arise not so much from their distrust of the procedures to be followed as from their deep uncertainties having to do with the possible outcome. To put the matter bluntly, many teachers are not too sure themselves how well or how poorly they are doing in the classroom. Moreover, they are not all that eager to learn. That condition may strike many non-teachers as puzzling or even paradoxical (it may seem so to some teachers as well) but it is true all the same, or at least I as a teacher have found it so, as have scores of others to whom I have spoken over the years. Why this should be so is a question soon to be addressed.

Another source of the wariness many teachers have at the prospect of being evaluated springs from what they know be true about the variability of their performance. Even though they may be genuinely uncertain when it comes to judging their own ability in some absolute sense, there is one thing that all teachers are sure of and agree upon, which is that teaching has its ups and downs. All teachers, it seems, have good days and bad, good classes and poor ones. Furthermore, these peaks and valleys of teaching sometimes last much longer than a single day or class session. They have been known to endure for weeks and sometimes months or even years.

Now the peculiar thing about much of this variability, particularly as it happens day-to-day, is that the teacher usually can't explain why it occurs. It just does, that's all. And there is not much to do about it except to ride the experiences out, enjoying the highs as they come along and trusting that the lows will not last for long. This is not to say that good or poor teaching is simply a matter or luck, but it is to acknowledge that it is partially so.

Returning to the question of how knowledgeable teachers are about the overall quality of their own performance, we might phrase the essential query this way: Do good teachers know they're good and poor teachers know they're poor? Doubtless the answer must be yes for some, especially those for whom the signs of success or failure are so obvious and so consistent as to be undeniable. But how numerous are those for whom all the signs agree? Not very, would be my guess. A small percentage at the top and an equally small percentage at the bottom. What, then, of the others? What do they know of how well they are doing?

As has already been said, my own teaching experience and my conversations with scores of teachers over the years makes me suspect that many, if not most, of us are often quite uncertain about how well or how poorly we are doing our work. There seem to be two major reasons for that uncertainty, each of them widely acknowledged in the professional literature on the subject, but neither as fully recognized by the merit pay people as they might be.

One has to do with the obvious and much-complained-about fact that teachers seldom get to see each other in action. Thus they often lack a comparative standard (save their memories of their own teachers) against which to judge their own performance. The other has to do with the equally troublesome fact that teachers often lack evidence of how the material they are teaching is getting across to their students. Furthermore, more often than not what *should* be getting across to them is itself questionable.

These uncertainties and instabilities that are, in a sense, natural to teaching take us a long way toward understanding why so many teachers are resistant to the idea of merit pay, or at least they do so for me. Successful teaching is a chancy affair under the best of circumstances and even for the most gifted of teachers. Judgments about which teachers are better or worse than others seem fraught with difficulty and vulnerable to all kinds of error, at least that's the way the situation often looks from the inside, from the viewpoint of teachers themselves.

The unease that many teachers may feel about such matters does not prevent professional evaluators from proceeding with their work, of course, though it should at least give them pause. The power of more or less random variables to throw even a good teacher off the track, the invisible character of the changes teachers seek to make in students, the unevenness of the signs of success from day to day and even from minute to minute, these are indeed real conditions teachers face and not mere figments of their imagination. They must be confronted and dealt with in any sound evaluation program, particularly if teacher approval is to be a pre-condition of its success.

There are technical solutions to some of these difficulties, as every evaluator knows. Increasing sample size, for example, reduces the probability of sampling error. In the case of quantifiable data, there are ways of estimating the reliability of the measurements, of checking for bias in the distribution of events, and so forth. The trouble is that all of these *are* "technical" solutions, ways of dealing with elusive and unstable phenomena. None of them directly affects the condition in question, it merely accommodates to it in one way or another. Accommodations of this kind may partially assuage the unease many teachers feel about being evaluated, but they are unlikely to eliminate it completely. The amount remaining after all reasonable technical assurances have been offered could well prove to be a severely limiting factor in the spread of merit pay practices.

III

Why should better teachers be paid more than others? That is the question occasioned by the third and final premise making up the bare outline of the merit pay argument. It has two answers, or, better, its answer can be given two different kinds of backing. One is ethical; the other, utilitarian. The first says that good teachers *deserve* to earn more than average. They have *earned* it. It is only *fair* for them to be treated in that way. Reward for merit is a fundamental form of *justice*. To see this to be so, we need but look around at what happens in other occupations. Good doctors, good lawyers, good tennis players, good plumbers — all receive more money than do their colleagues who, for one reason or another, have failed to make the grade. Why not teachers?

The second answer, the utilitarian one, approaches the question rather differently. It argues that it makes sense to reward the best teachers because of what if will do for the profession in general and for the schools in particular. Unless better teachers earn more than poorer ones, indeed, unless they earn as much or more than they might have earned in most alternative occupations, the argument continues, there will not be a sufficient incentive to attract good people into the profession and to retain the better ones already there. Good schools require good teachers. Merit pay is simply a way of keeping the best and attracting others like them.

Here, then, are two separate lines of reasoning, each supporting the practice of merit pay. What, now, shall we make of them? Which is the more attractive and why? What is the argumentative force of each?

We first must note that these two approaches to the question are by no means mutually exclusive. There is no reason why the justification of merit pay may not receive its backing from both arguments at once. The contention that better teachers *deserve* more money in no way interferes with the allied contention that the policy of paying them more may also serve to keep good teachers in the profession and to attract newcomers of similar talent.

We next need acknowledge that the ethical argument, regardless of its rhetorical force, is not the one being put forward by most of today's advocates of merit pay. This is not to say that they in any way disagree with that line of reasoning, but it is to point out that most take the side they are on not out of some altruistic desire to see that good teachers receive their just deserts, rather it is because they are deeply worried about the state of the teaching profession in our country and they want to do something about it. They see merit pay as a partial solution to a serious problem

The predominance of utilitarian considerations among advocates of merit pay is not something for which they need apologize. There is nothing at all wrong about wanting to make teaching attractive to newcomers or desiring to retain the best teachers already within the profession. If higher salaries for the most meritorious will do that, without at the same time having undesirable side effects of unacceptable proportions (by creating a disgruntled class of teachers, for example), so much the better. The question the utilitarians must face, however, is the pragmatic one: Will that happen? Will adding a few, even quite a few, thousand dollars a year to the salaries of our best teachers succeed in keeping them in teaching longer than they would normally stay? Will it at the same time attract to the profession talented young people who otherwise would have chosen to do something else?

Because that pragmatic question calls for an empirical answer, the only reasonable thing to do is to wait and see. We won't know whether merit pay plans will work as the utilitarians anticipate until we have tried them. Yet I can't help being skeptical about the likelihood of their success, all the same.

My skepticism derives chiefly from what I believe to be true about the nature of good teaching and from what I know for certain about some of the intrinsic rewards of teaching and some of the extrinsic ones as well, above and beyond those dispensed in pay envelopes. To treat these matters, albeit all too briefly, we must now turn from the merit pay argument, *per se*, though its premises will continue to serve as a kind of backdrop for what follows.

IV

There are many definitions of good teaching, that much has already been acknowledged. Common to all or most of them is the image of the good teacher possessing certain dispositions, traits, habits of action — call them what you will — that predispose him to perform his teaching duties not merely correctly but excellently. Now the question is whether there is some way of formulating these characteristics of a good teacher in a manner that brings to light their most common qualities, those shared by the largest number of teachers of all kinds. I believe there to be. I further believe that such a formulation may help to reunite teachers of today with a once-honored tradition from which many seem to have become separated.

The tradition of which I speak is one in which teaching is seen as entailing the exercise of virtue. In this view, the good teacher is a person who exhibits certain traits of character in the performance of his or her teaching responsibilities. It is the presence or absence of those virtues, rather than the mastery of a set of techniques, that ultimately sets apart the person of excellence in the teaching profession, just as it does in most other serious human undertakings.

This is not to say that technique is unimportant in teaching. On the contrary, a lack of rudimentary teaching skills doubtless accounts for the failure of many a would-be teacher and for the unhappiness of countless others who limp along from day-to-day and from year-to-year without realizing the deficiencies of such techniques as they employ. But it is to insist that teaching in general involves more than technique; good teaching, much more.

What are these so-called virtues that apply to teaching? There is no list of them that I have ever seen and yet I think I can name a few. Intellectual honesty and fairness in dealing with students must certainly be near the top of the list. So too must be a buoyant and optimistic outlook on life, a view in keeping with the fundamentally optimistic nature of the teaching process. Patience is a trait that I personally would rank high, as is perseveration, the kind of stick-to-it-iveness that keeps the teacher burning the midnight oil to get that set of papers back on time. And what about a genuine caring for the well-being of one's students? Solicitude, I suppose one might call it. Who would leave that off the list? And wouldn't we also want to describe the good teacher as a person dedicated to his work, convinced of its importance, and willing to give generously of his own time and energy in its enactment, even to the point of foregoing other of his desires and pleasures in the process?

The list could go on but I think the point has been made. There are many virtues commonly associated with the idea of good teaching and it doesn't take an awful lot of thought to specify a goodly number of them. People may disagree about the ones I have listed. Some may wish the order changed, others may insist upon certain additions or subtractions. But I would wager that no one would want to throw the list out entirely.

Now the question is what to make of such a list, with or without those corrections that some people might insist upon. Suppose we accept the fact that a set of virtues associated with good teaching can indeed be identified. Suppose we go so far as to acknowledge that the possession of some such set of virtues is fully as important to the success of teaching as is the mastery of technique, perhaps even more so. What then? What does that say to us about the way good teachers should be identified? What does it say about the way they should be treated by the public at large, by school administrators, by their teaching colleagues, and by the pupils they serve? Finally, what does the virtuous nature of teaching reveal about the rewards of teaching?

To begin, how does one know a virtuous teacher when one sees one? The answer is: one doesn't. Unlike techniques and other "surface" characteristics that often can be readily witnessed, virtues reveal themselves slowly. The only way to know for sure whether a person is virtuous, a teacher or anyone else for that matter, is to know that person well, to be in his or her company for a long time. The presence or absence of certain virtues, such as courage or cowardice, are sometimes revealed in a twinkling, true enough, but those that have been named as being associated with good teaching are for the most part not like that. Instead, they are qualities that one comes to appreciate in a person, sometimes quite slowly.

What this means for the identification of superior teachers seems to me quite straightforward. It says that the ultimate evaluation of a teacher's quality must come from within the community in which the teacher works and in which he or she is known. It must come from testimony. Teaching colleagues, administrators, students, parents, all may have something valuable to say about the matter and should be encouraged to say it. It also

Philip W. Jackson

says that the identification of such qualities is probably a slow process, taking years rather than weeks or months to make. Finally, it suggests something else about the process as well. It at least implies that good teachers gradually become *recognized* as such if they stay around for a sufficient time, rather than having to be *identified* through some sort of standardized procedure.

How should a virtuous person be treated? With respect and honor, Aristotle tells us, and with praise as well. Who can dispute that judgment? Who also can fail to acknowledge that as a nation we have become sorely remiss in the regularity with which virtuous teachers are treated as they deserve to be? Perhaps we never did honor our teachers as other countries have done and as some still do today, that I leave for experts in comparative education to settle. But my own experience here at home tells me that we honor them less today than we did as recently as a generation or two ago.

Why is that, I wonder? Is the public solely to blame or might teachers themselves be partially at fault? Could it be that teachers of today are really less praiseworthy, less virtuous as teachers, than were their predecessors in generations part? If so, how did that come about?

Without wishing to add to the many criticisms teachers are receiving these days, and while fully acknowledging the need for improved public opinion concerning the worth of teachers and of teaching, I confess to harboring the suspicion that significant numbers of today's teachers are indeed less virtuous, in the sense in which that term is being used here, than was true in generations past. For the former, teaching is more of a job and less of a "calling" than it might have been judged to be by teachers past. How might such a condition be explained, if it turned out to be true? More importantly, what, if anything, might be done about it?

Unfortunately, I lack an answer to both of those questions. Furthermore, I am convinced that there is none to be had, at least none simple enough to be stated straightforwardly. Each is broad enough to be the focus of almost endless conjecture and inquiry. At the same time I do have a hunch about where a piece of the answer to each question might lie.

I suspect that we who are in the business of training teachers and of conducting research into the teaching process may have unwittingly contributed to the low esteem in which teaching is held by the public at large and, sad to say, by many teachers themselves. We have done so, my suspicion tells me, by pretending to know more about teaching than we actually do — i.e. by too much talk about new and modern methods that are really neither, accompanied by boasts about "what research says" with respect to how to teach this or that — and, more importantly, by promoting a view of teaching as technique. In the process we seem to have failed to remind both teachers and the public at large — perhaps we have even forgotten it ourselves — that teaching is indeed a moral enterprise, one which, when performed well, is worthy of praise of a kind that money cannot buy.

The notion of praiseworthiness as contrasted with praise-received brings me near to the end of my remarks. All that remains is a word or two having to do with the intrinsic rewards of teaching.

One of the points that Aristotle also makes is that it is better to be praiseworthy than to be praised. Better, in short, to be worthy of praise than to receive it. Why so? For the simple reason that praise may be mistakenly given or denied, whereas praiseworthiness transcends that condition. To be self-sufficiently praiseworthy is to be above caring whether praise is received or not.

Why the absence of care? Because the praiseworthy person acts in a way that is intrinsically satisfying. The formula is as old as human wisdom: virtue is its own reward.

Apply this ancient adage to teaching and what do we have? It says that the teacher who is doing an outstanding job, in the sense of behaving virtously as a teacher, is already being rewarded and is well aware of that fact, whether or not public praise and even more concrete forms of approval are forthcoming. At least for the reflective teacher, which is to say the virtuous one, good teaching rewards itself.

But there are all kinds of problems with this formulation. For one thing, how does this observation about good teaching being its own reward jibe with the earlier one about teachers not knowing for sure how well or how poorly they are doing? Are the two reconcilable? They are, I believe, in the following way. Teachers may know that they are doing the best they can do and thus be rewarded by that knowledge, whether or not praise from anyone else is forthcoming. They may at the same time not be sure that what they are doing is good enough, in the sense of its having the effect they desire. Nor can they be certain that others are not doing it better than they. So even the virtuous teacher may be doubt-ridden in that sense.

But what about the public applause and the material rewards as well? Can we rest content with the belief that good teachers are or should be above such mundane matters? Will that not lead inevitably to the financial exploitation of teachers, as has happened in the past, and to the further debasement of their status by the public at large? Is not talk about the virtue of teaching merely today's version, limited in scope perhaps, of what used to be called "the opiate of the masses"?

The choice, in the final analysis, is not between sacrifice and reward. As usual, it is somewhere between the two. It calls for ways of convincing teachers, or reinforcing their own conviction, that they are engaged on one of the most significant tasks that humankind has yet conceived: that of making it possible for our society and all it stands for to continue. How might this be done? With bigger pay envelopes and lots of applause from the sidelines of course, but our efforts only begin there. We must help teachers realize, in concrete terms, the dignity of their undertaking. That means assisting them in coming to terms with the magnitude of their work, helping them keep its moral dimensions in focus, refusing, with them, to see it denigrated to some kind of a push-pull activity that any fool can do. It means, above all, making schools the kind of place where talented teachers can realize the personal fulfillment that the best of teaching has offered from the days of Socrates forward. Few enterprises are more challenging; none is more important.

Merit Pay and the Concerns of the Teaching Profession

Terry Herndon

Each generation of public school administrators and teachers has had to deal with various schemes and pressures to adopt merit pay plans for teachers. The stated goals have included the improvement of individual performance, the reduction of "turnover" in personnel, the enhancement of recruiting power, and the achievement of the simple justice of meritocracy. Sometimes the case was rationally made. Other times the case was politically imposed. As a result, our history is littered with a number of abandoned efforts.

This time is more difficult than the others because America's most powerful citizen has been promoting the idea. In 1983, President Reagan unleashed a formidable and unprecedented "jaw boning" campaign for merit pay as his only significant response to the National Commission for Excellence in Education. More recently, Secretary Ted Bell has begun offering grants for experimental ventures. This determined evangelism has created the impression that the President and his government believe merit pay to be a *sina qua non* for school improvement.

We do not know the extent to which this is believed by the public, but merit pay is no longer an isolated and abstract issue. Growing numbers of politicians are finding merit pay to be a politically useful response to the universal desire to improve the public schools. Therefore, the 1983-84 appearance is not just our turn to respond to an old question. It is a serious and difficult dilemma for the school establishment.

On the one hand, many citizens almost instinctively support the idea of performance-based compensation. It is, after all, very compatible with the spirit of competition and social Darwinism that undergirds our capitalistic culture and drives our free enterprise economy. Therefore, it is part of the day to day life that many experience in the workplace.

Having been acculturated to the notion of competitive pay, most citizens are not inclined to evaluate whether the system, as they experience it, truly protects public interests, provides economic justice for workers, enhances their personal productivity, or truly serves the long term interests of the employing institution. It is even more rare for them to evaluate the comparability of their institution and its business to schools and schooling, the comparability of their work to teaching or the probable impact of operating a merit pay system in a school. Most importantly, they do not carefully define the operational causes of unsatisfactory educational results and then evaluate proposed solutions according to their probable effect on the real problems.

Instead they say to themselves, "Some teachers are better than others. It's fair that better teachers get more pay. *Ergo*, we need a merit pay plan for teachers."

Moreover, large numbers of teachers do the same analysis and arrive at the same conclusions. Each assumes that the criteria will be both clear and relevant; that the evaluators will be both competent and objective; that the process will be both thorough and fair; and that none of these elements will be contaminated by personal, political or economic considerations.

The force of this public sentiment today is sufficient to create some desire among school people simply to accommodate and get on with other matters. This would be easy, popular, and efficient in the short term. Furthermore, in some political environments it would probably maximize short term support for increases in school spending.

On the other hand, the educational establishment has been schooled by experience and knows well that merit pay will not solve any of the real problems that they face and will create still more problems. Therefore, the short term political deal is a bad deal in that short term political gains will quickly dissipate amid larger, long term problems. They know further that, if they make the political deal, they and not the President will be held accountable for the old problems still unsolved as well as the new problems. For these reasons, many in the school community are reluctant to deal and to associate themselves with the creation of false expectations among the electorate.

In sum, school people would like to accommodate and thereby dispose of the "red herring" and get on to real stuff; but many see that the risks of doing so are unacceptable.

Specifically, why is it that they feel merit pay won't work?

(1) **Merit pay systems can institutionalize the acceptability of mediocrity and inferiority.** The ideal objective for a school system is to have an excellent teacher in every classroom. The only way to do this is to enact high standards for employment and performance, and to provide the administration and supervision which is necessary to enforce those standards. Most merit pay systems ignore recruiting pressure altogether and presuppose that most teachers will not attain the high standard. The majority is defined as sub-standard and paid less than the few who attain excellence. In most systems other than merit pay systems, the critical judgment in regard to performance is whether the work is satisfactory or is unsatisfactory. The criteria for satisfactory performance may be as high as the employer can justify but the supervisor must act to purge the unsatisfactory. Merit plans create a much more comfortable set of choices.

(2) **Merit pay systems can be driven more by political than professional considerations.** In fact, the teaching profession's passion for objective criteria for decisions is a result of the *Realpolitik* of local government employment. Nepotism, racism, sexism, chauvinism, and cronyism have all been powerful forces in the operation of local government. These created the force behind civil service and, in the schools, tenure and objective pay

schedules. If the defenses against these abuses are breached, then we should expect to see pay increments doled out for political merit as often as professional merit. Indeed, the popular press has chronicled that this has been too often true in the new federal system of merit pay.

(3) **Merit pay systems can complicate the remediation of performance problems among teachers.** The salaries of public servants are a matter of public record. As a result, the segregation of teachers into two pay categories, meritorious and not meritorious, is a matter of public record. The consequences of this declaration by a principal or school board can be horrendous. All parents want their children in the classes of the superior teachers and are, at best, ambivalent towards any other assignment. In addition, adolescents and teenagers can be merciless in the use of performance information in their relationships with teachers and in rationalizing their own performance. Reflecting performance (a private decision) in compensation (a public decision) can make a struggling teacher's success much less likely. The weight of this dynamic on a humane administrator can, in fact, become another distortion in the evaluation process. It has been a major factor in the failure of some earlier merit pay plans.

(4) **Merit pay plans might stifle extra effort.** Few will argue that excellence in teaching is sometimes related to personal, social and spiritual considerations as well as pedagogical. Many teachers involve themselves with students (including students not assigned to them) in a variety of personal and social ways that make major differences in lives but are totally divorced from any job description which is usable for merit pay administration. As a result, the very existence of the merit pay plan devalues these non-compensable activities. If one accepts the encouragement of productivity as a valid argument for merit pay, then he or she must conclude as well that lack of renumeration discourages performance.

(5) **Merit pay plans can require arbitrary comparison and contrast of functions.** A reasonable merit pay plan will set objective criteria for each teaching function and compensate each teacher who fulfills the criteria. Most observers would agree. However, most observers would not consider that this is nearly impossible. In fact, the kindergarten teacher, the K-6 music teacher, the 12th grade teacher of Advanced Placement Calculus and the 8th grade teacher of Industrial Arts are usually competing with one another for one of a limited number of merit increments. It's obviously an unfair competition in that each assignment is relatively unique. When one adds distinctions in social class, intelligence, physical capacity, emotional health and other student traits to the formulae, it is readily apparent that contrasts and comparisons are nearly meaningless. Yet, merit pay systems must arbitrarily homogenize teaching conditions and objectives or arbitrarily judge the differences. Neither is rational.

(6) **Merit pay systems can induce unpleasant competition within faculties.** This tendency is caused by the limitations that are virtually always placed on

a merit pay system. To force discriminating judgment by administrators, the systems invariably limit the number of increments. Even when the policy declares another practice, there is an operational limit imposed by economic or political realities. Therefore, if one person is included then another is excluded. An effort to be in is an effort to keep another out. The unsavory potential of such systems to divide faculties has caused teachers to refuse to cooperate with some earlier plans. Individuals preferred not to be set apart.

Experienced educators know of the failure of prior merit pay plans and know that the dynamics described above undermine the probability of success for new efforts. This cynicism combines with contemporary politics to create a real dilemma. The need to escape the dilemma has led to a number of artful schemes based upon the "career ladder" concept.

Most of these are rhetorically fancy merit pay plans and do not warrant independent analysis. Secretary Bell's scheme, for example, speaks to a probationary period followed by a "comprehensive evaluation of the new teacher's performance." If the new teacher meets the test, he or she would be "advanced in rank to the position of professional teacher" (the second step of the career ladder). Those failing the test could have an extended probationary period but would ultimately advance or be dismissed.

To this point, the scheme is a redefinition of the *status quo* as produced by tenure and the single salary schedule. If there is something new, if his essay proposes changes, then it must be found in the transition from step two (professional teacher) to step three (master teacher).

The attainment of this step would require "distinguished teaching performance." Dr. Bell notes, however, that "there will be more worthy applicants than there will be positions available. (Therefore), the evaluation and decision-making process must be as objective, fair, and as free from favoritism and political influence as possible." To resolve the problem of competition among non-comparable functions, he arbitrarily divides teaching activity into four classes: primary, intermediate, junior high and senior high. The next step is simple: The Board of Education will allocate a number of master teacher slots to each class.

One cannot avoid the observation that all of the adverse dynamics are, in fact, acknowledged. They are not, however, resolved. They are dismissed as unimportant. The plan is, in fact, a rhetorically fancy merit pay plan put forth amid assumptions that are more illusory than real.

For example, it is assumed that master teachers' salaries will be significantly higher than other teachers' salaries and this presumably means higher than administrative posts and other opportunities available to senior teachers; but Dr. Bell later notes that there will not likely be enough money to make the general salary schedule truly competitive and to fund the master teacher increments, and the legislatures must, therefore, prevent local competition between general schedules and special increments by allocating specified funds to each.

In other words, "merit pay" by any other name is beset with the problems of merit pay. The only career ladder schemes that escape the traps

Terry Herndon

will be schemes that are not merit pay. Such plans are possible but they will result from new ways of thinking about teaching and not from repackaging of old ideas about compensation. They will derive from a functional analysis of teaching assignments and a description of each assignment in terms of the specific skills that are required for its performance and the tasks to be performed.

Certain basic skills will be required for all teaching positions and certain basic tasks would be inherent in all positions. Some positions might require additional, higher order skills, more complex tasks and higher risk decisions than characterize most positions. Positions requiring higher skills or the performance of more sophisticated tasks would receive higher compensation. Only such an approach can produce a true "career ladder" as opposed to a "merit pay" cover-up.

There are many reasons why many professional educators believe that merit pay hasn't succeeded, lacks efficiency, and won't work. Its real danger, however, lies in the simple fact that it won't work, rather than any of the specific reasons. Merit pay simply does not address the problems of the school and will not enhance performance. If the public is led to believe that it will, then, with merit pay, comes the expectation of a more productive school. Soon thereafter the "piper will be paid." The politicians will have passed on and the educators will pay once again.

This point is best made in looking at The Report of the National Commission on Excellence in Education. The Commission finds that:

— Secondary school curricula have been homogenized, diluted, and diffused to the point that they no longer have a central purpose.

— Expenditures for textbooks and other instructional material have declined by 50% over the past 17 years.

— Compared to other nations, American students spend much less time on school work.

— Not enough of the academically able students are being attracted to teaching.

— Teacher preparation programs need substantial improvements.

— The professional working conditions of teachers are, on the whole, unacceptable.

— Given (the) freedom to choose half or more of their education, many students opt for less demanding personal service courses, such as "bachelor living."

There are many who categorize the problems differently, but, in any event, the lists are most always immune to remediation by merit pay.

The thirty-seven recommendation of the Panel are generally constructive and are responsive to the complexities of the problems. They speak to a more rigorous content in the curriculum; higher standards and expectations

---

of students; more time in study; improved teacher education; competitive, market sensitive, and performance based salaries at a higher level than we know today; more effective administrative leadership; more responsive politicians; expanded federal assistance; and more political and tax support for schooling.

If these recommendations were fulfilled, it would relieve the educators' principal anxieties about merit pay. Apart from this context, many see the whole issue as a hoax with no promise for good and much potential for evil.

The nation must address the real and serious problems associated with providing universal, free, high quality education for its children. It must not be diverted from this challenge by politicians who prefer simple solutions to non-problems or by the desire to scapegoat either politicians or educators.

Merit Pay for Teachers: The Implications of Theory for Practice

Gary Natriello

The recent wave of reform proposals for American schools has contained repeated calls for higher performance standards for both students and teachers (National Commission, 1983; Twentieth Century Task Force, 1983). Those focusing on the quality of the teacher corps have emphasized the need both to hold current teachers more accountable and to recruit new teachers of a high calithe subject of theoretical and empirical work in various branches of the social sciences. This paper considers several lines of theory and research in these areas and specifies the implications of each for the design and implementation of merit pay systems in public schools. The goal is to provide several perspectives with which to sensitize those who must confront the merit pay question first hand. The presentation proceeds first by considering theory and research in these areas to develop the implications for those charged with implementing merit pay systems, and then by examining some of these implications in action in a working merit pay system in a public school district.

Three major theoretical approaches are considered. First, the perspectives of psychologists as represented in the work of Lawler (1976) are reviewed. This work pays particular attention to the motivational implications of merit pay systems. Second, the perspectives of sociologists as represented in the work of Dornbusch and Scott (1975) are considered. Theory and research in this perspective focuses on the dimensions of authority and evaluation systems in organizations and the impact of merit pay processes on these systems. Third, the perspectives of political scientists represented in the work of Clark and Wilson (1961) are presented. This work calls attention to the options available to organizational executives who must devise systems to encourage individual participation in an organization.

I. A Psychological Perspective

In reviewing the literature on control systems in organizations, Lawler (1976:1249) proposes a seven element thermostat-like model to analyze such systems. These elements are: 1) a sensor to measure some kind of activity; 2) a device to set the standards for the activity; 3) a discriminator that compares the sensed information with the standard; 4) an effector that responds to the discriminator by increasing or decreasing the activity; 5) some communication process; 6) the activity itself; and 7) a source of energy or motivation for the activity.

Each of these elements might appear in a system for the evaluation and reward of teaching performance. There would have to be some way of measuring the teaching activity, e.g., through observations of teaching. There would also need to be some standard or standards of teaching performance, e.g., certain approved approaches or desired outcomes. Some process would have to be developed to permit the comparison of sensed information with the established standards, e.g., some type of rating scale. Some effector would have to be employed, i.e., some kind of action would have to be taken to increase or decrease or otherwise modify the activity, e.g., rewards and punishments might be used to motivate desired behavior. Communication concerning deviations from the standards would have to occur, e.g., teachers might be informed of the assessment of their performance. The activity itself would be teaching or some aspect of teaching such as maintaining control in the classroom. Some intrinsic or extrinsic source of motivation would have to be present such as professional satisfaction in a job well done or the receipt of merit pay.

Lawler uses this model of the control process to consider the factors that might cause control systems to produce extrinsic and intrinsic motivation and three types of dysfunctional behavior in organizations: bureaucratic behavior, the production of invalid data, and resistance to the control system. Lawler makes a distinction between the control system of an organization and the reward system, a distinction crucial for considering merit pay programs. According to him, the control system specifies the behavior that the individual employees are supposed to perform, while the reward system exists to reward those employees who perform in the desired manner (Lawler, 1976: 1250).

Lawler's discussion of the impact of control systems and reward systems on motivation is rooted in expectancy theory. Expectancy theory argues that an individual's motivation to perform a certain task is the result of his subjective probability that effort on his part will lead to successful performance (E — P), multiplied by the product of his subjective probability that performance will lead to an outcome (P — O) and the value of that outcome to the individual (V). This sum is then used to predict the effort that a person will devote to a task. Effort is combined with ability to produce a certain level of performance which, in turn, leads to a reward. The relationship between performance and reward as experienced by the individual influences subsequent probabilities that performance will lead to an outcome. Figures *1a* and *1b*, taken from Lawler (1976:1252), depict the models of extrinsic and intrinsic motivation:

Gary Natriello

Figure 1a – Extrinsic Motivation Model

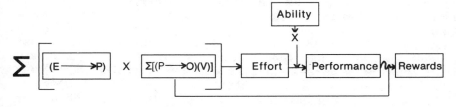

Figure 1b – Intrinsic Motivation Model

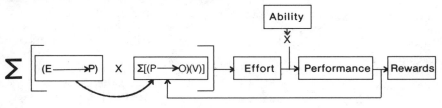

The model for intrinsic motivation differs in two major ways from that for extrinsic motivation. First, in the intrinsic motivation model the subjective probability of effort leading to successful performance is depicted as influencing the subjective probability that performance will lead to an outcome. That is because research has shown that feelings of achievement and accomplishment, which produce intrinsic motivation, are more likely to result when there is a less than perfect relationship between effort and performance. Second, in the intrinsic motivation model, the connection between performance and rewards is depicted as more direct than in the extrinsic motivation model because intrinsic rewards are given by individuals to themselves and are closely related to behavior (Lawler, 1976:1253).

These models carry implications for the design of control systems and reward systems that enhance extrinsic and intrinsic motivation. First, they imply that the relationship between performance and rewards is an important factor influencing the subsequent subjective probability that performance will lead to outcomes, which, in turn, affect subsequent effort on tasks. Thus attaching rewards to performance may increase motivation. Merit pay is one such reward. However, the models also suggest that the relationship between performance and extrinsic rewards such as merit pay may be less direct than the relationship between performance and intrinsic rewards such as a sense of professional accomplishment.

Lawler (1976:1275-1278) identifies certain conditions under which the relationship between performance and extrinsic rewards may be particularly problematic. These include situations where inclusive measures of an employee's performance are not available, situations where measures of employee performance must be subjective rather than objective and where the degree of trust between employees and superiors is low, and situations where the employee cannot influence the measures of performance employed in the control system either because of the nature of the technology involved in the tasks at hand or because of other organizational factors such as the size of the organization or the degree of centralization in the organization.

Many of these conditions will affect teachers in school organizations. The measures for assessing teaching performance are neither inclusive nor objective in most cases (Natriello and Dornbusch, 1982; Darling-Hammond, Wise, and Pease, 1983). In some circumstances, such as when evaluations of teaching performance are tied to measures of student outcomes (Daugherty and Dronberger, 1983), individual teachers have relatively little control over the measures of their performance since both outside factors and the work of other teachers contribute heavily to student learning.

Not only may certain conditions make it difficult to realize the motivational benefits of control and reward systems, these very systems may also lead to dysfunctional behavior in employees in the form of rigid bureaucratic behavior, the production of invalid data, and resistance to control systems. Rigid bureaucratic behavior occurs when individuals behave in ways that are called for by the control system, but that are dysfunctional in terms of the generally agreed upon goals of the organization (Lawler, 1976:1254). Such bureaucratic behavior is likely to occur: (a) when control system measures are not inclusive enough or do not adequately measure goal accomplishment; (b) when the standards are set too high and by someone other than the performer; (c) when the discriminator function is performed by an outsider with reward power; (d) when information from the control system goes to a person who uses it as a basis for distributing rewards; (e) when performers value the reward given by the control system; (f) when the goals of the organization are not clear and/or generally accepted; and (g) when there is a high level of performer identification with a subunit (Lawler, 1976:1259).

Each of these seven conditions must be addressed if control systems for the evaluation of teaching are to avoid increasing the level of bureaucratic behavior among teachers. Some of these seven conditions will be present in any system for evaluating teacher performance. Procedures for measuring teaching performance inclusively and adequately may be difficult to develop (Natriello and Dornbusch, 1982; Darling-Hammond, Wise, and Pease, 1983). Those measures which are thought to reflect most accurately some outcome of teaching performance (e.g. student scores on standardized tests) may fail to tap a variety of contextual factors which affect teaching and learning in classrooms. Earlier it was noted how such measures are not influenced by performance. Yet a system of measures with broad coverage may lack reliability. Moreover, it may be quite difficult to set standards that are challenging without being too high, and it may be impossible to set uniform standards that are not developed by someone other than the actor or teacher.

Other common conditions in schools are the lack of clarity surrounding the goals of the organization and the high level of identification of teachers with their subunits, their students and classrooms. School goals are often unclear (Weick, 1982) and teachers confined to their classrooms often develop closer identification with their unit than with the organization in general.

While the four conditions discussed immediately above may occur in any system for the control of teacher performance in schools, the other three conditions are most apparent when the control system is attached to the reward system in the form of merit pay. In merit pay systems the discrimination function is performed by an individual, often an outsider, who has reward power; the information from the control system goes to an individual who uses it as a basis for giving rewards; and the performers working under the control system presumably value the rewards, the merit pay. Thus, one problem administrators implementing merit pay systems will have to cope with is the potential increase in bureaucratic behavior as teachers seek to enhance their rewards.

A second dysfunctional outcome of control systems is the production of invalid data about the functioning of the organization. Valid data both about what can be done and what has been done is necessary for organizational effectiveness. The former permits useful planning, and the latter allows control of daily activities (Lawler, 1976:1259). Organizational control systems will tend to produce invalid data: (a) when performance data are subjective in nature; (b) when the data are measuring a dimension perceived by the performer as reflecting competence in an important area; (c) when performers are not allowed to participate in the setting of standards and the standards are perceived as unreasonable; (d) when the performer has control over the information gathering and the discriminator function; (e) when the information is given to the performer's superior for use as a basis for distributing rewards and punishments; (f) when the performer values the rewards and is alienated from the system; (g) when the activity being performed produces unclear outcomes that are difficult to measure; and (h) when the activity is not vital to the continued functioning of the organization (Lawler, 1976:1264-1265).

These conditions leading to the production of invalid data must be considered in the course of implementing merit pay systems if administrators wish to preserve and enhance the capacity to elicit valid information on the functioning of school programs, information important for school improvement. Certain of these conditions are inherent in the nature of the activities that comprise teaching and learning. The activity of teaching is not one that produces clear-cut outcomes that are easy to measure. Teaching and learning are complex tasks which are shaped by a variety of factors and result in a variety of outcomes (Darling-Hammond, Wise, and Pease, 1983). Moreover, much of the data on teaching performance are subjective in nature. The evaluation of teaching performance has typically involved the collection of data on the process of teaching. As Lawler (1976:1264) observes, the process a person goes through in order to obtain an outcome is more difficult to measure than the result itself. (See also, Blau and Scott, 1962.) The evaluation of teaching may thus not have the benefit of either clear outcomes, or easily measured processes. Information may not be valid under these conditions since it is easier to distort such data.

Since schools are not likely to cease functioning if certain teacher activities are not performed, information on teaching performance is more likely to be distorted than information on activities that directly affect the continued existence of an organization. When activities do not directly affect the continuation of an organization, performers can distort information and still be confident that the problems caused by the invalid data will not result in the loss of their jobs. Thus, there is no deterrent to reporting invalid data in schools.

The effects of several of the conditions that lead to the production of invalid data may be enhanced with the adoption of merit pay systems. For example, under merit pay, information on teaching performance will be given to the teacher's superior and used as a basis for distributing significant rewards and punishments. Moreover, individual teachers will place great value on the monetary rewards that are related to the performance data.

Individual resistance to the control system is the third dysfunctional consequence of certain conditions in control systems noted by Lawler (1976:1265). Such resistance may involve failure to cooperate with the functioning of the control system and failure to cooperate with other organizational demands. Such resistance is likely to arise: (a) when the control system measures performance in a new area; (b) when a new control system replaces a system which performers have a high investment in maintaining; (c) when the standards are set without performer participation; (d) when the results from the control system are not fed back to the performers; (e) when the results from the control system are fed to higher levels in the organization for use in distributing rewards; (f) when performers coming under the new system are relatively satisfied with current arrangements and see themselves as committed to the organization; and (g) when performers are low in self-esteem and authoritarianism (Lawler, 1976:1274).

Several of the conditions likely to provoke resistance to the control system are present in school organizations about to implement a merit pay program. A control system modified to be used in conjunction with a reward system such as merit pay inevitably replaces the existing control and reward systems. Teachers may have a heavy investment in the existing system. Those with years of experience may have adapted their teaching performance and other behaviors to maximize their satisfaction under the old system. Some of these adaptations may have been dysfunctional in terms of the goals of the school, but others may have been quite useful for achieving school goals. On the one hand, a teacher interested in maximizing his or her income may have taken additional jobs and so devoted less time to preparation for teaching. On the other hand, a teacher interested in maximizing his or her income may have acquired an advanced degree to move ahead on the salary schedule, in the process acquiring new skills and perspectives that lead to improved teaching performance. In either case, teachers may resist the move to a merit pay system since such a system would render their previous investment decisions less useful for securing additional income.

The implementation of a merit pay system would, of course, mean that results from the control system are fed to higher levels and used for distributing rewards. Thus, moving to a merit pay system carries with it the threat of increasing performer resistance to the control system.

Lessons for School Administrators

While the perspective of organizational psychologists such as Lawler suggests that administrators charged with designing and implementing merit pay systems will face numerous challenges, it does offer a number of implications concerning ways to make the process more successful. This work points out the fact that merit pay is a change in the reward system that may require changes in the control system. Administrators interested in developing control systems that enhance motivation must be concerned not only with the relationship between effort and performance but also with the relationship between performances and valued outcomes. Moreover, they must strive to avoid system features that lead to bureaucratic behavior, invalid data and individual resistance.

Three strategies would seem to lead to more successful systems. First, administrators should see to it that conditions enhance the relationship between effort and performance. In many instances this can be accomplished by examining the working conditions of teachers to make sure that such conditions do not force teachers to waste a great deal of effort in ways that do not contribute to the dimensions of teaching performance deemed most important by the control system. In some schools, current working conditions are so adverse that introducing a merit pay system will only result in higher levels of teacher frustration.

Second, administrators must work to enhance the relationship between performance and valued outcomes. This can be done both by making sure that teachers use techniques that will enable them to achieve desired ends and by designing a control system with measures that reflect teacher outcomes and tie them to the reward system. The former task implied here is one of more careful and sophisticated supervision to provide teachers with expertise to accomplish more efficiently their teaching tasks (Natriello, 1984b); the latter task is developing accurate measures of teaching performance and outcomes. Lawler cautions that appropriate measures of performance must be both inclusive (i.e., reflective of the major aspects of teaching) and relatively less subjective than the measures usually employed in evaluating teaching if administrators wish to avoid the negative consequences of control systems.

A third strategy that administrators could use to promote motivation and avoid negative consequences would be to encourage teacher involvement in almost all phases of the control system and the reward system. Teachers should be involved in developing the measures of performance and in setting standards, and they should receive feedback on their performance. They should be able to exert continuing influence over the control system.

II. A Sociological Perspective

The work of Dornbusch and Scott (1975) and Natriello and Dornbusch (1984) on evaluation and authority systems in organizations provides a slightly different perspective to guide the implementation of merit pay programs. While containing elements of the expectancy theory approach, this work moves beyond it systematically to consider more complex authority structures and organizational arrangements as they affect evaluation and control processes.

The theory of evaluation and authority begins with the assumption that evaluation is a primary mechanism for exercising control and authority in organizations. Evaluation is considered in terms of a six stage model of the evaluation process, not unlike the thermostat model proposed by Lawler. The six stages of the model are depicted in Figure 2, taken from Natriello and Dornbusch (1984:44).

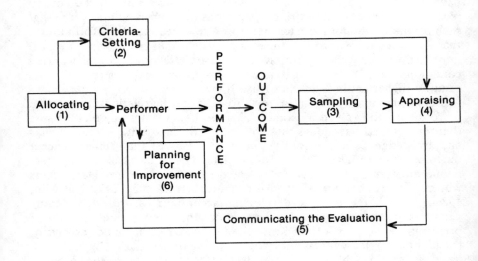

Figure 2 – A model of the Evaluation Process

The first stage, allocating, refers to the process by which tasks are assigned to individual performers in an organization. The second stage, criteria setting, refers to the process of determining which task properties will be taken into account in evaluating task performance. Sampling, the third stage, refers to the process of selecting information on the performance of the tasks. Appraising, the fourth stage, refers to the process of assigning an evaluation to a performance by comparing the information collected on the performance with the evaluative criteria established for the task. The fifth stage, communicating, refers to the process of informing the performer of the evaluation of the performance, and the sixth stage, planning for improvement, refers to the process of determining what steps need to be taken to insure future performance at an acceptable level. The model describes one complete cycle of the evaluation process.

The theory of evaluation and authority relies on three concepts to consider the conditions that promote individual effort on organization tasks. First, evaluations must be soundly based, that is, the quality of performances or outcomes as judged by the performer must be affected by the performer's level of effort and the performances or outcomes considered better by the performer must receive higher evaluations (Dornbusch and Scott, 1975:343). Second, evaluations must be influential, that is, performers must believe that evaluations have an effect on organizational sanctions (Dornbusch and Scott, 1975:338). Third, evaluations must be central, that is, they must be perceived by performers as influencing the distribution of those organizational sanctions performers consider more important. The theory argues that more soundly based, more influential, and more central evaluations lead performers to consider their tasks and the evaluations of them more important. More important tasks, in turn, lead to greater performer effort. With some slight differences to accommodate the concepts of evaluation and task importance, this approach embodies ideas like those of expectancy theory.

This approach suggests that great care must be taken in developing evaluation systems in which performer effort is reflected in evaluations which, in turn, affect the distribution of important organizational sanctions. Merit pay proposals in themselves focus on the connection between evaluations of teaching performance and valued organizational sanctions. But the theory of evaluation and authority suggests that such plans must also pay close attention to the connection between teacher effort and performance and evaluations of teaching. Studies of the processes by which teachers are evaluated (Dornbusch and Scott, 1975; Natriello and Dornbusch, 1982; Natriello, 1983; Natriello, 1984b) suggest that evaluation is a rare event in most schools. Administrators seldom have extensive training or experience in evaluating teacher performance.

Other concepts in the theory of evaluation and authority focus attention on the social character of organizations. Evaluation and control processes seldom involve a single evaluator and a single performer. Features of the evaluation system pertaining to multiple evaluators and multiple performers may also affect performer reactions to the system. Natriello and Dornbusch

(1984) note that evaluations should be reliable, that is, performers should believe that evaluations received for a given performance are based on the same criteria and standards as the evaluations received for similar performances by other participants in the same or similar positions. In addition, recent reformulations of the theory (Natriello, 1984a) have argued that evaluations should also be consistent, that is, performers should believe that evaluations received from multiple evaluators for the same tasks should be based on the same criteria and standards. The theory of evaluation and authority suggests that when evaluations are less reliable and less consistent, performers will consider them less proper, and the authority system of the organization will be weakened.

The problems of unreliable and inconsistent evaluations may be present in school organizations, particularly when merit pay systems are implemented. Teachers may quite naturally compare their performance and the resulting evaluations with the performances and resulting evaluations of their peers. When the criteria for performance are subjective, as they often are in the case of teaching, there may be much room for unreliability in the evaluation system. This condition could lead to teacher perceptions that the evaluation system is improper and to teacher resistance.

Inconsistent evaluations may occur for much the same reasons. Unless the evaluation process is structured so that all evaluators in the school or district apply the same criteria and standards when assessing teaching performance, teachers may quickly come to perceive the evaluation process as inconsistent. Teachers working under one principal may perceive other principals applying different criteria and standards. When this occurs, teachers will be less likely to perceive the system as proper, and so may resist compliance.

Like Lawler, Dornbusch and Scott also consider the negative consequences of evaluation systems. The theory of evaluation and authority argues that when performers consider their evaluations less proper or less soundly based, the organizational authority system will contain internal pressures for change. Incompatibilities in the authority system, i.e., system conditions that prevent performers from maintaining evaluations at or above a level which they find acceptable, are seen as leading to perceptions that the system is less soundly based and less proper.

Dornbusch and Scott develop a typology of authority system incompatibilities by considering the requirements of the simplest case of a compatible authority system. In a compatible system the performer, first, would receive an unambiguous task assignment which did not conflict with other assignments received for the same or similar tasks. Second, the performer's activities would affect the values of the relevant properties for performances and outcomes on which the performer would be evaluated. Third, the sample taken of the performer's work would provide valid information as to the values actually achieved in the full performance. Fourth, the standards for evaluation would be set appropriately so that the performer could expect to receive evaluations at the acceptance level by adjusting the level of effort.

The four types of authority system incompatibility discussed by Dornbusch and Scott (1975) involve the violation of one or more of these requirements for a compatible authority system. Contradictory evaluations occur when performers are in a situation in which in order to receive one evaluation at a level acceptable to them they must receive another evaluation below an acceptable level. Uncontrollable evaluations occur when performers are in a situation in which they receive evaluations below a level acceptable to them for performances or outcomes they do not control. Unpredictable evaluations occur when performers are in a situation in which they receive unacceptable evaluations because they cannot predict accurately the relationship between aspects of their performance and the level of evaluations they receive. Unattainable evaluations occur when the standards used to evaluate performers are so high that they cannot achieve evaluations at or above a level they find acceptable.

The theory (Dornbusch and Scott, 1975; Scott, Dornbusch, Busching and Laing, 1967) argues that incompatibility in authority systems leads to instability. Instability may take various forms, including performer dissatisfaction with part or all of the evaluation and authority system, communication of dissatisfaction with the authority system to others in the organization, suggestions for changes in the authority system, performer noncompliance with attempts by the organization to exercise authority over performer behavior, lowered expectations for performance and evaluations, and withdrawal from participation in the organization.

Teachers may be subjected to all of these incompatibilities in the evaluation and authority system. Contradictory evaluations may result when multiple evaluators such as principals and department chairpersons don't share the same criteria for performance or when single evaluators apply contradictory criteria such as a call for the use of creative teaching methods with high levels of student involvement but low levels of noise in the classroom. Uncontrollable evaluations may result when teachers are evaluated using measures they can't easily influence as when student scores on standardized achievement tests are the sole basis for evaluating teaching performance. Unpredictable evaluations may result if the criteria for effective teaching are not agreed upon and clearly communicated to teachers. Unattainable evaluations may result, particularly in the current climate of demands for excellence, when standards are set too high given the materials, work arrangements, and students with which a teacher has to work.

Many of these situations currently exist in schools, and they probably lead to some dissatisfaction, suggestions for change, noncompliance, lowered expectations, and withdrawal from the organization. Yet when evaluation systems with these problems are connected to a more powerful reward system such as merit pay, the theory of evaluation and authority would predict, first, that teachers would come to perceive the evaluations of their performance as more important and, second, that all of these indicators of instability would become more pronounced.

The theory of evaluation and authority also focuses on several other conditions of the workplace that affect the evaluation process. The visibility of task performance to evaluators is shown to affect the degree to which evaluations are perceived to be soundly based by performers (Dornbusch and Scott, 1975:343-345). When task performance is less visible to evaluators, performers perceive evaluations as less soundly based. The visibility issue involves the nature of the tasks, the working conditions, and the frequency of evaluations. Work may be less visible due to the nature of the task. For example, tasks where most of the work involves mental activity may not be visible to evaluators. Work also may be less visible due to the physical separation of performers and evaluators. On the other hand, more frequent efforts to evaluate through sampling of performances and outcomes may compensate for these conditions.

Visibility is an issue that certainly affects the evaluation of teaching. Teachers generally perform their tasks out of sight of their evaluators, sometimes even at home. Moreover, evaluation is an infrequent event in most schools (Natriello and Dornbusch, 1982). These factors suggest that unless administrators take special action to improve the visibility of teaching, teachers will tend to perceive the evaluations that influence the distribution of merit pay as less soundly based.

A second condition of the work of teaching that has an effect on the evaluation and authority system is the predictability of the tasks. Tasks may differ in terms of the extent to which participants believe that the resistance to carrying out task activities is predictable from performance to performance (Dornbusch and Scott, 1975:347-348). The theory argues that when tasks are less predictable, performers will prefer greater autonomy in order to respond to the changing circumstances that confront them. Accordingly, when tasks are less predictable and performers are not given autonomy, they will consider the evaluation and authority system less soundly based and less proper.

Many of the tasks of teaching, indeed the most important tasks of teaching, are quite unpredictable. It is usually not clear exactly how much resistance a teacher may encounter in teaching a particular set of materials to a particular group of students. As a result teachers will prefer greater autonomy than performers of more predictable tasks. If the evaluation and control system does not provide that autonomy, then teachers will tend to perceive their evaluations as less soundly based and less proper.

Lessons for Administrators

Several of the concepts employed by the theory of evaluation and authority call attention to the importance of the relationships between effort and performances and outcomes and between performances and outcomes and rewards, as did the work of Lawler. The theory also calls attention to certain features endemic to teaching that make sound, influential, and central evaluations difficult to achieve, features which must be addressed when implementing a merit pay system. The low visibility of teaching suggests that administrators must re-double their efforts to collect adequate samples of teaching performances and outcomes. In order to collect sufficient data administrators must be prepared to devote time and attention to this task. The cost in terms of administrative time is one of the hidden costs in merit pay systems.

The low predictability of many teaching tasks alerts administrators to a major problem in developing an adequate control system. One solution would be to emphasize those aspects of teaching that are most predictable and to strive to make the remaining aspects more predictable. However, as Wise (1979) has noted, this strategy may lead to hyperrationalization and to the trivialization of teaching which, in turn, may lead to serious negative consequences for teacher motivation (Braverman, 1974). The cure for low predictability may be worse than the problem itself.

Both the low visibility and low predictability of teaching may make it more difficult not only to develop soundly based, influential and central evaluation systems, but also to develop systems in which evaluations are reliable and consistent. Administrators must take care to avoid procedures which in either reality or appearance lead to differential evaluations of teachers from the same or different administrators. This means that the procedures must be replicable both across teachers in a single school and across schools in a district. Such procedures are likely to take a great deal of time to develop and are likely to require a substantial amount of administrator training. Moreover, continuous monitoring of the system and subsequent corrections in training and procedures may be necessary to maintain reliable and consistent evaluations.

The six-stage model of the evaluation process presented in the theory provides a guide to the activities that must be considered in developing a system. The sequence of the stages suggests that administrators must devote effort to seeing to it that the stages are not incongruous. For example, the criteria set for good teaching must be reflected in the sampling strategy used to collect data on teaching performance. Teachers must be informed not only about the results of their evaluation, but also about the criteria and measures used in developing the evaluation and about the activities they should engage in to try to improve their performance.

III. A Political Perspective

Clark and Wilson (1961) develop a theory of incentive systems in organizations which seeks to relate environmental trends, personality factors, patterns of expectations, and organizational history to the behavior of organizations. They argue that the incentive system utilized by an organization is the principal variable affecting organizational behavior and that the incentive system is altered in response to changes in the motives of contributors or potential contributors to the organization (Clark and Wilson, 1961:130). Moreover, the motives of contributors may change due: (a) to changes in the environment, (b) to changes in notions of what is possible, and (c) to changes in the organization itself (Clark and Wilson,

1961:131). Their analysis focuses on the role of the executive who must distribute incentives to members in order to maintain their continued cooperation with and support for the purposes of the organization. Thus, they deal with the political issue of maintaining participation in and compliance with the work of the organization.

Clark and Wilson (1961) classify incentives into three broad categories: material incentives or tangible incentives that have a monetary value (e.g. salary, fringe benefits); solidary incentives that derive from the act of associating with others (e.g. socializing, congeniality, sense of group membership and identification); and purposive incentives that derive from the stated ends of the association rather than from the simple act of associating (e.g. suprapersonal goals of the organization). They point out that a single organization may utilize a mix of all three incentives but argue that many organizations may be distinguished by the type of incentives upon which they primarily rely. Accordingly, they distinguish three types of organizations: utilitarian organizations which rely primarily on material incentives (e.g., business firms); solidary organizations which rely largely upon solidary incentives (e.g., service-oriented voluntary associations, colleges); and purposive organizations which rely mainly on their stated purposes to attract and hold members (e.g., reform organizations).

Public schools have utilized all three types of incentive systems. In the nineteenth century public education was a purposive activity, imbued with a sense of mission or destiny (Tyack and Hansot, 1982). Educational leaders and teachers were participants in a great and noble experiment which would transform the society. As public education became more firmly rooted among American institutions and as schools spread throughout the nations, they became more bureaucratic organizations with incentives based primarily on solidarity.

Despite the fact that the majority of public schools have relied upon solidary incentives, as Johnson (1983) points out, from time to time there have been a large number of school districts that have experimented with material incentives such as merit pay. Johnson cites NEA surveys which showed that 48 percent of the 309 districts surveyed used merit to determine salaries in 1918-1919, 33 percent of 941 districts used it in 1923, and 18 percent relied on it in some manner to determine salaries in 1928 (Johnson, 1983:177). Johnson notes that the impetus for this round of merit pay programs came from growing concern about the country's competitive position in the world, intensified by World War I. She also notes that a more recent round of merit pay programs in the fifties and sixties was influenced once again by concern about the position of the U.S. in the world, this time fueled by Sputnik and the space race and cites an Educational Research Service survey which showed that 10 percent of school districts used some form of merit pay in the 1960s.

The point is not that one form of incentive system has triumphed over others in the history of American public education, but rather that all three of the forms specified by Clark and Wilson have been relied upon from time to time. While Clark and Wilson see schools as solidary organizations, and while for much of their history most schools have relied upon solidary incentives to secure and maintain cooperation from teachers, there are more than a few examples of schools relying on purposive and material incentives.

Each type of organization has a different mix of challenges and opportunities for executives and members. In utilitarian organizations, the fundamental conflicts center around the distribution of material resources such as salary. The executive will see his or her major responsibility as obtaining material resources to provide incentives from the environment. In such circumstances the executive will pay little attention to the substantive goals of the organization, and members will rarely reflect upon or question the value of the organization's activities. Such organizations will be flexible about the actual activities carried out as long as the flow of material incentives continues. Internal conflicts may be readily settled by bargaining since material benefits are readily divisible (Clark and Wilson, 1961:139-141).

If Clark and Wilson are correct in their analysis then the adoption of merit pay plans as the primary system of incentives for teachers in certain school districts may bring both benefits and costs to public education. Their analysis suggests that in schools where teachers are subject to merit pay systems, the major areas of conflict will revolve around the distribution of merit increments to various teachers or groups of teachers. While some may doubt the contribution of such conflicts over salary to the educational process, shifting the domain of conflict to material incentives may make it easier to settle internal disputes by redistributing such resources in response to shifting demands from teachers and groups of teachers.

The theory proposed by Clark and Wilson also suggests that principals and central district administrators will devote more time to securing material resources while devoting less attention to substantive goals, and that teachers will spend less time reflecting on the basic purposes of education. This may have both positive and negative effects depending upon one's point of view. Some may decry a less professional attitude on the part of teachers, while others will welcome a less propriety approach from educators and an enhanced willingness to be responsive to the large community from whom they must secure important material resources. Schools which rely on merit pay systems may be more flexible in meeting changing demands from the community and the society.

These observations on schools as utilitarian organizations rely on an implicit contrast with the current operation of schools as solidary organizations. In solidary organizations, executives must be primarily concerned with obtaining incentives in the form of organizational prestige, publicity, and good fellowship through activities such as public speeches and recruiting additional high status members. Such organizations will act on their environment when the opportunity arises to improve their public image. Executives and members of such organizations will devote a great deal of conscious attention to the purposes of the organization. The ability of such organizations to alter their activities is more constrained than in utilitarian organizations since the activities of the organization are more central in the thinking of members. Compared to utilitarian organizations, solidary organizations will experience more severe internal tensions, and these tensions will occur over the distribution of personal prestige and organizational status. Moreover, such tensions will not be easily assuaged by material compensation (Clark and Wilson, 1961:141-146).

Schools that operate as solidary organizations should experience more severe internal tensions about the distribution of prestige and status, tensions that will be more difficult to settle than those over material incentives in utilitarian organizations. School leaders will spend more time dealing with these less tractible conflicts. They will also have to devote considerable effort to securing organizational prestige in the larger environment by communicating the purposes of the school in order to bolster the capacity of the school to offer meaningful incentives to teachers. Finally, constrained by the image of their traditional role held by both teachers and the larger community, schools which rely on solidary incentives will tend to be less flexible than those operating with material incentives.

In purposive organizations the primary efforts of the executive are devoted to creating and stating organizational purposes in order to maintain contributions of effort. Most external acts concern the achievement of goals or giving the appearance of doing so. Internal conflicts typically derive from conflicts over purposes or over the failure to attain goals and attempts to assign blame for the failure. While the incentives themselves are usually derived from organizational goals that imply change, the goals are usually inflexible, sometimes general and inapplicable to real issues and sometimes specific and sacrosanct. In such organizations a great deal of the executive's time is devoted to producing a sense of accomplishment, real or otherwise, to maintain the force of the incentives (Clark and Wilson, 1961:146-149).

Schools that rely on purposive incentives may experience the most severe and least tractible internal tensions and may have the least flexibility to respond to changing external conditions. Administrators of such schools will devote considerable attention to stating the traditional purposes of the organization and managing deep-seated internal conflicts over basic purposes.

Lessons for Administrators

Clark and Wilson (1961:149) argue that executives modify incentive systems in response to changes in the organizational environment and in response to changes in contributor motives. While executives will generally avoid purposive incentives because they result in less stable and less flexible organizations, such incentives may be resorted to in times of crisis, during the formative stage of the organization and when the group involved has few material or solidary incentives at its disposal. They thus suggest that executives will, by and large, shift between solidary and material incentives as environmental and motivational changes occur (Clark and Wilson, 1961:156-164).

Applied to changes in the use of incentives by school organizations in the past and more recently, the analysis of Clark and Wilson provides an explanation for the movement of school organizations from reliance on purposive to solidary and lately to material incentives. Schools relied on purposive incentives in their formative stages (Tyack and Hansot, 1982). As they became more established in the American institutional context, school leaders shifted to a reliance on solidary incentives which allowed greater stability and flexibility in dealing with both internal and external problems. For most schools solidary incentives served quite well for a long time.

However, in recent years changes in both the external environment and in the values of those who might consider teaching as a career have severely diminished the capacity of schools to function effectively as solidary institutions. First, the diminished reputation of public education as a prestigious institution in American society, due in part to the very success of the public school movement (Cohen and Neufeld, 1981) has severely constrained the ability of school leaders to offer solidary incentives. Second, the opening up of alternative and more lucrative paths to success for vast numbers of women and minorities and for those with a desire to enter the middle class in American society have deprived the school of the large cohorts of competent individuals who might be particularly sensitive to even the less potent solidary incentives left for the schools to offer. These conditions, which seem unlikely to pass soon, may leave administrators little choice but to consider material incentives such as merit pay.

IV. Merit Pay in Action: The Lawnview District

Administrators in the school district of Lawnview decided to adopt a merit pay plan for teachers and for administrators in 1953. Today in Lawnview, teachers and administrators still receive merit pay. Lawnview is a small affluent district in the suburbs of a major metropolitan area in the midwest. While its size and socio-economic status make it unlike many American school districts, its relatively homogeneous population and highly regarded school system afford the opportunity to examine a merit pay system under almost optimal conditions. Lawnview demonstrates how the factors noted by the theorists present themselves to administrators who manage an operating merit pay system. The material that follows on the Lawnview merit pay system comes from interviews with teachers and administrators conducted for a larger study of the system. More complete descriptions of the Lawnview merit pay system can be found in Natriello and Cohn (1983) and Cohn and Natriello (1984). Brief descriptions of the program are presented here to illustrate some of the factors noted by the social theorists.

Both Lawler and Dornbusch and Scott argue that the relationship between effort and performance is a crucial link in establishing a successful control or evaluation system. Lawler points out that working conditions must permit performers, in this case teachers, to convert their effort into desired performance and that administrators should see to it that such conditions exist. Dornbusch and Scott point out that the low predictability of many of the tasks of teaching make this particularly problematic. In Lawnview, some of the conditions that foster the connection between effort and performance exist naturally while others must be planned by administrators. Since most of the students in the Lawnview system come from middle and upper middle class backgrounds, Lawnview teachers are confronted with less diversity in learning abilities and less severe learning problems than teachers in more heterogeneous districts. Beyond this advantage, administrators in Lawnview have worked to develop and maintain good working conditions. Teachers are provided the latest in supplies and equipment, and the average class size is the lowest in the metropolitan area.

Lawler and Dornbusch and Scott also point out the importance of the relationship between performance and rewards. Their analyses suggest that this relationship can be enhanced through a careful and sophisticated approach to supervision which provides teachers with knowledge of appropriate techniques of instruction. Administrators in Lawnview report devoting a great deal of time and attention to supervision, and teachers view the quality of the supervision they receive as a strength of the system. One teacher reported finding her principal helpful because "he keeps up on research — he keeps me informed about developments in my field I don't know about." Another teacher sees her principal as a "resource." The principal at one elementary school in the district is respected by one teacher for his "expertise" on students, by another for his "knowledge of curriculum" and by numerous others for simply knowing what's going on with every child. A teacher planning to retire reflected on her experience with the observation that, "Lawnview has given me an education that no college could give me."

The crucial relationship between performance and rewards can also be enhanced by the development of a good evaluation system, one that is inclusive of the most important aspects of teaching and one that provides accurate and relatively objective assessments of teacher performance. The criteria for evaluation have been one of the central features of the Lawnview system since its inception. The original criteria developed in 1953 were fairly inclusive, as evidenced by their organization under three broad headings: "Personal Qualities of the Superior Teacher," "Professional Training and Growth Leading to Superior Teaching," and "Evidence of Superior Teaching." These criteria have been revised several times. In 1966 the criteria were re-written in more behavioral terms. The document describing these criteria makes reference to the work of Bloom (1965), Gagne (1965), and Mager (1962) as it seeks to provide a more behaviorally oriented and objective treatment of criteria for teaching. The criteria were revised again in 1981 to be more specific about the evidence of teaching performance used in the evaluation process.

Gary Natriello

District administrators described the changes in the criteria for the evaluation of teaching over the years as a process of clarifying and explaining more precisely just what is expected of teachers. As might be expected from the work of Lawler, educators in the district, both administrators and teachers, have felt the need to move from criteria involving higher inference levels on the part of evaluators to criteria involving lower inference levels.

The attention to precision in the criteria for teaching has carried over into other aspects of the evaluation process. Administrators have received training in how to collect data on teaching performance to support their appraisals. The problem of the limited visibility of teaching performance noted by Dornbusch and Scott has been attacked in a number of ways. All principals are required to make at least three formal observations during the school year, but most rely on a variety of techniques for collecting information on performance, from parent reports to informal weekly conference, to monitoring student work. One principal explained how even artifacts such as the amount of certain supplies used by a teacher could be a clue to the kind of work going on in a particular classroom. The pressure on principals to collect adequate information on teacher performance, i.e., to perform Lawler's sensor function, comes from both teachers concerned about their merit increments and from administrative superiors. The written evaluations that principals make of teacher performance are subject to challenge from teachers appealing their increments and to review by central office administrators who examine them to see if appraisals are justified by evidence from observations or other sources.

Studies of the appraisal process have been conducted by members of the administrative team. A study based on evaluations of teachers in 1964-65 and 1970-71 found these evaluations offered little in the way of specific detail on either the source of evidence for the judgment or the specific criteria against which the evidence was compared in the discriminator function noted by Lawler (Shaughnessy, 1976). A second study based on evaluations of teachers from 1977 through 1979 found that progress had been made in connecting appraisals to criteria and evidence (Faulk, 1983).

The involvement of performers in the design and implementation of control and reward systems has proven valuable in the Lawnview system. A key element in the program from the beginning has been the Committee on Evaluation. This committee, consisting of the superintendent, a representative from the administrative staff, and one teacher representative from each elementary school and two from each secondary school, has been the main vehicle for staff participation in the design and operation of the program. The Committee on Evaluation conducted a survey which led to the original criteria for evaluation, and a sub-committee of this committee drafted the 1966 revision of the criteria in more behavioral and objective terms. Building representatives to the committee solicit the views of teachers about he evaluation process and serve to orient new staff members to the valuation and merit pay system. Administrators credit members of this committee with handling many of the problems reported by the teaching staff.

As the analysis of Clark and Wilson would suggest, many of the internal tensions in the district concern the distribution of material resources in the form of merit pay. Some charges deal with alleged favoritism within a school, a problem in the reliability of evaluations in the terminology of Natriello and Dornbusch. One teacher interviewed accused the principal of having favorites, while another teacher, reputed to be on the favored list, felt that, "the favorites are the ones who do the best job." Other charges deal with differences between evaluators in different buildings in line with Natriello and Dornbusch's concept of consistency. One teacher who felt that the inconsistencies were far too great across buildings suggested that evaluators work across buildings. Central office administrators noted another type of problem regarding consistency. They observed that some principals are more effective than others in building a case in support of their teachers. These principals are able to secure higher increases for the teachers in their schools.

Another major area of conflict in recent years has concerned the way in which teacher effort in extracurricular activities is rewarded. Sponsorship of extracurricular activities is currently included in the regular teacher evaluation process and the regular merit pay program. There is no extra compensation for sponsoring activities. This is viewed as unfair by many of the elementary teachers who argue that they don't have the opportunity to do as much outside of school as junior and senior high teachers. Some elementary teachers feel that the only way to obtain the highest rating and the highest increment is to become a coach. On the other hand, those teachers who do coach feel that their extra work is often not reflected in their merit increments; they have argued for extra compensation.

While internal conflicts appear to revolve around the issue of the distribution of material rewards, there appears to be little use of the non-monetary rewards used by principals in other schools. For example, while deCharms and Natriello (1981) found that principals sometimes used things such as scheduling preferences and class assignments to reward and punish teachers in schools without merit pay programs, teachers in Lawnview report that such decisions are made solely on the basis of educational reasons, never to reward and punish teachers.

While the Lawnview merit pay system has encountered problems over the years, it has endured by adapting to pressures from teachers, administrators, and the community. Administrators in Lawnview have learned to deal with some of the critical factors suggested by the social theorists. This brief examination of their experience provides a more graphic example of some of the dilemmas that those about to design and implement merit pay programs might expect and the ways in which these dilemmas have been addressed in one district.

Conclusions

The implications of the social science theories for the implementation of merit pay programs for teachers are mixed. On the one hand, the perspectives of Lawler and of Dornbusch and Scott point up the various problems that merit pay will pose for teachers and administrators along with some strategies to minimize, but not eliminate, those problems. On the other hand, the perspective of Clark and Wilson suggests that school administrators must still secure the cooperation of teachers at a time when the traditional solidary incentives offered by schools are becoming less effective.

The future of merit pay programs in the public schools may depend far less upon the internal workability of such plans (the severe problems identified earlier not withstanding) as some have suggested (Johnson, 1983), and upon their effectiveness and efficiency as others have noted (Murnane, 1981), than upon the capacity of school leaders and schools to regain powerful solidary incentives to make schools viable solidary organizations. While the analyses suggested by the perspective of Lawler and that of Dornbusch and Scott point to the difficult internal problems that must be confronted by those instituting merit pay programs for teachers, the analysis suggested by the theory of Clark and Wilson points up the dilemma of school administrators who resist merit pay programs in the face of changes in environmental conditions and in the values of potential teachers.

These social science theories give some sense of the options open to school leaders interested in improving schools through strengthening the incentives available for use in recruiting and retaining competent and highly skilled teachers. One option would be to seek to enhance the capacity of schools to utilize material incentives by securing sufficient resources to institute programs such as merit pay. The other would be to seek to enhance the store of solidary incentives available to the schools by restoring some of the lost prestige to public education and public school teaching. As the theorists have pointed out, school administrators will confront substantial challenges in pursuing either course of action.

References

Blau, P.M. and W.R. Scott. *Formal Organizations.* San Francisco: Chandler, 1962.

Bloom, B. (ed.) *Taxonomy of Educational Objectives* New York: Longmans, Green, 1956.

Braverman, H. *Labor and Monopoly Capital.* New York: Monthly Review Press, 1974.

Clark, P. and J. Wilson. "Incentive Systems: A Theory of Organizations." *Administrative Science Quarterly*, 6, 1961:129-166.

Cohen, D. and B. Neufeld. "The Failure of High Schools and the Progress of Education." *Daedalus*, 110, 1981:69-89.

Cohn, M. and G. Natriello. "Critical Issues in the Development of a Merit Pay System." Paper presented at the Annual Meeting of the American Educational Research Association. New Orleans, LA: April, 1984.

Darling-Hammond, L., A.E. Wise, and S.R. Pease. "Teacher Evaluation in the Organizational Context: A Review of the Literature." *Review of Educational Research*, 53, 1983:285-328.

Daugherty, G. and G. Dronberger. "A Merit Pay Program that Works: The Seiling Oklahoma Experience." *Spectrum*, 1, 1983:3-10.

deCharms, R. and G. Natriello. "Evaluation and Teacher Motivation," Report Submitted to the Spencer Foundation, St. Louis, MO: 1981.

Dornbusch, S.M. and W.R. Scott. *Evaluation and the Exercise of Authority*. San Francisco: Jossey-Bass, 1975.

Dowd, M. "A Course in Politics: Reagan and the Democrats Try for High Marks on Education." *Time*, July 20, 1983:14-15.

Faulk, L. "A Comparative Analysis of Teacher Evaluations Written by Administrators." Unpublished Doctoral Dissertation, Columbia University, 1983.

Gagne, R. *The Conditions of Learning*. New York: Holt, Rinehart and Winston, 1983.

Johnson, S.M. "Merit Pay for Teachers: A Poor Prescription for Reform." *Harvard Educational Review*, 54, 1984:175-185.

Lawler, E.E. "Control Systems in Organizations." pp. 1247-1291 in M.D. Dunnette (ed.), *Handbook of Industrial and Organizational Psychology*. Chicago: Rand McNally, 1976.

Mager, R. *Preparing Instructional Objectives*. Palo Alto, California: Fearon Publishers, 1962.

Murnane, R.J. "Seniority Rules and Educational Productivity: Understanding the Consequences of a Mandate for Equality." *American Journal of Education*, 89, 1981:14-38.

National Commission on Excellence in Education, *A Nation at Risk: The Imperative for Educational Reform*. Washington, D.C. U.S. Government Printing Office, 1983.

Natriello, G. "Evaluation Frequency, Teacher Influence, and the Internalization of Evaluation Processes: A Review of Six Studies Using the Theory of Evaluation and Authority." Eugene Oregon: Center for Educational Policy and Management, University of Oregon, 1983.

Natriello, G. "A Reformulation of the Theory of Evaluation and Authority." Baltimore, Maryland: Unpublished Paper, 1984a.

Natriello, G. "Teacher's Perceptions of the Frequency of Evaluation and Assessments of Their Efforts and Effectiveness." *American Educational Research Journal*, 21, 1984b:579-596.

Natriello, G. and M. Cohn. "Beyond Sanctions: The Evolution of a Merit Pay System." Paper presented at the Annual Meeting of the American Educational Research Association. Montreal, Canada, 1983.

Natriello, G. and S.M. Dornbusch. "Pitfalls in the Evaluation of Teachers by Principals." *Administrators Notebook*, 29, 1982:1-4.

Natriello, G. and S.M. Dornbusch. *Teacher Evaluative Standards and Student Effort*. Longman, 1984.

Scott, W.R., S.M. Dornbusch, B.C. Busching, and J.D. Laing. "Organizational Evaluation and Authority." *Administrative Sciences Quarterly*, 12, 1967:93-117.

Shaughnessy, J.T. "Merit Pay: A Functional Analysis of Teacher Evaluations Written by Administrators." Unpublished doctoral dissertation, Columbia University, 1976.

Tennessee State Department of Education. "Tennessee's Better Schools Program: A Summary of Governor Lamar Alexander's State of Education Address." Nashville, Tennessee, 1983.

Twentieth Century Fund. *Report of the Twentieth Century Fund Task Force on Federal Elementary and Secondary Education Policy*. New York, 1983.

Tyack, D. and E. Hansot. *Managers of Virtue*. New York: Basic Books, 1982.

Walton, S. "Florida Teachers Union to Offer Alternate Merit Pay Plan to Council." *Education Week*, 30, October 26, 1983:8.

Weick, K. "Administering Education in Loosely Coupled Schools." *Phi Delta Kappan*, 63, 1982:673-676.

MANAGERIAL EXPERIENCE WITH MERIT PAY: A SURVEY OF THE BUSINESS LITERATURE

David F. Wood

Dan S. Green

Merit in the Business Literature

Since 1983, the issue of merit pay has received more attention from the mass media and politicians than any other issue in education in the last few decades. Among professional educators, merit pay stands out as the issue of the era. The National Commission on Excellence in Education, in its recent report, "A Nation at Risk: The Imperative for Educational Reform" (1983), called for "performance-based pay" for teachers. One of the recommendations of the recent Congressional Task Force on Merit Pay was that "despite mixed and inconclusive results with performance-based pay in the private sector and in education, we support and encourage experiments with performance-based pay."

The concept of merit pay, generally defined as pay for performance, is nearly as old as the concept of work for pay. The use of merit pay in the business world is a time-honored practice. Although not a new practice to education, recently many school systems have considered or have implemented some type of merit pay system.

The recent concern regarding the quality of public education, bolstered by President Reagan's call for merit pay for teachers to remedy the problem, has elevated the term merit pay to a household word. The literature on merit pay, both theoretical and empirical, is vast and complex and is found primarily in three disciplines — business, education, and psychology. Because of the overall and increasing importance of merit pay systems, and because many of the ideas regarding merit pay in the educational literature are based on the use of merit pay systems in the business world, we have surveyed the business literature on merit pay from 1970 to the present. It is our hope that the results of this survey will be instructive to those thinking about or considering a merit pay system.

Our survey is based on 66 articles that appeared in the business literature between 1968 and 1983 that discussed some facet of merit pay. Some articles discussed the concept or issue of merit pay in general; others described specific cases of the implementation of merit pay programs. A third category of articles reported surveys of employee responses regarding merit programs. Generally there is agreement that merit pay programs, properly implemented, will result in improved motivation among managers and a higher level of effort among employees. Also, the authors generally agree that merit pay systems are consistent with current theories of motivation, especially Victor Vroom's (1964) expectancy theory.

Vroom's expectancy theory is built around three variables: valence of needs satisfied, want-need instrumentality, and effort-want expectancy. Valence refers to the attractiveness of the needs that might be satisfied. Want-need instrumentality is defined as the perceived relationship between actual need satisfaction and obtaining specific rewards. Effort-want expectancy refers to the perceived relationship between effort expended and desired specific rewards. More simply, expectancy theory posits that if employees want higher pay and they believe that working harder will bring them more pay, they will work harder to gain more pay. It is this expectancy that most authors cite as the reason that merit pay systems should be successful.

Problems with Merit Pay in Business

Although most of the authors support the general concept of merit pay, many disadvantages with the current implementation of such pay-for-performance systems are noted. Some of the disadvantages were found in the underlying assumptions of merit pay itself; however, most focused on the organizational climate, the implementation process, or the specific managers involved. It is of interest to note that, as important as the assumptions are, no article explicitly lists them; they appear casually, in part, in only a few articles. It seems as though it is assumed that they are well known and valid. The disadvantages cited can be grouped into four major categories. The first category deals with the individuals responsible for merit evaluations. The second focuses on overall organization policies and procedures. The third deals with the implementation and operation of merit systems, and the fourth category considers problems with the specific instruments used to evaluate personnel.

Adequacy of Evaluators

A merit pay system is essentially an evaluative process. As an evaluative process, it is a social phenomenon, governed by the norms which govern human interaction and subject to the patterns and fallacies of human behavior. Employee assessment is the key process of a merit pay system. Several questions have been raised about the behavior of supervisors charged with initiating and performing merit evaluations. Authors who discussed the adequacy of evaluators include Burke (1972), Carey (1980), Winstanley (1980), Lawler (1978, 1981). and Mihal (1983). Several concerns were noted in these articles. Lawler (1978), commenting on employee performance appraisal, characterized it as a "fairly crude" process: "It's probably the most difficult area in terms of relating pay to performance."

First, the administrators responsible for performing the evaluations have little formal training in evaluation and are generally ill-prepared for the complex task of evaluating their employees. It seems that most organizations assume that, once one is a supervisor, he or she is capable of conducting an accurate and adequate merit evaluation. Secondly, since few if any rewards are given for being a proficient evaluator, there is little incentive to improve. Burke (1972) especially emphasizes that the skill requirements for being a successful evaluator are opposed to those required for day-to-day management, hence it is unlikely that most managers will become capable evaluators without special training.

Thirdly, the problem of subjective evaluations or favoritism is frequently mentioned. Herbert Meyer (1975) believes that typical supervisors in organizations with merit pay systems give employees about the same size merit increase except for differences based on personal factors such as length of service, future potential, or perceived need to boost an employee's ego. Burke (1972) suggests that a partial reason for perceived favoritism may be that a superior's frame of reference is likely to be different from most subordinates, which may encourage them to perceive favoritism, even if it does not exist. This is especially noticed in the tendency for most people to believe that they are above average in performance even if they in fact are not. Thus they would perceive a "fair" merit increase as inconsistent with their perceptions.

A final issue regarding the evaluator and the evaluation process deals with the human consequences of the evaluation. Very simply, it may be difficult for a manager to evaluate his employees without considering the consequences of the evaluation; this means that the evaluation may be less than objective. As Thompson and Dalton (1970) claim, "Performance appraisal touches on one of the most emotionally charged activities in business life — the assessment of a man's contribution and ability. The signals he receives about this assessment have a strong impact on his self-esteem and on his subsequent performance." Meyer (1975) also writes that a merit system is likely to threaten the self-esteem of the great majority of employees because they will not receive the reward that they feel their performance justifies.

Organizational Problems

The second major category of problems with merit systems in the literature relates to organizational policies and procedures, including strategic planning, organization design, and control policies and procedures. Authors who have discussed organizational concerns include Costello and Zalkind (1962), Burke (1972), Lupton and Gowler (1972),

Zand (1972), Farmer (1978), Carey (1980) Belcher (1980), Winstanley (1980), Lawler (1981), Hubbartt (1982), Bushardt (1982), Winstanley (1982) and Mihal (1983). An essential part of planning a merit pay system is the formulation of goals. These authors present a strong argument that the goals of merit pay systems are often fuzzy or conflicting. Merit pay system designers generally claim that the motivation of employees is a (or the) major goal, yet, when one examines the implementation of merit systems in detail, it often seems that the primary intent is to provide a social control system to insure that certain tasks are done in specific ways. Lupton and Gowler (1972) point out that these two goals are conflicting.

Furthermore, if one examines a firm from a systems approach, there are several control subsystems which affect any manager. The technological subsystem is typically designed by industrial engineers to insure production efficiency. The workflow administration subsystem controls deadlines and schedules to accomplish certain tasks, and the supervision and personnel subsystems are designed to develop, train, and promote managers. A merit pay system becomes yet another form of control system added to these. Lupton and Gowler (1972) stress that little thought is generally given to make these systems consistent with each other. This is especially relevant to merit pay in that merit evaluations are typically conducted annually, while the other systems exert their control on a much more frequent basis. Thus, it is argued, the merit system is likely to be ineffective if it is inconsistent with the other control systems.

Organizational design can also be a factor. Lawler (1981) highlights that matrix organizational structures are inherently in conflict with merit systems since in a matrix organization individuals have more than one evaluator for different portions of their activity. Often a project leader will evaluate an employee for a given period of time or job in addition to a functional superior who is usually responsible for the individual's merit evaluation. Lawler (1981) points out that evaluations based on multiple evaluators present a serious problem when they are combined. Another problem related to the organizational structure has to do with the interdependence of tasks between individuals and across organizational subdivisions. In this case, judging an individual by performance measures becomes extremely difficult, if not inappropriate. First, the organization must be redesigned to contain significant task interdependence within departments and within an individual's scope of authority. Lawler (1981:53) states the problem succinctly:

"It is impossible to have an effective merit pay system if, for example, jobs are poorly designed and the organization is poorly structured. What this means is that a necessary part of a merit system is performance evaluation, and performance can be evaluated accurately only if all of the parts of a particular task can be ascribed to one individual.

Another point emphasized by these authors, especially Zand (1972), is that if individuals don't trust each other and the organization, no merit pay system will be perceived as fair. Favoritism will be inferred, and motivation will not be improved.

Implementation and Operation of Merit Systems

A third major category of problems consists of specific environmental obstacles to the implementation and operation of merit pay systems. Sources which have dealt with this type of problem include *Banking* (1975), Johnston (1978), *Across the Board* (1978), Farmer (1978), Hills (1979), Piamonte (1979), Spencer (1980), Lawler (1981), Silverman (1981), Goodale and Mouser (1981), and Bushardt (1982).

One problem in this category has to do with the result of supervisors' beliefs and needs. A belief often cited is that "everyone deserves something." Secondly, Lawler (1981) points out that giving disparate raises causes conflict, and managers often desire to avoid conflict. This leads to rather narrow differences in merit increases, even in the face of wide differences in performance. The idea of merit pay, or pay-for-performance, seems to run contrary to current societal norms which emphasize equality and the widely held notion that seniority and longevity ought to be rewarded.

A major factor which impacts on a merit pay system is the external environment. In an inflationary period, cost-of-living raises often dwarf merit raises, minimizing an employee's perception of the merit raise. Also, in a similar manner, external equity adjustments cause similar problems because the job market has dictated higher entry level salaries. A further concern in many cases is that there are limited financial resources which can be devoted to merit increases. Exacerbating this limitation are fringe benefits like hospitalization, which have become much more expensive yet are not perceived by employees as a "raise." Finally, Silverman (1981) notes that often an organization's promotion policies lead to "automatic promotions," and hence to pay increases which have little to do with merit, thus obscuring the function and perception of a merit increase.

Piamonte (1979:597) has observed that operating managers are much less in favor of merit than senior managers who institute such systems: "Senior managers of countless firms demonstrate an amazing resistance to the news that their merit-pay schemes are not working. The want merit pay in spite of the following facts: (1) Their operating level managers find their roles in a merit-pay program distasteful. (2) Fashionable theories of motivation tend to denigrate the worth of money as a motivator. (3) More employees are upset than uplifted at merit-pay time when expected pay allotments fail to materialize. (4) There is little (if any) hard evidence linking the introduction of a merit-pay program to either increased motivation or to the presumed ultimate objective — increased work force productivity." However, Piamonte believes that these attitudes proceed from faulty implementation, not the nature of merit pay. He concludes positively, claiming that: "Administered correctly, it's still the best way to encourage high performance."

Adequacy of Instruments

The fourth major category of merit pay problems focuses on the validity and use of the specific evaluation instruments. Authors who mention this category include Evans (1970), Burke (1972), Mobley (1974), Johnston (1978), Brinks (1980), Carey (1980), and Goodale and Mouser (1981).

Evans (1970:729) unequivocally points out that "Most performance evaluation programs do not attempt to measure true performance." Instead, they measure traits and personalities. An examination of typical instruments used to evaluate managers for merit increases include factors such as "cooperation" and "commitment to the goals of the organization." These particular factors are less related to performance than they are to a manager's personality. Lawler (1981) believes that "merit pay plans that don't truly link pay to performance will become less and less acceptable."

A second major objection is that the instruments focus on a subset of an individual's activity. Evaluative instruments also tend to emphasize quantitative measures over qualitative ones, and more visible activities over less visible ones. Individuals whose tasks are less measurable or whose jobs contribute only indirectly to measurable output are thus slighted. It is also noted that the instruments reward individual rather than group accomplishments. An important example of this is that typically an individual's socioemotional roles in groups are ignored, yet these roles have been widely cited for the last thirty years as an important and necessary component of group performance (Homans, 1950).

The question of the adequacy of the evaluative instrument cannot be minimized. Athough as important as the instrument is, according to Evans (1970), "the objectivity or subjectivity of the appraisal device itself is not nearly as important as the objectivity or subjectivity of the factors that are evaluated."

Problems with the Merit Concept Itself

There have also been some objections to merit pay systems on the more fundamental level of the concept itself — e.g., Patten (1976) and Johnston (1978). The same objections are also raised by Brinks (1980).

Perry and Pearce (1983) claim that although the purpose of merit pay systems is to motivate employees, in practice they do not seem to lead to increased motivation. One reason they cite is that the majority of people see themselves as above average. This causes a negative reaction, hence negative motivation, when roughly 50% of employees are rated as below average by a merit scale. Another side of this problem is that merit systems are typically norm-referenced. That is, a person's rating is relative to the others in his unit. Thus, it is quite possible that a large majority of employees can exceed an expected or standard criterion, yet the merit raise distribution will be forced to be symmetric, with only a few individuals receiving high raises. According to Meyer (1975) "The fact that almost everyone thinks he is an

David F. Wood & Dan S. Green

above-average performer lies at the root of most of our problems with merit pay plans."

Another consequence of having a norm-referenced system is that due to the usual fixed-total merit budgets, the merit process becomes a "zero-sum" game. Thus, for any one employee to receive more, someone else must receive less. This can lead to reduced cooperation and mutual trust, causing the entire system to be less effective.

Hills (1979) suggests that pay may be a demotivator: "Pay for performance may actually decrease employee satisfaction with the work, resulting in lower motivation and performance in the long run." Regarding motivation, Deci (1976) argues that if one uses rewards as an extrinsic motivator of performance, the rewards must be directly contingent upon performance. However, in doing this, intrinsic motivation will be decreased. Accordingly, Deci claims,

> Making rewards noncontingent upon performance will not interfere with intrinsic motivation; but neither will it motivate extrinsically. Thus there is a trade-off between the effects of rewards on intrinsic motivation and extrinsic motivation — in other words, is the increment in extrinsic motivation greater than the concomitant decrement in intrinsic motivation?

Similarly, Meyer (1975) writes that "merit pay emphasizes the direct relationship between job performance and dollar rewards, thereby detracting from intrinsic motivation in the work itself."

Merit systems are also often seen as costly to administer. Miller (1979), especially, points out that managers view the cost of turnover and retraining due to the loss of marginal employees when they are dissatisfied with their merit increase as greater than the savings in the organization resulting from performance improvements.

Management by Objectives

To deal with some of the problems with evaluator training and bias, and with inadequate standardized evaluation instruments, it has been suggested that Management by Objectives (MBO) be used in conjunction with merit pay programs. The basic thrust of a Management by Objective program is that supervisors and subordinates jointly set goals and agree on specific ways to measure their accomplishment(s). It therefore seems natural that merit pay systems could be based on MBO evaluations. MBO allows each individual to be rated on the performance attributes which are most relevant to him/her rather than on a standardized set of factors purported to describe everyone's job. This idea has been examined by Tosi and Carroll (1972), Kirkpatrick (1973), Mobley (1974), Hunady and Varney (1974), Patten (1976), Murray and Kuffel (1978), and Brumback and McFee (1982).

MBO is also promoted because it allows more objectives to be considered than would otherwise be the case. It also improves communication between manager and employee about the salary determination process since it involves periodic meetings to evaluate progress on specific, quantified objectives. There are also some disadvantages with tying merit pay to an MBO system. Mobley (1974) notes many of the arguments against linking MBO to merit compensation, but concludes that the positive arguments seem to outweigh the negative arguments. Since in an MBO program subordinates initiate the goal formation process, there may be a tendency to reduce the level of goals. Secondly, MBO tends to highlight quantitative goals rather than qualitative ones. Because of the personalized and individualized nature of an MBO evaluation, comparing individuals becomes more difficult. Especially troublesome is measuring the degree of challenge or difficulty inherent in accomplishing a particular goal. Finally, MBO typically emphasizes individual goals over group goals which may or may not be a concern.

All of the authors who examine MBO as a beneficial base for merit pay recognize these difficulties, but only Patten (1976) concludes that MBO is inappropriate for merit pay. He believes than an MBO-merit pay relationship would interfere with the overall mutual trust level of groups within a firm. Patten further believes that pay should not be given only for results, but also for loyalty and longevity. Murray and Kuffel (1978) agree that there are disadvantages with an MBO-merit pay linkage and that any MBO program will fail unless it is consistent with and supported by the firm's salary structure. Mobley (1974) is a bit more positive and suggests MBO and merit should be tied together in those situations where the advantages outweigh the disadvantages. Brumback and McFee (1982) simply believe that MBO alone is not enough; they coin the term MBR — Management of Behavior and Results — which incorporates MBO (performance or results analysis) and adds evaluation of behavior (efforts and activities) to a person's performance analysis.

The Definition of Merit

Virtually none of the articles cited above attempts to define merit. It was universally assumed that an individual's superior would somehow evaluate him or her. In an MBO situation, merit would be given to those who surpassed the agreed-upon goals. In articles concerned with a universal evaluation instrument, it was assumed that merit would be defined by categorizing individuals into approximately four broad categories, perhaps quartiles of the employee population as measured by the evaluative instrument.

Five articles dealt with specific examples of merit systems which have been implemented in sufficient detail to enable us to gain an insight into how merit has been defined in practice. Johnson and McCloskey (1978) describe a merit system at the Red River Army Depot, where merit was defined as Ability, Skill, and Knowledge (ASK) and was determined by testing individuals. This differs from the usual performance-related definition of merit, although the authors showed a correlation between employee test scores and supervisory judgments about their performance. Xerox (1978) carefully specifies the management review levels for recommending merit (bonus) awards, but the criteria used were not specified. AT&T (Tomasko, 1982) gives a lump sum award to employees who are defined as meritorious by exceeding corporate goals. A given percentage of the evaluation is focused on operational results, and a percentage is based on superceding strategic milestones. Tomasko (1982) stresses that the stage of a given product life cycle affects how high the goals should be set. Hubbell (1974) showed that merit at Allis Chalmers was represented by an employee's quartile score on a comprehensive rating instrument.

The Mechanics of Merit Pay

Many of the articles were not concerned with the advantages and disadvantages of merit pay, but dealt with the mechanics of effective implementation. It was generally assumed that there should be ranges of salary with minimums for entry level employees and an established maximum for each grade. Goldberg (1977) summarized the operation of many plans. The midpoint of the salary range for a grade is the amount an employee would expect to earn after he had spent enough time in the position to learn the duties well. The upper half of the salary range would be reserved for merit increases.

Other authors recommend varying percentage increases to reflect degrees of merit (Matichuk, 1977; Fleuter, 1979; Brinks, 1981). Still others were more concerned with eliminating such side effects of merit pay systems as leap-frogging salaries of employees with equal ratings. Stokes (1981) and Fleuter (1979) both offered detailed proposals to accomplish this. Krefting and Mahoney (1977) investigated the smallest meaningful pay increase and its determinants.

Results of Research Studies

Twelve articles were found which reported actual experience with merit pay systems. The articles focused on several different points. Rappold (1981) and Siegel (1981) reported results from the Federal Government's first experience with merit pay. Performance was evaluated by each supervisor, categorizing subordinates into five broad categories. The authors believed that, while evaluations tended to cluster in the higher categories, the experiences were positive. What can be learned from these experiences is detailed by Siegel (1981) as follows:

(1) Management should set the writing of performance appraisal standards as a top priority. (2) Figure out a merit pay plan now, and test it. (3) Allow time for employees to work under these standards. (4) Review the reviewers. Differences in rating philosophy among supervisors in a pool was a problem in most agencies in 1980. (5) Establish your training needs and meet them. (6) If you need help at step 1, get it.

Three studies actually tested the impact of merit pay systems on effort expended. Perry and Pearce (1983) found that managers in the U.S. Federal Civil Service did not expect that a large amount of effort would lead to a high performance rating, and further they did not expect that a high rating would lead to a significant pay increase. The result of this is, at least in the given case, that the merit pay system had not fulfilled the purpose for which it was designed. Thus, in Vroom's terms, they found that, while the valence of a pay increase was relatively high, the instrumentality of a high rating leading to the reward and the expectancy of receiving a high rating were both quite low. Belcher (1980) also tested Vroom's theory as applied to merit pay and found that effort applied to a job was only related to its consequences (expectancy, instrumentality and valence of rewards) for those with a high perception of their own ability. With those having a low perception of their ability, or with those employees who had performed the same job for a long period of time, effort seemed to be unrelated to consequences. Winstanley (1979, 1982) found that half of a sample of managers surveyed at Xerox thought that merit raises and effort were unrelated.

Kopelman and Reinharth (1982) also examined the relationship between merit pay systems and performance. In their study, there seemed to be a much higher substantiation of Vroom's model. They found that the higher the correlation between performance evaluations and rewards received, the higher the performance level was likely to be. Their study found that the larger the range of pay increases, the higher the actual performance level. Also, they found that rewards had a higher correlation with future performance levels than with the current level. This finding suggests that rewards may act as future motivators, rather than recognizing past motivation. It may be that employees need to see the results of the merit system before they actually begin to believe in it. Once they are convinced that it works as intended, they alter their behavior accordingly.

The second question asked by surveys was the extent to which merit pay is perceived as such during an inflationary period. The AMA Forum (1982) found that there has been a larger percentage increase in inflationary adjustments at the low end of salary ranges than there has been in average merit increases. This suggests that the basic entry level salary for many positions has been increasing faster than the pay of more experienced employees, even with merit increases. The result of this tendency is a situation leading to severe salary compression. Krefting and Mahoney (1977) surveyed individuals in various occupations and organizations to determine the factors which influence the size of the smallest meaningful pay increase. They found that inflation rate, last pay increase, expected pay increase, and pay satisfaction were most significant. Supporting the influence of inflation, Giles and Barrett (1971) concluded that the marginal utility of merit increases is increasing. Patten (1968:38) concluded his survey of a large unnamed corporation with the observation that, "The facts of organizational life clearly affect merit increases in such a way that pay-for-performance cannot be viewed as a pure concept... Salary indexes, salary grades, employee ages, length of service, and performance of divisions all affect merit appraisals."

The third question asked by surveys was whether or not merit pay systems led to happy (presumably highly motivated) employees and better organizational performance. Smith (1972) found that, by and large, employees under merit systems were not appreciably more satisfied than they had been without such systems. He also found that organizations with merit systems did not perform appreciably better financially than those without.

Finally, two articles evaluated the definition of merit used in actual merit pay systems. Both Evans (1970) and Winstanley (1975) found that an overwhelming number of companies claimed to have merit pay systems (between 90% and 93%) but that only a very few actually measured performance in a systematic way. What most companies measured were personality traits or attitude. This is perhaps the key issue surrounding the concept and/or implementation of merit pay — many systems are simply not based on merit (performance) and rely too much on subjective attributes, rather than objective, performance factors.

Conclusion

What then can be said to summarize the results of the studies? The business literature clearly shows, with few exceptions, that the concept of merit pay is praised. Also, with few exceptions, the use of a properly designed and implemented merit pay system is said to be a valuable management tool. The issue of merit pay is, however, not without its critics. Meyer (1975), one of the most vocal critics of merit pay, believes that most of the problems with merit pay systems is based on the fact that the great majority of employees feel that their own job performance is above average — the consequence of this is that the self-esteem of those whose performance is rated average or below will be threatened. In turn, this can lead to employees demeaning the importance of the job or disparaging management.

Also, "merit pay emphasizes the direct relationship between job performance and dollar rewards, thereby detracting from intrinsic motivation in the work itself" (Meyer, 1975). Meyer suggests that, in lieu of a merit pay system, both the individual and organizational goals would be more effectively served by "a system that would switch the emphasis to rewards for self-development and opportunities for greater responsibility."

Lawler (1981) notes that "nearly all organizations claim that they use merit pay systems. Unfortunately, most of these systems have failed." Most have failed, he argues, because of poor performance measures, poor communication of salary determination practices, a poor delivery system, and poor managerial behavior, primarily in the failure to recommend widely different pay increases given a wide range of performance differences. He concludes that "they are clearly trying to avoid the unpleasant task of explaining a low raise to their subordinates."

Yet Lawler, one of the most ardent advocates of merit pay, still claims that "today, organizations need motivational tools more than ever. Clearly, paying for performance can't solve all motivational problems. But it can help, and this fact makes continuing efforts to develop effective merit pay systems both likely and important." Farmer (1978) reinforces this, stating that "in a private enterprise system, a good merit pay program is the best motivator organizations have."

In considering the use of a merit pay system, the business literature strongly suggests that the system be thoroughly deliberated and planned. One should not merely propose or decree a system. It must be emphasized that a great deal of time and effort must be expended in the design stage to insure that the system can be implemented as conceived. According to Lawler (1981): "It seems clear that many companies have latched on to the concept of merit pay without being aware of what is needed to make a merit system work."

Accurate and adequate performance appraisal is vital to the success of any merit pay system. Managers must be trained to accurately evaluate their employees. Again, according to Lawler (1981): "In order for appraisal to be effective, people need to be trained, systems must be developed, and time must be invested in the process by both appraisor and appraisee." Burke (1972) argues that it is unlikely that most managers will become competent evaluators without special training. Performance evaluations should be objective, valid and performance-based. Extra care must be taken not to allow subjective considerations or favoritism to enter into the evaluation: "A merit pay plan rests on the assumption that a supervisor can make objective and valid distinctions between the performances of various individuals who report to him. That the validity of this assumption is so often questioned probably explains why merit pay is not used more widely than it is" (Meyer, 1975).

Many problems and concerns with merit pay relate to organizational policies and procedures. For example, Lawler (1981) notes that "often, a poor merit pay system is a symptom of other problems and cannot be improved until they are solved. It is impossible to have an effective merit pay system if, for example, jobs are poorly designed and the organization itself is poorly structured."

Also at the organizational level, the literature urges that several steps be taken during the design stage to insure that the merit pay system will be effective. First, an organization must see to it that most major task interdependencies are contained under a single supervisor's jurisdiction. Secondly, the organization must devote the necessary resources, namely time and expertise, to the planning of the salary system. Next, jobs must be correctly classified by responsibility, external job market, and the like. Also, thorough, up-to-date job descriptions must be available. A specific performance-oriented, not trait-oriented, evaluative instrument must be formulated for each job. The design and development process should be participative and involve review and feedback at several levels of the organization. Generally, the more that employees are involved in the process, the more they will accept the final plan. Finally, communication about the criteria for setting salary and evaluating performance should be open in the extreme.

Communication about salary practices and the results of the merit evaluation is emphasized in the literature as a crucial point. Lawler (1981) comments that "organizations have traditionally kept salaries and pay practices secret." "Thus," he continues, "the typical employee is often asked to accept as an article of faith that pay and performance are related." Similarly, Farmer (1975) notes that "the age of salary secrecy has almost passed," claiming that to have a vital merit pay program, "organizations should improve their salary communications. They should inform employees what level of merit increase is normal at a given time . . . ." In short, a large part of the effectiveness of a merit system hinges on the employees' specific knowledge about why they received the salary increase they did. A concurrent requirement, related to the above, is that there be a high degree of trust throughout the organization. Zand (1972) emphasizes the point that, if individuals don't trust each other and lack trust in the organization, the merit system is likely to be considered as unfair which, in turn, is likely to lead to undesired consequences. If these points are adequately implemented, the literature suggests that a merit pay system can work.

Thus, the literature suggests that although pay-for-performance systems are not without problems, well-designed and implemented systems can be a worthwhile addition to an otherwise well-managed and prosperous firm. But like so many other techniques, the compensation system is likely to have unintended negative consequences if implemented in a firm with problems in planning, structure, supervisory ability, or trust. Farmer (1978) aptly writes that "merit pay programs have the capacity of being developed to do the right job for both organizations and their employees. But this will not happen by itself."

In speaking of the future of merit pay, Lawler (1981) writes that "it is going to be more difficult to administer merit pay systems in the future. Organizations are becoming more difficult to manage, society is more complex, and the workforce is more demanding. But it is also more important than ever that pay should be tied to performance."

References

AMA Forum, "New Survey Shows Salary Compression Remaining a Major Problem, But It May Be Easing," *Management Review*, 71, May 1982, 35-36.

Belcher, David, "Pay for Performance," *Compensation Review*, 12, Third Quarter 1980, 14-20.

Brinks, James, "Is There Merit in Merit Increases?," *Personnel Administrator*, 25 May 1980, 59-64.

Brinks, James, "Merit Pay Delivery Systems for Banking," *Bankers' Magazine (Boston)*, 164, *May/June 1981, 43-46.*

Brumback, Gary and McFee, Thomas, "From MBO to MBR," *Public Administration Review*, 42, July/August 1982, 363-371.

Burke, Ronald, "Why Performance Appraisal Systems Fail," *Personnel Administration*, 35, June 1972, 32-40.

Bushardt, Stephen and Fowler, Aubrey, "Compensation and Benefits: Today's Dilemma in Motivation," *Personnel Administrator*, 27, April 1982, 23-26.

Carey, James, "A Salary Administration Program for Today's Economy," *SAM Advanced Management Journal*, 45, Summer 1980, 4-11.

Costello, Timothy W. and Zalkind, Sheldon S., "Merit Raise or Merit Bonus: A Psychological Approach," *Personnel Administrator*, 25, June 1962, 10-17.

Cowan, Paula, "How Blue Cross Put Pay-for-Performance to Work," *Personnel Journal*, 57, May 1978, 250-255

DeSanto, John, "Higher Pay for Good Performance, the Average Grade Approach," *Public Personnel Management*, 9, Fourth Quarter 1980, 282-284.

Deci, Edward L., "The Hidden Costs of Rewards," *Organizational Dynamics*, 4, Winter 1976, 61-72.

Dyer, Lee and Theriault, Roland, "The Determinants of Pay Satisfaction," *Journal of Applied Psychology*, 61, 1976, 596-604.

Evans, William, "Pay for Performance: Fact or Fable?", *Personnel Journal*, 49, September 1970, 726-731.

Farmer, C. Richard, "Merit Pay: Viable?", *Personnel*, 55, September/October 1978, 57-67.

Fleuter, Douglas, "Different Approaches to Merit Increases," *Personnel Journal*, 58, April 1979, 225-232.

Giles, Brian, And Barrett, Gerald, "Utility of Merit Increases," *Journal of Applied Psychology*, 55, 1971, 103-109.

Goldberg, Myles, "Another Look at Merit Pay Programs," *Compensation Review*, 9, Third Quarter 1977, 20-28.

Goodale, James, and Mouser, Michael, "Developing and Auditing a Merit Pay System," *Personnel Journal*, 60, May 1981, 391-394.

Greene, Robert, "Which Pay Delivery System is Best for Your Organization?", *Personnel*, 58, May/June 1981, 51-58.

Hills, Frederick, "Pay for Performance Dilemma," *Personnel*, 56, September/October 1979, 23-31

Homans, George C., *The Human Group*, New York: Harcourt and Brace, 1950.

Hubbartt, W. S., "Ten Commandments of Salary Administration," *Administrative Management*, 43, April 1982, 24-25 .

Hubbell, Roger, "Making a Top-level Performer Out of your Merit Increase Program," *Administrative Management*, 35, July 1974, 45-48

David F. Wood & Dan S. Green

Hunady, Ronald, and Varney, Glenn "Salary Administration: A Reason for MBO," *Training and Development Journal*, 28, September 1974, 24-26.

Hunter, Richard and Silverman, Buddy, "Merit Pay in the Federal Government," *Personnel Journal*, 59, December 1980, 1003-1007.

"Icing on the Cake," *Across the Board*, 15, March 1978, 70-71.

Johnson, Michael and McCloskey, Kenneth, "ASK-ME -- A Merit Promotion System," *Personnel Journal*, 57, August 1978, 430-433.

Johnston, James, "Merit Pay for College Faculty?", *SAM Advanced Management Journal*, 43, Spring 1978, 44-47.

Kirkpatrick, Donald, "MBO and Salary Administration," *Training and Development Journal*, 27, September 1973, 3-5.

Kopelman, Richard, "Linking Pay to Performance is a Proven Management Tool," *Personnel Administrator*, 28, October 1983, 60-68.

Kopelman, R. E. and Reinharth, L., "Research Results, the Effect of Merit-Pay Practices on White Collar Performance," *Compensation Review*, 14, Fourth Quarter 1982, 30-40.

Krefting, Linda, and Mahoney, Thomas, "Determining the Size of a Meaningful Pay Increase," *Industrial Relations*, 16, February 1977, 83-93.

Lawler, Edward, "Comments on Meyer's Pay for Performance Dilemma and Rejoinder," 4, *Organization Dynamics*, Winter 1976, 73-77.

Lawler, Edward, "New Approach to Pay, Innovations That Work," *Personnel*, 53, September/October 1976, 11-23.

Lawler, Edward, "Merit Pay: Fact or Fiction?" *Management Review*, 70, April 1981, 50-53.

Lupton, Tom and Gowler, Dan, "Wage Payment Systems: A Review of Current Thinking," *Personnel Management*, 14, November 1972, 25-28.

Matichuk, William, "How to Reconcile the Merit Principle with Anti-inflation Regulations," *Compensation Review*, 9, Second Quarter 1977, 72-75.

McMillan, John and Williams, Valerie, "The Elements of Effective Salary Administration Programs," *Personnel Journal*, 61, November 1982, 832-838.

"Merit-Pay Plans make a Comeback," *Banking*, 67, June 1975, 16 .

Meyer, Herbert, "The Pay-for-Performance Dilemma," *Organizational Dynamics*, 3, Winter 1975, 44-49.

Mihal, William, "More Research is Needed, Goals May Motivate Better," *Personnel Administrator*, 28, October 1983, 61-67.

Miller, Ernest, "'Administering Pay Programs . . . ' An Interview with Edward E. Lawler III," *Compensation Review*, 25, First Quarter 1977, 8-16.

Miller, Ernest, "Pay for Performance," *Personnel*, 56, July/August 1979, 4-11.

Mobley, W., "The Link Between MBO and Merit Compensation," *Personnel Journal*, 53, June 1974, 423-427.

Murray, Stuart and Kuffel, Tom, "MBO and Performance Linked Compensation in the Public Sector," *Public Personnel Management*, 7, May/June 1978, 71-76.

Patten, Thomas, "Linking Financial Rewards to Employee Performance: The Roles of OD and MBO," *Human Resources Management*, 15, Winter 1976, 2-17.

Patten, Thomas, "Merit Increases and the Facts of Organizational Life," *Management of Personnel Quarterly*, 7, Summer 1968, 30-38.

Patten, Thomas, "Pay for Performance or Placation," *Personnel Administrator*, 22 September, 1977, 26-29.

Perry, James and Pearce, J., "Initial Reactions to Federal Merit Pay," *Personnel Journal*, 62, March 1983, 230-237.

Piamonte, John, "In Praise of Monetary Motivation," *Personnel Journal*, 58, September 1979, 597-599

Rappold, Steve, "The Merit Pay Payout: CAB's Experience the First Year," *Management*, 5, Spring 1981, 10-11.

"Recognizing Merit at Xerox," *Management Review*, 67, June 1978, 44.

Schwartz, Jeffrey, "Maintaining Merit Compensation in a High Inflation Economy," *Personnel Journal*, 61, February 1982, 147-152.

Siegel, Efstathia, "Eight Agencies Link Pay to Performance: Will Merit Pay Work?", *Management*, 5, Spring, 1981, 15-17.

Silverman, Buddy, "Developmental Pay: Forerunner to Merit Pay in the Federal Government," *Compensation Review*, 13, Second Quarter 1981, 25-36.

Smith, James, "Merit Compensation: The Ideal and the Reality," *Personnel Journal*, 51, May 1972, 313-316.

Spencer, George, "Keeping Salary Scales in Tune with Merit," *Personnel Management*, 12, March 1980, 40-42.

Stokes, Douglas, "A New Mathematical Approach to Merit-Based Compensation Systems," *Compensation Review*, 13, Fourth Quarter, 1981, 43-55.

"The Trouble with Merit Increases," *Management Review*, 71, October 1982, 60-61.

Tomasko, Robert, "Focusing Company Reward Systems to Help Achieve Business Objectives," *Management Review*, 71, October 1982, 8-12.

Thompson, Paul, and Dalton, Gene, "Performance Appraisal: Managers Beware," *Harvard Business Review*, 48, January/February 1970, 149-159.

Tosi, Henry and Carroll, Stephen, "Management by Objectives: Its Implication for Motivation and Compensation," in Tosi, House, and Dunette (eds), *Managerial Motivation and Compensation*, East Lansing, Michigan: MSU Business Press, 1972.

Troutman, Lawrence, "Motivating Compensation: An Interview with Dr. Edward E. Lawler III," *The Mortgage Banker*, 38, August 1978, 62-65.

Vroom, Victor, *Work and Motivation*, New York: John Wiley, 1964.

Winstanley, Nathan, "Use of Performance Appraisal in Compensation Administration," *Conference Board Record*, 12, March 1975, 43-47.

Winstanley, Nathan, "A Personnel Perspective on Pay for Performance," *Personnel Journal*, 58, November 1979, 758.

Winstanley, Nathan, "How Accurate are Performance Appraisals," *Personnel Administrator*, 25, August 1980, 55-58.

Winstanley, Nathan, "Legal and Ethical Issues in Performance Appraisals," *Harvard Business Review*, 58, November/December 1980, 186-188

Winstanley, Nathan, "Are Merit Increases Really Effective?", *Personnel Administrator*, 27, April 1982, 37-41.

Zand, Dale, "Trust and Managerial Problem Solving," *Administrative Science Quarterly*, 17, June 1972, 229-239.

Possibilities

Measuring Teacher Merit: What We Can Learn from Business and Industry

Robert E. Rumery

Introduction

Several years ago, two colleagues and I published an extensive critique of existing methods for evaluation of teaching (Johnson, Rhodes & Rumery, 1975a). The methods examined included the use of achievement tests to determine the extent to which teaching objectives were met, the assessment of teachers characteristics as reported by students, peers, supervisors, or other observers, and the observation of pedagogical behavior by any of the same sets of observers. Both assessment of teacher characteristics and observation of pedagogical behavior commonly involve the use of rating scales. Another article published about the same time considered only the use of student ratings in the evaluation of college and university teaching (Rumery, Rhodes & Johnson, 1975). The focus of both articles was the assessment of teaching merit in colleges and universities, but the issues raised are much the same in elementary and secondary school.

The use of rating scales to evaluate teaching performance parallels the use of rating scales in business and industry for the appraisal of job performance. In fact, it has been suggested (Landy & Farr, 1980) that appraisal of job performance is more often accomplished through the use of rating scales than through any other method. This fact has led to the suggestion that an appropriate response to current pressure for identifying teachers of unusual merit would be to adapt the methods so widely used in business and industry to educational environments.

There is a considerable body of literature on job performance appraisal, much of it concerned directly with appraisal of teaching performance. One part of this literature, dealing exclusively with appraisal of teaching performance, is most frequently published in a few journals dedicated to educational research: the *Journal of Educational Psychology, Educational and Psychological Measurement*, and the various journals published by the American Educational Research Association and the National Council on Measurement in Education. Articles on the use of rating scales as vehicles for job performance appraisal in general are typically published in the *Journal of Applied Psychology, Organizational Behavior and Human Performance* and *Personnel Psychology*. Little cross-referencing is apparent between these two bodies of literature, even though many of the articles in the latter set of journals deal directly with assessment of teaching merit in colleges and universities. In addition, common theoretical underpinnings of job performance appraisal and teacher evaluation may be found in articles typically published in such journals as *Psychometrika*, *Psychological Review*, and *Psychological Bulletin*.

It is the intent of this paper to assess the current state of the art in the use of ratings as vehicles for performance appraisal in order to arrive at some conclusions about the feasibility and manner of use of rating scales in various educational environments. This will be done by reviewing the research literature concerned with performance appraisal — chiefly in the *Journal of Applied Psychology*, *Organizational Behavior and Human Performance* and *Personnel Psychology* — for about the last ten years, as well as foundational material from other, sometimes older sources. The review is not intended to be exhaustive; articles cited have been chosen on the basis of their possible contribution to recommendations about whether and how ratings might be used to assess teacher merit, principally in the common schools.

Rating Scale Methodology

Scale Development

The development of rating scales follows a fairly consistent sequence. The first step in the process involves generating a pool of items, usually using the "critical incident technique" (Flanagan, 1954). In the critical incident technique, respondents are asked to think of a highly successful job incumbent and a highly unsuccessful one. Where the technique has been applied in development of teacher performance rating scales, respondents have been asked to think of the best teacher they ever had and the worst teacher they ever had (Ryans, 1960). The respondents are then asked to identify specific behavioral incidents that exemplify highly successful or highly unsuccessful performances. The desired outcome of this step is the production of clear descriptions of concrete and specific behavior.

The identification of critical incidents is commonly followed by a procedure to organize these incidents into a set of categories or dimensions which characterize the entire pool of examples. For example, the following dimensions are prevalent in evaluation of teaching in colleges and universities (Abrami, Note 1): "Knowledge of Subject Matter, Stimulation of Students' Interest, Ability to Explain Clearly, Enthusiasm for the Subject or for Teaching, Preparation and Organization, Availability and Helpfulness, and Concern and Respect for Students." Either of two methods might be used to arrive at these dimensions or categories. The first method requires an independent panel of judges to sort the examples into a set of categories whose members are alike. The number and content of the categories may be specified prior to the judgments. Usually, in this stage, the pool of examples is substantially reduced on the basis of failures to meet standards of agreement set in advance. In the second method, an independent sample of judges rates the examples according to any of several sets of instructions. The ratings might be judgments of the critical nature or utility of the several examples or they might be ratings of the degree of proficiency indicated by each example. Alternatively, the pool of unclassified examples might be used to rate the performance of job incumbents. Whatever the procedure, the result is the assignment of a numerical score to each incident. Intercorrelations between incident scores are then obtained and reduced to a set of dimensions by application of factor analysis or other similar data-reduction technique. The pool of examples may be further reduced in this stage on the basis of *a priori* selection standards. Sometimes, the definition of dimensions is followed up by estimation of their internal consistency and intercorrelations among dimensions.

Either the descriptions of behavior arrived at in the application of the critical incident technique or paraphrases of these descriptions constitute the items in a provisional rating scale. The rating scale is not complete, however, until a mode of response is provided for each item. Two modes of response are common: graphic rating scales and category-response rating scales. Category responses may be evaluative adjectives — excellent, good, average, poor, unsatisfactory and the like; they may be frequency adverbs — usually, sometimes, rarely, never, or others; or they may be verb phrases indicating assent to the statement presented in the item — strongly agree, agree, disagree, strongly disagree. Graphic rating scales usually provide a horizontal or vertical line of the same length for each item. Numerals may be placed at the ends of the line or at equally spaced intervals along the line. Numbered points on a graphic rating scale may be "anchored" by categorical labels corresponding to those used in category-response scales. Often, the items of graphic rating scales consist of category or dimension names, sometimes with definitions of the categories or dimensions. Raters then locate individual ratees on the graphic rating scale with an "x" or checkmark. This mark may then be translated to a numerical value on the basis of comparisons with numerical values identifying points on the graphic scale or by measuring the distance from the end of the scale designated as the "low" end. Of these two response modes (category and graphic), the category scale is far more commonly used. Other response formats are possible and some of them will be considered later.

Psychometric analysis may be undertaken as part of the process of scale development, or it may occur after the final form of the scale is achieved; more commonly, it takes place during and after scale development. General methods for psychometric analysis of rating scales or performance rating data are discussed in the next section.

Psychometric Analysis

Psychometric analysis of data obtained from use of rating scales is intended to provide quantitative information about reliability of ratings, the relative absence of certain kinds of rating errors, and the validity of specific interpretations of these data. Reliability estimation assesses the extent to which rating data are free from random variation. Rating errors are non-random variations in ratings — either variations between raters or between obtained individual ratings and some ineluctable true or correct value. The types of rating errors most often cited are halo, leniency or severity errors, contrast errors, central tendency errors and restriction of range errors. These various rating errors were initially defined at various times between 1920 and 1940. Of these, halo and leniency/severity errors are most common. Conceptual definitions of these various errors are given below, along with citations indicating sources of these particular definitions. In general, these definitions represent a modal contemporary view of the nature of these rating errors.

Halo. A rater's failure to discriminate among conceptually distinct and potentially independent aspects of a ratee's behavior (Saal, Downey & Lahey, 1980).

Leniency/severity. A rater's tendency to assign a higher or lower rating to an individual than is warranted by that ratee's performance (Saal & Landy, 1977).

Contrast. A tendency for a rater to rate others in the opposite direction from himself on a trait (Murray, 1938).

Central tendency. A tendency for ratings to cluster around the midpoint of a rating scale, avoiding extreme categories (Korman, 1971; Saal, Downey & Lahey, 1980).

Restriction of range. A tendency of ratings to cluster around any point on a rating scale, high, low or midpoint (Saal, Downey & Lahey, 1980).

Current methodology for assessing the psychometric quality of performance ratings draws mainly on the work of Hoyt (1941), Ebel (1951), Guilford (1954), Stanley (1961) and Cronbach, Gleser, Nanda & Rajaratnam (1972). Guilford, Stanley and Cronbach et al. proposed evaluation of performance ratings by collecting data in the framework of a Raters x Ratees x Dimensions design. Consider, for example, evaluation of a rating scale for appraising the performance of secondary-school or college instructors that embodies the dimensions previously offered: Knowledge of Subject Matter, Stimulation of Students' Interest, Ability to Explain Clearly, Enthusiasm for the Subject or for Teaching, Preparation and Organization, Availability and Helpfulness, and Concern and Respect for Students. (While these dimensions are representative of those commonly found in student rating vehicles used for appraising teacher performance in colleges and universities, different dimensions might be more typical in common schools or when raters are other than students.) A study for estimating the reliability of ratings or for estimating the contribution or rating errors would entail obtaining ratings of all of these dimensions for a sample of teachers in the sample on all dimensions. Using this strategy, if 20 raters rated 10 ratees on the seven dimensions above, the result would be a total of 1400 distinct ratings. Each of these ratings could be considered to be composed of several independent components:

Robert E. Rumery

Rating of ratee i by rater j on dimension $k =$ universe score halo leniency or severity contrast range restriction random error.

Analysis of variance of these ratings leads to estimates of variance from sources indicated in Table 1. The interpretations given are in terms of the components represented in the formula above.

Table 1

Source	Interpretation
Raters	Leniency/severity bias.
Ratees	"True score" or "Universe score" variation, contributing to reliability of ratings. A nonsignificant contribution from this source indicates range restriction error.
Dimensions	Uninterpreted.
Raters x Ratees	Halo.
Raters x Dimensions	Contrast error.
Ratees x Dimensions	Uninterpreted.
Raters x Ratees x Dimensions	Random error.

Variance from the source Raters x Ratees x Dimensions can be estimated directly only if ratings of the same ratees by the same raters using the same set of dimensions are repeated. Otherwise, variance from this source is estimated as residual variation and interpreted as being due to random error. Estimates of reliability of ratings are obtained by computation of intraclass correlation coefficients. The extent of contribution of the various rating errors is indicated by the magnitude of appropriate F-ratios. Formulas for intraclass correlation coefficients and the appropriate F-ratios are as follows:

Intraclass correlation coefficient for reliability of a single rater's rating:

$$\frac{\text{MS(Ratees)} - \text{MS(Raters x Ratees)}}{\text{MS(Ratees) (j-1)MS(Raters x Ratees)}}$$

Intraclass correlation coefficient for reliability of the average of raters' ratings:

$$\frac{\text{MS(Ratees)} - \text{MS(Raters x Ratees)}}{\text{MS(Ratees)}}$$

F-Ratio for halo:

$$\frac{\text{MS(Raters x Ratees)}}{\text{MS(Raters x Ratees x Dimensions)}}$$

F-Ratio for leniency or severity:

$$\frac{MS(Raters)}{MS(Raters \times Ratees)}$$

F-Ratio for range restriction (Error indicated by nonsignificant F):

$$\frac{MS(Ratees)}{MS(Raters \times Ratees)}$$

The use of a complete Raters x Ratees x Dimensions analysis, described by Saal, Downey & Lahey (1980) as the ideal data collection strategy, is usually impractical outside of a rigorously controlled laboratory situation. Alternative strategies include a partial Raters x Ratees x Dimensions design, a Raters x Dimensions design or a Ratees x Dimensions design. In the partial Raters x Ratees x Dimensions design, some of the raters rate some of the ratees on all of the dimensions. In the Raters x Dimensions design and in the Ratees x Dimensions design, several or many raters rate individual ratees on all dimensions, although the same sets of raters rarely rate the same sets of ratees. These two strategies, principally the former, are widely used in research on student evaluation of teaching in colleges and universities. The former strategy focuses on the within-ratee structure of data; the latter strategy focuses on the between-rater structure of data. All of the strategies except the complete Raters x Ratees x Dimensions strategy are limited in the information they can reveal about the dependability of ratings. For example, the Raters x Dimensions strategy is incapable of providing independent information about interrater reliability, halo errors and restriction of range errors. In fact, halo and range restriction errors are confounded with universe scores, spuriously inflating estimates of reliability obtained from the use of this strategy. When the complete Raters x Ratees x Dimensions strategy is impractical, or for other reasons, *ad hoc* indices of psychometric quality are often used. These *ad hoc* indices are generally neither equivalent to one another nor to indices obtained from the complete Raters x Ratees x Dimensions analysis. Saal, Downey & Lahey (1980) list three distinct operational definitions of leniency/severity errors (two subdivided into three similar definitions involving, respectively, Raters x Ratees x Dimensions, Ratees x Dimension, and Raters x Dimensions data matrices), four distinct operational definitions of halo, including one requiring the complete Raters x Ratees x Dimensions strategy, four distinct definitions of central tendency and range restriction errors and six distinct operational definitions of interrater reliability. Although most rating errors are conceptually defined in terms of the activity of an individual rater, all but two of the operational definitions are based on pooled data from multiple raters. Moreover, in the complete Raters x Ratees x Dimensions strategy, interrater reliability and range restriction errors are not experimentally independent; they both make use of the same data and are probably negatively correlated. Furthermore, interrater reliability and interrater agreement do not refer to the same state of affairs (Lawlis & Lu, 1972;

Tinsley & Weiss, 1975); the intraclass correlation coefficients cited do not exhaust the possibilities for computation of that index (Shrout & Fleiss, 1979); and there are at least a half-dozen constructions of the concept of reliability beside interrater reliability. Lawlis & Lu have demonstrated the possible joint occurence of high interrater reliability and high interrater agreement, high interrater reliability and low interrater agreement and low interrater reliability and high interrater agreement. Most introductory books in psychometrics refer to reliability in terms of stability, equivalence, and internal consistency. While the conceptual definitions given above might lead us to believe that we understand the various hypothetical components of ratings, the multiplicity of operational definitions, the lack of congruency between conceptualization and operationalization and the lack of congruency among operationalizations of a single concept present serious obstacles to any clear interpretation of the results of any inquiry in which the data collection vehicle is a rating scale.

In recognition of all the difficulties cited above, Saal, Downey & Lahey (1980) have proposed standardizing operational definitions of reliability and the various rating errors using a modification of the Raters x Ratees x Dimensions strategy. A logical difficulty with this "ideal" strategy is that it treats the various dimensions of performance as different levels of a single independent variable. They propose the more logical alternative of viewing dimensions as multivariate and performing multivariate analysis of variance on dimension within a Raters x Ratees design. The difference between this strategy and the Raters x Ratees x Dimensions strategy lies in the mode of analyzing the data rather than in the mode of collecting the data; in terms of what data are collected and how they are collected, there is no difference between the multivariate Raters x Ratees strategy and the univariate Raters x Ratees x Dimensions strategy. Similar proposals have been made by LaForge (1965) and by Cronbach et al (1972).

Significant halo and leniency/severity errors are encountered with such regularity in performance ratings that some industrial or organization psychologists take a "Where there's smoke, there's fire" posture: "Where there are ratings, there are halo or leniency/severity errors." Contemporary views of halo effect suggest that it is ubiquitous because it originates in the peculiar constraints encountered in the general context of performance appraisal (Borman, 1978; Cooper, 1981). Borman has suggested four problematic constraints.

1. Raters' opportunities to observe relevant job-related behavior are an obvious prerequisite for obtaining satisfactory performance ratings. Yet, when supervisors are asked to rate subordinates, they often lack an opportunity to rate all job behavior relevant to job effectiveness. Under these conditions, raters might be required to provide ratings on dimensions of behavior they have not had an opportunity to observe. They are likely to comply with this requirement on the basis of presumed covariation between observed dimensions and unobserved dimensions, or between general impressions and unobserved dimensions.

---

2. Raters' knowledge of common rating errors and of methods for reducing them are important ingredients for obtaining high-quality ratings. Yet ratings are often required of raters who are inexperienced in performance appraisal and ignorant of common sources of error or of ways to reduce them.

3. The content or format of rating vehicles may not allow raters to translate readily the work-related behavior they observe to a specific level on a specified dimension. Rating scales with insufficiently concrete items or response categories may force raters to lump vaguely related observations together.

4. Organizational constraints may cause ratings to reflect organizational demands rather than true levels of performance exhibited by raters. For example, a supervisor might hesitate to provide a deserved low rating to an employee in order to avoid confrontation with a disgruntled employee or the burden of replacement.

Random measurement errors and nonrandom rating errors are important because they compromise the interpretability of the results of performance rating. The term "validity" is most widely used to refer to the interpretability of any quantitative information. Contemporary psychometricians view validity as evidence that a specified interpretation of data is warranted and alternative interpretations are not. When ratings or other information tell us that a teacher is unusually competent or incompetent, validity requires evidence that this conclusion is not reached as a result of irrelevant behavior or extraneous environmental factors or the occurence of any of the several rating biases. Such evidence is provided when psychometric analysis shows relatively small contributions due to rating errors or when significant Ratee x Dimension effects (discriminant validity) are observed.

Improving the Psychometric Quality of Ratings

There are two methods of improving the psychometric quality of rating. The first of these is training of raters. The premise is that if raters are aware of the possible sources of error and familiar with the job requirements of whatever performance they are to appraise, the distortions outlined by Borman and Cooper are likely to be minimized. The second approach is to rely on more rigorous strategies in the development of rating scales. These may involve greater reliance on concrete descriptions of job behavior or the use of formats which minimize the contribution of general impressions to rating on relevant dimensions.

Training Raters

In reviewing research on training of raters, Landy & Farr concluded, "Rater training has generally been shown to be effective in reducing rating errors, especially if the training is extensive and allows for rater practice." There are some apparent contradictions of this conclusion, however.

Bernardin & Pence (1980) provided two types of training to potential raters. In the first type of training, leniency and halo errors were defined and illustrated with graphic illustrations and numerical examples. In the second type of training, potential raters heard lectures on the multidimensionality of job performance (teaching) and were given the opportunity to generate and define dimensions of performance, discuss behavioral examples of each dimension, and to attempt to develop stereotypes of effective and ineffective performance. Their ratings of hypothetical ratees, described in written vignettes, were compared to the ratings of untrained raters. This experiment examined the effect of training on three dependent variables — leniency, halo and accuracy. Accuracy was defined in terms of discrepancies of the ratings produced by the raters from ratings given the hypothetical ratees by a panel of experts. Raters receiving the first type of training showed significantly less leniency than raters in the control group, but both of the groups receiving training produced less accurate ratings than the control group. Bernardin & Pence attributed this result to a response set (attempting to avoid rating errors) which decreased attention to critical behaviors. Comparison of two experiments, both reported after Landy & Farr's review might help to resolve the apparent contradictions exemplified by the Bernardin & Pence results among others (Bernardin, 1979; Ivance-vich, 1979). Zedeck & Cascio (1982) investigated the joint effects of purpose for rating and training on performance appraisal ratings. McIntyre, Smith & Hassett (1984) studied the effects of the perceived purpose for rating and of different kinds of training on performance appraisal ratings. Zedeck & Cascio employed training called rater-error training, similar to the first type employed by Bernardin & Pence; that is, common rating errors were described and illustrated and raters were admonished to try to avoid them. After training, raters rated written descriptions of job performance according to one of two purposes: job development or assignment of merit salary increases. Zedeck & Cascio found that there was less differentiation of hypothetical ratees when the purpose of rating was assignment of merit salary increases than when the purpose of rating was job development. Training had no effect on ratings. McIntyre, Smith & Hassett employed two separate types of training and a combination of the two. One of the training methods was the rating-error method used by Zedeck & Cascio; the other was designated as frame-of-reference training and resembled the second method used by Bernardin & Pence. The frame-of-reference training involved providing subjects with information describing the performance to be evaluated, in this case a bogus lecture to be given by a theater student represented as a graduate teaching assistant, and describing to them the 12-item rating scale to be used and the four dimensions represented by the 12 items. Next, a practice videotape was viewed and rated by the subjects. "True scores" arrived at by a panel of expert raters were represented to the subjects along with behavioral rationales for those ratings. After this training, three purposes for rating were established for three groups of raters. The perceived purposes were research purposes (research on students' abilities to evaluate accurately classroom lectures), course-improvement purposes (feedback to instructors about their performance) or hiring decision purposes. Each of these three groups was further divided into four groups according to type and extent of training (see above), including a no-training group. Rating quality was assessed using four dependent variables: halo (measured with a variance measure corrected for "true halo" (Cooper, 1981)), leniency/severity (measured as the mean deviation over items and raters of "true" ratings from obtained ratings), correlation accuracy (the mean correlation between individual raters' ratings and true ratings over three rated performances), and distance accuracy (the mean absolute deviation of obtained ratings from true ratings). When halo was corrected for true halo, the frame-of-reference training produced a significant reduction in halo. When an uncorrected halo measure was used, rater-error training was more effective in reducing halo. For both measures of accuracy, frame-of-reference training and the combination of rater-error and frame-of-reference training were more effective than either rater-error training alone or no-training, but the difference between frame-of-reference training and the combination of frame-of-reference training and the combination training was so small as to make the combination cost ineffective. Variations in purpose of rating had no effect. These results are consistent with Landy & Farr's conclusion in that more extensive training (frame-of-reference training was more extensive than rater-error training) and practice in rating led to reduction in halo errors. Question about the long-term effects of training, the effect of rater training on the validity of ratings and the optimal content of training programs remain unanswered.

Development Strategies

It has been suggested that a possible cause of halo errors could be vagueness or ambiguity in the language used in rating scales, or ambiguity in the behavioral events to be rated. In order to avoid this ambiguity, Smith & Kendall (1963) proposed a method for developing performance-appraisal rating scales called "retranslation of expectations." The method involves using four independent samples of judges to develop the dimensions to be rated and the definitions of these dimension, to develop and subgroup behavioral examples of various levels of these dimensions, and to assign scale values to the behavioral examples as part of the scale anchoring process. The resulting scales are called "behavioral expectation scales" (BES) or "behaviorally anchored rating scales" (BARS). BARS are normally presented as graphic rating scales, with the name of each dimension and its definition at the top of a single page. Along a vertical scale, behavioral examples are spaced at intervals arrived at during the development process. A rater then locates a ratee with a mark on the graphic scale. A refinement of this method of scale development has been proposed which provides greater potential redundancy of ratings, thus presenting the possibility of evaluating the consistency of individual raters (Blanz & Ghiselli, 1972). The result of this refinement is called a mixed standard scale (MSS). The process of developing a MSS is essentially equivalent to the Smith-Kendall procedure but does not result in a graphic rating scale with behavioral examples as anchors. Instead, the behavioral examples are presented in more or less random order and the raters are to respond whether a ratee's performance on a particular dimension is better than, about the same as or worse than the behavioral example.

Although BARS and MSS are often regarded as distinct types of scales, it is probably more appropriate to view them as different scale formats. In a study intended to compare the BARS format with the MSS format, the retranslation of expectations procedure was used to produce both scale formats (Dickinson & Zellinger, 1980). The scale construction procedure is described in some detail in order to familiarize the reader with the requirement of the Smith-Kendall procedure and to provide a basis for subsequent discussion. In this study, the retranslation-of-expectations procedure was used to construct rating scales in three formats for evaluation of teaching in nonlaboratory courses in the college of Veterinary Medicine at Colorado State University. In this application, the retranslation-of-expectations procedure was composed of five phases.

In Phase 1, a group of judges composed of students and faculty in the College of Veterinary Medicine were instructed to produce five examples of behavior illustrating effective courses/instructors and five examples of behavior illustrating ineffective courses/instructors. All of the behavioral descriptions were pooled and the participants in this phase sorted these "critical incidents" into relatively homogeneous categories, labeled the categories, and suggested definitions. Eleven categories or dimensions resulted.

In Phase 2, a second group of participants were given two tasks: 1) Write ten critical incidents describing five effective and five ineffective instructors/courses and 2) Write behavioral statements of similar specificity to exemplify low, medium and high amounts of each of the 11 dimensions identified in Phase 1. Over 700 statements were produced in Phases 1 and 2. These examples were edited for redundancy and clarity and reduced to 287 statements.

In Phase 3, the 287 statements were rewritten in expectation format. For example, the following expectations statement (Harari & Zedeck, 1973) indicates a high degree of professor rapport with and sensitivity to students: "This professor could be expected to answer the student's questions about learning and conditioning without making the student feel stupid and without making the student feel that he's bothering the professor." The 287 statements in expectation format were then given to a third group of participants for retranslation into dimensions. Statements were retained only if 70% of the participants in this phase matched the examples to the dimensions in which they had originally been classified. A dimension was retained only if 70% of its statements were reassigned to the original dimension and if the dimension was represented by a range of examples (low, medium, high) to anchor it. In this phase, 164 examples and one dimension were eliminated.

In Phase 4, a fourth group of participants rated each example on its dimension using a 5-point scale. A dimension was eliminated if it was not defined by a range of scale values and an example was eliminated if the standard deviation of ratings given by this group of participants was greater than one. Three dimensions and 24 examples were eliminated in Phase 4.

In Phase 5, scale values from Phase 4 were subjected to multiple-group factor analysis. Examples were separated into two sets by the position of their scale values relative to the mid-point (3) of the five-point scale. An example was eliminated if its factor loading on the hypothesized factor (the category identified in Phase 1) was less than .40 or if less than 60% of its communality fell on the hypothesized factor. A dimension was eliminated if it was not represented by a range of examples.

The five phases yielded six dimensions anchored by 65 scaled examples. These factors are listed below, along with their definitions.

1. **Student-faculty interaction**: The faculty member and students are in a cooperative, interpersonal environment conducive to learning.

2. **Teaching methods**: The degree to which all available media sources (slides, live animals, videotapes, illustrations during lectures) involving all senses are used.

3. **Correlation of course with overall curriculum**: The content of this course relates sequentially to other courses in the program.

4. **Enthusiasm**: The excitement in the subject matter generated by a faculty member, which stimulates student thought.

5. **Competence**: The quality of being recognized as thoroughly knowledgeable in a specific subject-matter area.

6. **Testing**: The evaluation procedures are consistent with course objectives, requiring thought more than memorization, and can be viewed as a learning experience.

The products of this process were used to construct rating vehicles in three formats: the mixed standard scale format (MSS), the behaviorally anchored format (BAR), and a Likert format (LT). In the MSS format, 18 behavioral examples were presented in random order. The response to each example was to indicate whether the ratee's performance was poorer than, about equal to or better than the behavioral example. In the BAR format, 29 behavioral examples were used as anchors for the six dimensions on a 5-point scale. Space was provided for comments supporting a rating value. On the LT format, a 5-point scale was given for each of the dimension titles and its definition with frequency anchors of "always," "very often," "about as often as not," "very seldom," and "never."

The purpose of the Dickinson-Zellinger study was to compare the convergent and discriminant validity of the BAR format and the MSS format when a common procedure was used for development of scales in the two formats. A third scale format, the Likert (LT) format, was used to facilitate comparisons of the BAR and MSS formats. Ratings were obtained from the 86 students in the veterinary medicine program. (Note: Whether these students all rated the same or different instructors/courses is not specified; the data collection strategy was apparently a Raters X Dimensions Strategy.) Convergent and discriminant validity were then assessed from a multitrait-multimethod correlation matrix (Campbell & Fiske, 1959) generated from these ratings. In this matrix, each element represented the correlation between one factor-format combination and another. A significant correlation between two ratings of the same factor using different formats is interpreted as convergent validity. Discriminant validity is indicated when correlations between ratings of different factors using the same format are approximately equal to corresponding correlations between different factors using different formats. Discriminant validity is also indicated by a significant Ratees X Dimensions effect in the Raters X Ratees X Dimensions analysis of variance.

Dickinson & Zellinger concluded that the discriminant validity of the MSS format was as high as the discriminant validity of BAR and LT, but that the convergent validity was somewhat lower. Method bias, however, was lower for MSS than for either BAR or LT. Preference ratings of the forms suggested lower acceptance of MSS than of either BAR or LT. Dickinson & Zellinger speculated that an alternative scoring system (Saal, 1979) might increase user acceptance. An advantage offered by MSS over both BAR and LT is that this format provides for error counts that can be used to determine inconsistencies in ratings given by individual raters to individual ratees.

Conclusions

A consistent pattern emerges concerning the effectiveness of training and rigorous scale development strategies in improving the psychometric quality of ratings. It is clear that both training of raters and rigorous development strategies do lead to reduction of the contribution of rating errors, especially leniency and halo. In the case of training, the effect of training appears to be small, but this conclusion is constrained by two aspects of the research on training. The first aspect is that the training of raters in the experiments cited was extremely brief. In the McIntyre, Smith & Hassett study, the most extensive training, involving a combination of rater-error training and frame-of-reference training, required less than an hour. The second aspect is that the rating situations in training experiments are highly artificial, providing very small sample of behavior. Smith, McIntyre & Hassett used 6-minute bogus lectures; Bernardin & Pence and Zedeck & Cascio used written descriptions of job performance. In the case of scale development strategies, the use of the retranslation of expectations strategy seems to lead to reduction in rating errors, especially when the scales produced are in the behaviorally anchored rating format or the mixed standard scale format. This reduction is achieved at great cost, however, leading some authorities to question its cost effectiveness (Landy & Farr, 1980; Dickinson & Zellinger). Nevertheless, both training of raters and rigorous development procedures produce benefits beyond improvement of psychometric quality of ratings. These will be discussed later.

The Rating Process

The Psychometric Error

The evaluation of the psychometric quality of ratings, and the attempts to improve this psychometric quality, are predicated on acceptance of rating scales as instruments of measurement, a view that is widely accepted in educational research circles. In industrial/organizational psychology, on the other hand, rating scales are commonly referred to as vehicles (e.g., Landy & Farr, 1980). This usage suggests acceptance of a view advanced by a noted educational researcher over 20 years ago (Remmers, 1962). Remmers argued that the measuring instrument in a rating situation is the rater, not the rating scale. The rating scale is a medium or vehicle for recording the output of the rating process. This view clarifies the use of interaction effects involving raters to represent the rating errors discussed earlier in this paper. If any measurement is to be interpreted in a reasonable fashion, it is essential to understand the principles underlying the use of the instrument that produced the measurement. For example, nearly everyone understands that the use of a thermometer to measure temperature depends upon the principle that fluids expand in volume in proportion to an increase in temperature in the medium surrounding the thermometer. It is widely understood that the measurement of elapsed time depends on certain principles of periodic motion; the swinging of a pendulum or the vibration of a quartz crystal. If we did not understand these principles, we would be somewhat less confident of our ability to measure these quantities; therefore, less confident of the meaningfulness of the measures themselves.

Likewise, confidence in the meaningfulness of ratings depends upon our understanding the principles by which raters as measuring instruments produce quantitative classification of ratees. Many researchers in the area of job performance appraisal have proposed that any substantial improvement in the quality of performance ratings can only be the result of detailed study of the processes by which raters arrive at these quantitative assessments (Borman, 1978; Cooper, 1981; Feldman, 1981; Landy & Farr, 1980). Some efforts have been made in this direction by extending the methods of classical test theory. The formula offered earlier in this paper is an example of such an extension and is very similar to a psychometric model of performance rating offered by Wherry in 1952 in an unpublished paper and summarized by Landy & Farr. Another extension of test theory (LaForge, 1961) proposes that there might not only be multiple sources of error, but of "true" ratings or universe scores as well. Each of these separate universe scores might be viewed as a distinct point of view or frame of reference about the events being observed or rated. An important feature of psychometric models such as these is that the components of ratings are statistical decomposition products rather than products of analysis of the information processing that is presumed to be associated with performance appraisal judgments. Psychological analysis of the components of the

Robert E. Rumery

appraisal judgment process has emerged from cognitive psychology and social psychological research in attribution theory.

Psychological Models of the Rating Process

Two models of the performance appraisal process have been offered in recent years. The first may be described as a traditional model (Borman, 1978; Cooper, 1981). Borman has proposed that performance evaluation judgments proceed through three steps. In the first step, a rater must observe the ratee's relevant job behavior. In the second step, the rater evaluates each ratee's behavior in terms of the effectiveness it represents. In the third step, the rater must combine the evaluations of many behaviors into a single rating on a specified dimension. To this a fourth step could be added calling for the rater to combine judgments of performance in several dimensions or categories into an overall global judgment. Each step of the process provides several opportunities for rating error. In the first step, rating errors can arise from raters' differential opportunities to observe relevant work behavior, from tendencies of different raters to attend to different behaviors even if they have the same opportunities to observe a ratee, and from differences among raters in the criteria for evaluative judgments. In the second step, rating errors arise from idiosyncratic approaches to the evaluation task. Raters may form an opinion about a behavior on the basis of prior contact with a ratee or they may make a global evaluation of the ratee rather than an evaluation of individual behaviors. The global evaluation in turn may not even be based on direct observation of specific behaviors. In the third step, rating errors may arise from interrater differences in the specification of critical incidents: A critical incident for one rater may not be critical for another. Some raters may weight recent events more heavily when combining ratings; others may weight "first impressions" more heavily. Finally, raters may differ in the "composition rules" they use to combine information from multiple dimensions or from multiple incidents. Some might effectively add information from multiple dimensions or categories; others might employ a conditional combination rule of some sort.

Cooper (1981) has elaborated Borman's model by separating observable from unobservable parts of the process and by adding steps in which information might be lost or error introduced. The result is an 11-step process:

1. Observation of ratee actions.
2. Encoding of observed actions, and aggregation and storage in short-term memory.
3. Random and systematic decay of information in short-term memory.
4. Transfer of encoded information to long-term memory.
5. Random and systematic decay in long-term memory.
6. Presentation of rating categories to the rater.

7. Retrieval in varied detail of stored observations and impressions from long-term memory.
8. Recognition of observations and impressions relevant to rating categories.
9. Comparisons of observations and impressions to rater's internalized standards.
10. Incorporation of extraneous considerations.
11. Rating.

Rating errors might be introduced in steps 3, 5, 7, and 10 in obvious ways; or they might be the result of interrater differences in steps 2, 4, 6, 8 and 9. Efforts to improve the psychometric quality of ratings are therefore attempts to standardize various aspects of the hypothesized process. "Frame of reference" training attempts to standardize steps 1 & 2 by directing attention to a common set of actions and standard interpretations of action categories. The use of behavioral anchors standardizes steps 8 and 9 by providing concrete and specific instances of levels of behavior in various dimensions. Diary-keeping by raters during observation (Bernardin & Walter, 1977) attempts to reduce decay in memory by reducing reliance on memory when judgment is called for.

Cooper's view of the rating process could be described as a stimulus-based view; that is, the process begins with information that is complete and immediately available. The term rating "errors" used to describe halo, leniency and the like, suggests unspecified malfunctions at various stages. Feldman (1981) has outlined a memory-based model which links research in the psychometric tradition with a social-psychological tradition concerned with attribution of causes of behavior and stereotyping processes and their influence on evaluation of other persons' behavior. In Feldman's approach, the stages proposed by Borman are viewed as tasks to be completed. These tasks call for the operation of several clusters of memory-based processes which are commonly automatic but which, under certain circumstances, may be consciously controlled (continuously monitored) by the rater. These process clusters are attention and recognition processes, information organization and storage, organization of information seeking and recall, and integration and judgment processes.

When attention and recognition processes are automatic, certain characteristics of persons — race, sex, cues of dress and speech, height and so on — are recorded without intention, but with future consequences in the interpretation of behavior. For example, the height and gender of a seven-foot-tall adolescent male are immediately registered without conscious reflection and later behavior is likely to be interpreted in terms of these features. Attention and recognition processes are likely to be controlled only when behavior occurs which is inconsistent with expectations triggered by the availability of these features; for example, the tall adolescent male is found to prefer basket-weaving to basketball.

Categorization is generally considered to be basic to perception and information storage. Categorization of a person or that person's behavior involves evaluation of the extent of overlap between personal or behavioral features and those of a category prototype. Automatic categorization implies that once a person or his/her behavior has been classified, it is represented in memory by the prototypic features rather than the personal or behavioral features that led to the classification. As with attention, categorization is consciously monitored only when categorization is in some way problematic; for example, where there is no immediately available prototype to which a person can be satisfactorily matched. In performance appraisal, automatic categorization is functionally equivalent to stereotyping, leading to underevaluation or overevaluation by producing false memories of the behavior of the person being rated. Some of the biases which might be introduced by controlled categorization are a tendency to underestimate the importance of situational factors and overestimate that of dispositional factors (ratee characteristics) as causes of behavior, a tendency to see ratees as more responsible for acts with serious as opposed to trivial consequences and a tendency to attribute good actions by liked persons to the persons and bad actions to the situation. The reverse would hold for unliked persons.

In the overall performance appraisal process, the appraiser is frequently called upon to compare current behavior with prior behavior, calling for recall of stored information about that prior behavior. Information about prior behavior is stored in terms of prototypic features associated with particular categorizations; and the memorial information will be false to some degree. Hence, even though the recall process is thought to be a controlled process, the information available at the time of preliminary judgments is largely determined by automatic and controlled processes operating during earlier stages of attention, recognition, categorization and storage. The conscientious appraiser may seek to verify earlier impressions of the job performance to be evaluated, but herein lies another problem. Generally a search for new information is a search for information consistent with a prior prototypic categorization rather than the logically more appropriate search for information that might disconfirm the prior impression. Thus, the various biases that influence categorization also operate to limit the availability of information that might correct prior errors. This does not mean that raters never change their first impressions; but recategorization is thought to require new information which is incompatible with earlier prototypes. The discrepancy between new information and previously stored prototypic information must exceed some threshold level characteristic of the individual evaluator, and once recategorization occurs, future information search is presumed to be biased toward information consistent with the prototypic basis of the recategorization.

The final stage of the appraisal process as Feldman has construed it consists of information integration and judgment. Integration of information may be either cognitive or evaluative; in either case, the information to be integrated is information previously stored in memory. The result of cognitive integration is a belief statement or a prediction of future behavior.

The result of evaluative integration is an affective response. Under some circumstances integration may consist simply of recall of earlier integrations. In other circumstances, the information to be integrated is biased by the availability of disparate information which is determined in turn by prior considerations of selective attention, and automatic and controlled categorization processes, and by other factors affecting availability such as salience of categories, recency of recalled information and moods or affective states of perceivers at the time of integration or at the time of storage. It should also be pointed out that all of the biases thought to occur in attention, categorization, storage, and recall are as likely to be present in the definition of critical incidents in the development of rating scales as they are in the course of using these rating scales.

It would be easy to conclude from the analyses of Borman, Cooper and Feldman that performance ratings are inevitably and hopelessly biased, but Feldman has cautioned against such pessimism. Automatic selective attention and categorization are valuable in the sense that they reduce the complexity of information that enters into human decisions. Moreover, they do so in a way that results in good decisions with sufficient frequency to reject the null hypothesis (that the promotion and reward of the truly competent is a random event). This is so in part because categories and the prototypes associated with them reflect covariances among naturally occurring events; hence, they are frequently accurate. Moreover, models as explicit as the Borman-Cooper model and especially Feldman's model, offer the hope, if adequately supported by empirical data, of ability to manage the appraisal process in ways that minimize the intrusion errors that seem to be indigenous to the process.

Feldman's account of the course of the performance appraisal process has led Lord (1983) to propose an alternative approach to measurement of the accuracy of ratings that is based on signal detection theory. In this view, two kinds of rating errors might occur: recall of behavioral incidents that did not occur (false present errors, sometimes called "false alarms") and failure to recall behavioral incidents that did occur (false absent errors, sometimes called "misses"). Correct recall of incidents that did occur are referred to as "hits." Within the framework proposed, it is possible to obtain measures of behavioral accuracy, classification accuracy and leniency/severity bias by examining relative magnitudes of hit rates (proportion of behaviors correctly identified) to false alarm rates (proportion of absent behaviors identified as present). Accuracy of recall of behavioral events is proposed to be associated with hit rates considerably higher than false alarm rates. Accuracy of recall of categories is assumed to be associated with high hit rates and high false alarm rates for prototypical items and low hit rates and low false alarm rates for antiprototypical items. Leniency bias is thought to be associated with high hit rates and high false alarm rates for all items. Severity bias is thought to be associated with low hit rates and low false alarm rates for all items. Although these methods seem to provide a more adequate base for assessing accuracy of ratings than traditional psychometric methods, their use is at present largely confined to experimental situations in which the availability of information can be controlled.

Empirical Results

The hypothetical processes associated with both the Borman-Cooper model of performance appraisal and the Feldman model are based upon empirical data which are consistent with the elements of the two models — evidence not cited in this review. The two models are sufficiently recent that very little research testing the consequences of either model is yet available. One of two recent studies of cognitive processes in performance appraisal explicitly tests predictions of the Borman-Cooper model against those of the Feldman model (Nathan & Lord, 1983); the other is a more general examination of the consequences of schematic information processing in memory-based judgments of leadership in problem-solving groups (Phillips & Lord, 1982). In the Phillips & Lord study, student observers completed specially constructed leader behavior description questionnaires after viewing a videotaped interaction of a four-person problem-solving group. A male member of the group, designated the leader, had been coached to exhibit five clear instances of prototypically good leader behavior, five instances of prototypically bad leader behavior, and five instances of nonprototypic behavior to be evenly distributed throughout a 15-minute session. After viewing the videotape and before completing the questionnaire, subjects were given bogus feedback that the group viewed had performed either second best or second worst of 20 groups engaged in the problem-solving task portrayed on the videotape. The questionnaire completed after viewing and feedback consisted of 10 statements describing prototypically effective leader behavior, 10 statements describing prototypically ineffective behavior, and 10 nonprototypic statements. Half of the behaviors of each subset of 10 were present in the videotaped segment; the other half were absent. Phillips & Lord found that subjects had less difficulty distinguishing present nonprototypic items from absent nonprototypic items than in distinguishing present prototypic items from absent prototypic items. Moreover, subjects in the group given good performance feedback exaggerated the number of prototypically effective behaviors occurring and those given bad performance feedback exaggerated the number of prototypically ineffective behaviors. The bogus feedback had no effect on the reported number of nonprototypic behaviors. These results are consistent with Feldman's prediction that memory-based reports of behavior are likely to call forth prototypic examples rather than the details of the behavior actually observed, and that integration of information is likely to bias recall in the direction of confirmation of prior categorizations.

In the Nathan & Lord study, student subjects viewed one of two videotapes of a college lecturer in which three of five dimensions of performance were manipulated to be opposite of the lecturer's overall performance. In the good performance videotape, 6 prototypically good incidents of behavior were incorporated to represent the dimensions of delivery and organization. The dimensions of relevance, interpersonal

---

Measuring Teacher Merit   157

relations with students, and depth of knowledge were each represented by 2 prototypically good incidents and 4 prototypically bad incidents. The sampling was reversed in the bad performance videotape. The lecturers on the videotapes were rated either immediately following presentation of the videotaped lecture or 2 days later. Subjects were asked to rate the lecturer on all five dimensions and on overall performance. Nathan & Lord reasoned that if the Borman-Cooper model is an accurate representation of the cognitive processes associated with rating then the proportion of good to poor behavioral incidents within a performance dimension will determine performance ratings on each dimension independent of the overall proportion of good to poor behavioral incidents represented in each videotaped lecture. If the Feldman model is correct, then the overall proportion of good to poor behavioral incidents will determine the performance ratings made across all performance dimensions regardless of the proportion of good to poor incidents in each dimension. In fact, the dimensional ratings did reflect the proportion of good to poor incidents in each dimension, supporting the traditional model; but it was also the case that a significant portion of the variation in dimensional ratings was predicted by general impressions of the lecturer, supporting the categorization model. The categorization model was further tested by comparison of correlations between overall performance ratings and the frequency of occurrence of four distinct types of reporting errors. The prediction of the categorization model is that the correlations between overall performance ratings and favorable false-present and unfavorable false-absent errors should be positive, while the correlations between general impression and favorable false-absent and unfavorable false-present errors should be negative. The predicted negative correlations were obtained, and the predicted positive correlations were obtained between general impression and frequency of favorable false-present errors, but not between general impression and unfavorable false-absent errors. Although these results do not provide a clear basis for choice between the Borman-Cooper model of the rating process and the Feldman model, they provide very strong support for the contentions of both that halo results from engulfing of ratings by an overall impression and from cognitive distortions of stored observations. The finding that dimensional ratings were stable over time despite a decrease in memory accuracy for specific behavioral incidents suggests that the stability of dimensional ratings commonly found in educational research is maintained by distortions associated with raters' global impressions. While these results are more equivocal than might be hoped, they provide sufficient information when combined with other data within a theoretical framework to make some suggestions about designing a program for identification of exceptional teachers which has some chance of success.

Recommendations

The review so far has focused on problems encountered in the use of ratings in job performance appraisal and on solutions of limited success.

The time has come for recommendations. In this concluding section, most of the recommendations will originate in the research reported in this review. Other recommendations will arise from theoretical considerations either of the nature of performance appraisal or of the nature of teaching. Some of the recommendations in this category will be from papers published by two colleagues and myself (Johnson, Rhodes & Rumery, 1975b; Rumery, Rhodes & Johnson, 1975). A third category of recommendations will cover concerns outside the scope of the research reviewed for this paper, and will be original material or will be drawn from a recent textbook in the area of job performance appraisal. The general content of the various recommendations will concern the development of rating vehicles, including the rationale for specific recommendations; choice and training of raters; rating strategies; sources of data other than ratings; and the integration of data from various sources.

Development of Rating Scales

In spite of the number of problems attending the practice of performance ratings, and the limited success realized in reduction or elimination of those problems, it appears that rating methods will continue to be the major source of data in performance appraisal situations. In a recent textbook on performance appraisal and review systems (Carroll & Schneier, 1982), over 150 of 248 pages of text were devoted to discussion of raters and ratings. Landy & Farr and Feldman, among others, have suggested that the most fruitful locus for addressing the egregious defects of rating methods is in the developmental stage.

In an earlier section, we saw that the use of behaviorally anchored rating scales was sometimes effective in reducing halo and other rating errors, although the reduction in error was often found to be extremely small. Other studies have found the BARS approach no better, or sometimes worse than other methods (Atkin & Conlon, 1978; Fay & Saari, 1979). Bernardin & Smith (1981) have argued that many studies of the efficacy of BARS in reducing rating errors overemphasize the summary rating aspects of their use. They suggested that appropriate appraisal of the BARS approach should emphasize the entire Smith-Kendall procedure, which had as its original intent the standardization, not only of the rating process but of the observation process as well. In early applications, behavioral anchors provided were intended only to be illustrative, and the user of BARS was to record a brief notation of the specific behavior observed on any dimension in justification of interpolated ratings. Perhaps the most important aspect of the technique is to minimize the contribution of memory to any resulting summary ratings. Both the Borman-Cooper and Feldman descriptions of the performance appraisal process identify biases at the time of memorial storage and retrieval as important sources of rating errors.

With all of the cautionary warnings stated and implied by the research cited in this paper, the first recommendation is that development of rating scales be accomplished by some variant of the Smith-Kendall procedure. The method illustrated by Dickinson & Zellinger shows promise for several reasons. First, the teams of judges used in various stages of the process represented several roles relative to ratees. This circumstance provides optimal protection against biases which might originate in schemata or category systems characteristic of occupants of particular roles. Second, the process applied by Dickinson & Zellinger provides multiple indicators of the content validity of items and of categories or dimensions. Finally, the approach is not tied to any particular rating scale format. In the application reported, the same procedure was used to produce behaviorally anchored scales, mixed standard scales and Likert scales with a common set of response categories. The same procedure might be used to produce category scales with behavioral examples as response categories.

The Smith-Kendall procedure is recommended for rating scale development for reasons other than possible improvement of psychometric quality. The first reason is that the provision of specific behavioral description either as provided by anchors or as supplied by observers provides a source of feedback to the teacher being rated which should facilitate efforts at improvement of performance. A study by Ivancevich (1980) verified that the performance of engineers was indeed improved following the use of BARS. A second reason is that when deficiencies of job performance are described in specific behavioral terms, those being rated are more likely to accept the results of performance appraisal. This result was also found in the Ivancevich study. A third reason is predicated on the possibility, not always realized, that BARS can be constructed in such a way that more or less independent judgments are made on the separate dimensions with summary ratings arrived at on the basis of algorithmic combination of dimensional ratings. Lyness & Cornelius (1982) found that algorithmic combination of decomposed ratings led to more accurate results than either holistic (undecomposed ratings of overall job effectiveness) or dimensional rating followed by clinical combination of dimensional ratings to obtain an overall evaluative rating. The superior outcome of the decomposed-algorithmic method was found in terms of interrater reliability across occasions, convergence of ratings between rating methods (typical numerical ratings and estimation of appropriate salary increases within a specified range) and agreement among raters within and between occasions, rating methods and levels of information (three dimensions, six dimensions, or nine dimensions), using both correlation and mean absolute difference as measurers of interrater agreement. (It is perhaps significant that the raters had less confidence in the decomposed-algorithmic approach than in the holistic approach.)

Although there have been high hopes for the potential value of mixed standard scales because of their similarity to well-understood Guttman scales (Arvey & Hoyle, 1974), with the exceptions noted above (Dickinson & Zellinger), the results have been somewhat disappointing. The disappointing results might be due to the fact that the two schemes for arriving at numerical scores (Blanz & Ghiselli, 1972; Saal, 1977) allow response patterns inconsistent with the Guttman scale structure. A recent variation on the "standard" MSS technique (Rosinger, Myers, Levy, Loar, Morhman & Stock, 1982) defined items in terms of proficiency levels of specific job tasks rather than in terms of abstract dimensions. In their specific application, the content of the appraisal system was used to describe highway patrol task clusters such as general patrol performance, accident investigation and court behavior. For example, three items in a subscale titled "Stop Vehicles for a Variety of Violations" were "Stops vehicles for a variety of traffic and other violations," "Concentrates on speed violations, but stops vehicles for other violations also," and "Concentrates on one or two kinds of violations and spends too little time on others." The importance of each task was determined by its place in a two-dimensional decision matrix representing the criticality and frequency of the various tasks. The authors claim that the same method could be used to develop scales to appraise job tasks associated with other occupations. Finally, an alternative to the "better than, about the same as, worse than" response strategy in mixed standard scales is possible. That would be to provide items in the format usually used for MSS scales, but representing more than three levels of proficiency. If such items were independently scaled and raters merely checked those behaviors that had been observed, numerical values could be assigned on the basis of the highest scale value of a checked behavior. Such an approach has been used (Johnson, Rhodes & Rumery, 1975b) but the psychometric properties of such an approach have not been studied. This variation on the MSS procedure is consistent with Bernardin & Smith's observation that superior job performance rarely involved appearance of a single behavior with a high scale value, but a distribution of behaviors over some range of values on any dimensional scale.

In short, although the general developmental process outlined by Smith & Kendall is recommended, the recommendation is somewhat conditional and does not extend to unequivocal recommendation of any particular scale format. The condition attached to the recommendation is that panels of judges used in development of dimensions and items include at least three constituencies: supervisors, peers and parents. The research of Dickinson & Zellinger suggests the superiority of either the BARS format or the MSS format, with the BARS format preferred slightly because of its greater acceptance by ratees. New formats might be tried and evaluated with special attention to reduction in rating errors, availability of feedback to ratees and acceptance by ratees.

Choice and Training of Raters

Consistent with the view cited above that, in a rating situation, the raters rather than rating scales are the instruments for measurement of behavior, the selection of raters and their training are of approximately equal importance with scale development. In business and industry, ratings are usually provided by supervisors of peers. There are conceivable advantages and disadvantages in the use of either group. Clearly, peers have more opportunities to observe job-relevant behavior than supervisors do, although that might not be the case in educational settings. Against this advantage is poised the disadvantage that peers might be subject to leniency bias. Supervisors might be better informed than peers about critical job requirements. Moreover, for good or ill, evaluation of employees is likely to be a prescribed part of their jobs. Supervisors, however, usually have far less opportunity to observe job-relevant behavior than peers; hence, their ratings are more likely to be subject to halo. A suggestion offered by Feldman that multiple raters be used should result in reduced rating biases produced by selective attention, automatic and controlled categorization, and selective information search. In higher education the use of multiple raters entails putting the rating task in the hands of students with peers or supervisors making personnel decisions on the basis of that data. The use of students of common schools in this way seems intuitively to be unacceptable whatever its acceptability in higher education. Students in common schools might, however, be able to report on the occurrence or nonoccurrence of critical incidents developed by previously described procedures.

Research results cited above suggest that training of raters is sometimes effective in increasing reliability of ratings and reducing rating errors, although the suggestion has been offered that this is done at the cost of accuracy. Frame of reference training is apparently more effective than rater error training in the reduction of rating errors, with the suggestion offered that more extensive training might be still more effective. Unfortunately, the content of any more extensive training has not been specified; but research by Lord and others (Phillips & Lord, 1982; Nathan & Lord, 1983) suggests training which increases the accessibility of a wider range of categories (Srull & Wyer, 1979) or which induces more automatic processing in attention, recognition, categorization, and storage.

Rating Strategies

This section discusses recommendations about how the recommendations in the previous two sections might be implemented. Several authors have suggested that biases in cognitive processes reflect, in part, unspecified individual differences in information processing (e.g., Cooper, 1981; Feldman, 1981). This is part of the justification of frame-of-reference training of raters. Evidence suggests that frames of references of raters are related to their positions relative to ratees — students, peers, supervisors, etc. or to the perceived purposes of rating (Rumery, 1969; McIntyre, Smith & Hassett, 1984). Carroll & Schneier have argued for the use of rating teams representing various points of view or frames of reference. Formation of rating teams representing several constituencies would achieve the goal of controlling for possible sources of bias.

Another recommendation is to eschew a practice widely found in evaluation of teaching in higher education. That practice is to confine ratings to a single occasion usually near the end of a course. Such a practice maximizes the reliance of ratings on memory; hence it maximizes the contribution of various rating errors referred to above. An alternative is offered by Bernardin & Walter (1977); namely, multiple occasion rating with raters keeping a diary of incidents observed on each occasion. This might be accomplished by having rating teams visit classrooms frequently at random and unannounced intervals or by assigning rating teams the task of rating videotapes of classroom activity obtained on multiple occasions. The latter practice would allow more careful rating by raters, but might be obviated by practical considerations.

Data Sources Other than Ratings

The use of ratings for job performance appraisal is likely to be most effective when the job to be appraised is totally and precisely defined by a finite set of accurately specifiable behaviors. For many jobs, no doubt including teaching, this is usually not the case. Rating scales cannot possibly capture such elements essential to teaching performance as continuing education relevant to teaching performance, study of material to be taught, planning of sequences of presentation, development of examinations and so on. In business organizations, the same problems exist in evaluating the performance of managers. A widely used source of data in evaluation of performance of managers is a technique described as "management by objectives" (MBO). In application of this method, managers specify management objectives to be accomplished during an evaluation period and provide evidence of the accomplishment of those objectives at the end of the evaluation period. A variation of this procedure has been used to evaluate the performance of attorneys in a law firm (Hough, 1984). In this variation, a Record of Accomplishments Questionnaire was developed making use of the critical incident technique and incorporating relevant biodata. The method was found to be highly reliable and to show gratifying convergent and discriminant validity. One objection to the management-by-objectives technique is that, when rewards are contingent upon satisfying most goals, those to be evaluated are likely to specify goals that they are certain can be achieved (Mucczyk, 1972). One safeguard against this tendency is to require that some objectives specify problems or deficiencies in current performance to be improved. In addition, there is evidence that setting difficult goals may lead to higher performance (Locke, Shaw, Saari & Latham, 1980). MBO-type measures might incorporate objective documentation of achievement: certificates of training, lesson plans, handouts, quizzes, examinations and the like. This is an approach which has received very little attention in the literature dealing with evaluation of teaching performance.

Integrating Data

The total data base for establishing exceptional merit for a teacher might include ratings on anywhere from 3 to 12 dimensions, "Accomplishment record" data, information about the level of class learning obtained from standardized achievement tests, and data from teacher-made tests or other assignments which would provide evidence of student learning. (Difficulties with the latter sources of data are discussed in Johnson, Rhodes & Rumery, 1975a). Given the earlier recommendation that ratings should not include a global evaluation, how are we to combine such manifold data to make decisions about who is entitled to exceptional rewards and who is not? Although other possibilities are available, there is none which shows consistent advantages over a weighted linear combination. Differential weights for individual variables might be established statistically or by negotiation. A suitable statistical basis for selecting weights would be to weight variables according to some measure of their variability, usually the standard deviation. An alternative statistical procedure might be to employ a variation of policy-capturing methods (Wherry & Naylor, 1966), selecting a set of weights which optimally differentiates teachers, or some other basis. A negotiated method might be to make a preliminary estimate of differential utility using a variation of the procedure used by Rosinger et al. (1982), then adjust those weights according to a negotiated consensus.

Concluding Remarks

In discussions of complex scale development practices such as the development of behaviorally anchored rating scales or mixed standard scales, the question of cost effectiveness regularly arises. It is obvious that these methods of scale development are expensive and the question will be asked whether the benefits justify the cost. The same question could be asked about the proposals made in this paper; the recommended procedures would indeed be very expensive. No apology is offered for making proposals without considering the potential costs; the title suggests that we look for the best we can do based on outcomes of research on performance appraisal. As is usually the case, the choice of a practical procedure to be implemented involves informed compromise between what is ultimately possible and what is within institutional means. But in cost-benefit analysis, it is nearly always the case that the costs of implementing a new system are quite easy to estimate, while the benefits of a change are more difficult. It is also usually the case that costs of not changing are difficult to estimate or simply ignored. The net result of these two assertions is that cost-benefit analysis is likely to be biased toward one of the following courses of action. (1) Implement a new system if the costs are the same as or slightly higher than the obvious costs of an existing system on the assumption that a projected increase in benefits will be sufficient to justify the change. (2) If the difference in cost between an old system and a new system exceeds some unkown and perhaps variable threshold, retain the old system without considering possible benefits of the new system. The time to give serious consideration to the benefits to be achieved and the losses to be avoided by changing to new performance appraisal systems may be at hand.

Reference Notes

1. Abrami, P.C. *The dimensions of effective college instruction.* Presented at annual meeting of the American Educational Research Association, Montreal, 1983.

Robert E. Rumery

2. Mucczyk, J.P. *A controlled field experiment comparing management by objectives to existing practices in two organizations.* Unpublished doctoral dissertation, University of Maryland, 1972.

3. Locke, E.A., Shaw, K.N., Saari, L.M. & Latham, G.P. *Goal setting and task performance: 1969-1980.* Technical Report GS-4, Office of Naval Research (Contract N00014-79-6-06800, 1980).

4. Rumery, R.E. *Cognitive systems as mediators of ratings of teaching performance.* Unpublished doctoral dissertation, University of Illinois, 1969.

References

Arvey, R.D. & Hoyle, J.C. (1974). A Guttman approach to the development of behaviorally based rating scales for systems analysts and programmer/analysts. *Journal of Applied Psychology*, 59, 61-68.

Atkin, R.S. & Conlon, D.J. (1978). Behaviorally anchored rating scales: Some theoretical issues. *Academy of Management Review*, 3, 119-128.

Bernardin, H.J. (1978). Effects of rater training on leniency and halo errors in student ratings of instructors. *Journal of Applied Psychology*, 63, 301-308.

Bernardin, H.J. & Pence, E.C. (1980). Effects of rater training: Creating new response sets and decreasing accuracy. *Journal of Applied Psychology*, 65, 60-66.

Bernardin, H.J. & Smith, P.C. (1981). A clarification of some issues regarding the development and use of behaviorally anchored rating scales (BARS). *Journal of Applied Psychology*, 66, 458-463.

Bernardin, H.J. & Walter, C.S. (1977). Effects of rater training and diary-keeping on psychometric error in ratings. *Journal of Applied Psychology*, 62, 64-69.

Blanz, F. & Ghiselli, E.E. (1972). The mixed standard scale: A new rating scale. *Personnel Psychology*, 25, 185-189.

Borman, W.C. (1978). Exploring the upper limits of reliability and validity in job performance ratings. *Journal of Applied Psychology*, 63, 135-144.

Carroll, S.J. & Schneier, C.E. (1982). *Performance appraisal and review systems: The identification, measurement and development of performance in organizations.* Glenview, IL: Scott, Foresman.

Cooper, W.E. (1981). Ubiquitous halo. *Psychological Bulletin*, 90, 218-244.

Cronbach, L.J. Gleser, G.C., Nanda, H. & Rajaratnam, N. (1972). *The dependability of behavioral measurements: Theory of generalizability for scores and profiles.* New York: Wiley.

Dickinson, T.L. & Zellinger, P.M. (1980). A comparison of the behaviorally anchored rating and mixed standard scale formats. *Journal of Applied Psychology*, 65, 147-154.

Ebel, R. L. & Zellinger, P. M. (1980). A comparison of the behaviorally anchored rating and mixed scale formats. *Psychometrika*, 16, 407-424.

Feldman, J.M. (1981). Beyond attribution theory: Cognitive processes in performance appraisal. *Journal of Applied Psychology*, 66, 127-148.

Flanagan, J.C. (1954). The critical incident technique. *Psychological Bulletin*, 51, 317-358.

Guilford, J.P. (1954). *Psychometric methods.* New York: McGraw-Hill.

Harari, O. & Zedeck, S. (1973). Development of behaviorally anchored scales for the evaluation of faculty teaching. *Journal of Applied Psychology*, 58, 261-265.

Hough, L.M. (1984). Development and evaluation of the "accomplishment record" method of selecting and promoting professionals. *Journal of Applied Psychology*, 69, 135-146.

Hoyt, C.J. (1941). Test reliability estimated by analysis of variance. *Psychometrika*, 6, 153-160.

Ivancevich, J.M. (1979). Longitudinal study of the effects of rater trainers on psychometric error in ratings. *Journal of Applied Psychology*, 64, 502-508.

Ivancevich, J.M. (1980). A longitudinal study of behavioral expectation scales: Attitudes and performance. *Journal of Applied Psychology*, 65, 139-146.

Johnson, H.C., Jr., Rhodes, D.M. & Rumery, R.E. (1975a). The assessment of teaching in higher education: A critical retrospect and a proposal. Part I: A critical retrospect. *Higher Education* (Amsterdam), 3, 173-199.

Johnson, H.C., Jr., Rhodes, D.M. & Rumery, R.E. (1975b). The assessment of teaching in higher education: A critical retrospect and a proposal. Part II: A proposal. *Higher Education* (Amsterdam), 3, 273-303.

Korman, A.K. (1971). *Industrial and organizational psychology*. Englewood Cliffs, NJ: Prentice-Hall.

LaForge, R. (1965). Components of reliability. *Psychometrika*, 30, 187-195.

Landy, F.J. & Farr, J.L. (1980). Performance rating. *Psychological Bulletin*, 87, 72-107.

Latham, G.P., Fay, C. & Saari, L.M. (1979). The development of behavioral observation scales for appraising the performance of foremen. *Personnel Psychology*, 32, 299-311.

Lawlis, G.F. & Lu, E. (1972). Judgment of counseling process: Reliability, agreement and error. *Psychological Bulletin*, 78, 17-20.

Lyness, K.S. & Cornelius, E.T., III (1982). A comparison of holistic and decomposed judgment strategies in a performance rating simulation. *Organizational Behavior and Human Performance*, 29, 21-38.

McIntyre, R.M., Smith, D.E. & Hassett, C.E. (1984). Accuracy of performance ratings as affected by rater training and perceived purpose of rating. *Journal of Applied Psychology*, 69, 147-156.

Murray, H.A. (1938). *Explorations of personality*. New York: Oxford University Press.

Remmers, H.H. (1962). Rating methods in research on teaching. In N.L. Gage (Ed.), *Handbook of research on teaching*, pp. 329-378. Chicago: Rand McNally.

Rosinger, G., Myers, L.B., Levy, G.W., Loar, M., Mohrman, S.A. & Stock, J.R. (1982). Development of a behaviorally based performance appraisal system. *Personnel Psychology*, 35, 75-88.

Rumery, R.E., Rhodes, D.M. & Johnson, H.C., Jr. (1975). The role of student ratings in the evaluation of teaching in higher education. *Higher Education Bulletin*, 3, 93-99.

Ryans, D.G. (1960). *Characteristics of teachers: Their description, comparison and appraisal*. Washington, DC: American Council on Education.

Saal, F.E. (1979). Mixed standard rating scale: A consistent system for numerically coding inconsistent response combinations. *Journal of Applied Psychology*, 64, 422-428.

Saal, F.E., Downey, R.G. & Lahey, M.A. (1980). Rating the ratings: Assessing the psychometric quality of ratings. *Psychological Bulletin*, 88, 413-428.

Saal, F.E. & Landy, F.J. (1977). The mixed standard rating scale: An evaluation. *Organizational Behavior and Human Performance*, 18, 19-35.

Shrout, P.E. & Fleiss, J.L. (1979). Interclass correlation: Uses in assessing rater reliability. *Psychological Bulletin*, 86, 420-428.

Smith, P.C. & Kendall, L.M. (1963). Retranslation of expectations: An approach to the construction of unambiguous anchors for rating scales. *Journal of Applied Psychology*, 47, 149-155.

Srull, T.K. & Wyer, R.S., Jr. (1979). The role of category accessability in the interpretation of information about persons: Some determinants and implications. *Journal of Personality and Social Psychology*, 37, 1660-1672.

Stanley, J.C. (1961). Analysis of unreplicated three-way classification with applications to rater bias and trait independence. *Psychometrika*, 26, 205-219.

Tinsley, H.E.A. & Weiss, D.J. (1975). Interrater reliability and agreement of subjective judgments. *Journal of Counseling Psychology*, 22, 358-376.

Vance, R.J., Kuhnert, K.W. & Farr, J.L. (1978). Interview judgments: Using external criteria to compare behavioral and graphic scale ratings. *Organizational Behavior and Human Performance*, 22, 279-284.

Wherry, R.J. & Naylor, J.C. (1966). Comparison of two approaches—JAN and PROF—for capturing rater strategies. *Educational and Psychological Measurement*, 26, 267-286.

Zedeck, S. & Cascio, W. Performance decision as a function of purpose of rating and training. *Journal of Applied Psychology*, 67, 752-758.

Improving Teacher Salaries: Merit Pay Isn't Enough

Barry D. Anderson
Jonathan Mark

I. Introduction

There is an emerging belief that the salaries of American public school teachers have become too low. That this is a relatively new phenomenon is suggested by the fact that, in 1972, authors such as Moynihan were arguing that it would not be desirable to spend more on education because the money would go to teachers, who were already well paid.

Low pay is a serious problem to the extent that it drives talented teachers out of the profession and makes it difficult to attract high-quality people to teaching as a career. It is believed that these outcomes would lead to reduced performance in the school system. Poor performance erodes public confidence which leads to reduced financial support and further reductions in teacher salary levels. A growing belief that this complex chain of cause-and-effect exists has resulted in attention to finding ways to increase teacher salaries.

To those who believe in the chain of cause-and-effect described above, it is most desirable to improve the salaries of only high-quality teachers. This line of reasoning leads to some form of merit pay or performance contracting as a means of selectively increasing salaries. But, a considerable body of evidence suggests that the teaching profession neither attracts nor retains the most academically talented college students (Koerner, 1963; Schlechty and Vance, 1981; Vance and Schlechty, 1982; Weaver, 1978). There is also evidence that there have been problems retaining people in the profession for many years (Charters, 1970; Mark and Anderson, 1978). These factors suggest that, in order to make long-term improvements to the profession, it may be advantageous to improve salary levels in general, without immediately directing increases to only the most qualified teachers. However, raising general salary levels would be expensive, and one might reasonably ask if increases of sufficient size could be afforded.

Several ways to solve the salary problem have been suggested, but most suggestions seem to ignore a situation which may have led to low salaries in the first place. There are far more teachers per pupil in today's schools than in the schools of even six or seven years ago. This fact suggests that a comparatively simple way to increase teacher salaries would be to reduce the number of teachers while holding total salary expenditures at a constant level. Compared to the complex systems of pay and promotion now being suggested as methods of raising teacher salaries, shrinking the size of the teaching force may turn out to be a very attractive procedure, if only because it is one procedure which offers real hope of delivering enough money to enable significant salary increases.

II. Finding Funds for Salaries

Four frequently suggested ways of increasing teacher salaries are the provision of additional money to the school system, especially in the form of state and federal aid; unionization; implementation of merit pay systems; and the development of career ladders for teachers. While the latter two proposals are intended to improve the quality of the school system by providing incentives to the teachers, they are also relatively low-cost methods of increasing the salaries of some teachers.

II.1 Provision of Additional Money

The suggestion that more money be given to the schools is usually coupled with a call for more state or federal funding, the need for which is made obvious by local taxpayers resistance to school tax increases. But how much money is required to raise teacher salaries to a more appropriate level? Increasing every teacher's salary by 20% would be very expensive. For instance, in the United States in 1981, there were 2,172,600 teachers earning an average salary of $18,987. Increasing that average salary by 20% to $22,784, would cost an additional 8.25 *billion* dollars. This cost, coupled with current economic conditions, the declining political influence of families with children (because of their declining numbers), and the fact that wholesale salary increases will not rid the schools of poor teachers, implies that the funds required for large salary increases will not be forthcoming. As a result, alternative methods of providing teacher salary increases have been sought. Typically, these involve maintaining the existing salary budget and adding marginal increases for improved quality. Two common examples of this are the provision of career ladders and merit pay for teachers.

II.2 Provision of Career Ladders

The provision of career ladders for teachers is unlikely to result in an improved system because career ladders are already in place. A career ladder exists if promotions, with both additional responsibility and salary, are possible. Our data indicate that in recent years, increasing percentages of the teaching force have been allocated to positions such as instructional aid, department head, or instructional supervisor. For example, in the St. Louis metropolitan area, the number of teachers in administrative and support positions grew from 11.9% of the teaching force in 1969 to 15.8% in 1982. The number of people in these positions was increased from 2,121 to 2,989 or 40%, during a period when enrollment fell 30% from 378,680 to

Barry D. Anderson & Jonathan Mark

263,350 and the total number of teachers increased by 220 or 1% from 15,-760 to 15,980.

Despite the increased use of non-teaching positions as a career ladder, average teacher salaries fell in real dollars. Further, the claim that there is "no incentive for good performance" has grown louder, and public confidence in schools has fallen. There is no evidence to suggest that continuing the trend of adding new non-teaching positions will improve either salaries or school performance. Nor is it likely that providing salary increments for levels of training and experience not now recognized in school district salary grids would successfully deal with the problem. This strategy would not increase the salaries of new teachers and the problems of attracting new people into teaching would remain.

II.3 Unionization

Another strategy which is sometimes suggested as a means of increasing the funds available to teachers, unionizing the teaching force, would not necessarily result in general salary increases. For example, Brown's (1975) results suggest that collective bargaining has had, at most, a minimal positive effect on teacher salaries. This result is confirmed by Balfour (1974) in his analysis of interstate differences in mean teacher salaries.

This finding, however, is not universally accepted. For example, Holmes (1975) found that collective negotiations had a significant positive impact on salaries. Increases were achieved by "inflating the per unit payment of the two teacher characteristics, educational attainment and years of service in the district" (page 13). For our purposes, it is only important to note that salary increases, however they may be attained, will not result automatically from collective bargaining.

II.4 Merit Pay

Merit pay is unlikely to be a good solution to the problem of low teacher salaries. Because merit pay would be awarded to only a limited number of teachers, it would not solve the salary problems of the majority. If it could solve the salary problem of most teachers, the system would be at least as costly as a general pay increase.

Independent of their effects on salaries, merit pay systems could cause additional problems for schools. The work of Natriello and Dornbusch (1982) suggests that merit pay may require administrative skills which are not normally demonstrated in school systems. Murnane (1981) has argued that the very nature of teaching is such that contracts based on seniority may be the most efficient type that are available. Introduction of merit pay systems may reduce the efficiency of school systems.

Two fundamental problems will exist even if schools solve the difficult problem of how to evaluate teachers for merit pay. Since merit pay would create an elite in a profession which is supposed to offer equal service to all, teachers' organizations will likely resist setting some teachers apart from others. Also, if merit pay schemes are implemented, it will be hard to gain acceptance from parents whose children are assigned to the "non-meritorious" teachers. The potential for legal challenges based on parental demands for equal access to quality service is obvious. Finally, comprehensive reviews of the virtues of merit pay systems do not suggest that it is a simple answer to problems of school quality (see Calhoun and Protheroe, 1983; Johnson, 1984).

III. An Alternative Approach

Another way to solve the problem of low teacher salaries is to reduce the number of active teachers and use the savings to increase the salaries of those who remain. This suggestion does not require a radical change in schooling: If the public school system simply returned to the pupil-teacher ratios which prevailed in 1975, teachers salaries could be increased substantially. If they returned to the pupil-teacher ratio which prevailed in 1969, then teacher salaries could be increased even more. It is a simple, workable solution which public opinion polls suggest would receive support. Plisko (1984), for example, reports that over 50% of people surveyed favour reducing the administrative and support components of school staffs. Approximately 20% favour increasing class sizes by reducing the number of teachers.

Two pieces of data which support this contention have been collected. The first is a detailed description of the metropolitan St. Louis teaching force over a fourteen-year period. The second is a set of data from the U.S. Government which permits a replication of much of the St. Louis study on a state-by-state basis and, consequently, for the entire United States.

III.1 The Metropolitan St. Louis Example

Data obtained from the Missouri Department of Elementary and Secondary Education are presented in Tables 1 and 2. The data were drawn from all active certified teachers, including support staff and administrators, in the school districts of the five-county Missouri portion of the St. Louis Standard Metropolitan Area (SMSA). The data cover the period 1969 through 1982 and involved between 50 to 55 districts, depending on the year.

The assumption made in calculating the potential average salaries in Table 1 is that the 1969 pupil-teacher ratio (hereafter denoted PTR) represents an acceptable level of service and that this ratio is held constant in subsequent years. The first two columns of the table present the actual number of students and certified personnel each year, while column three presents the actual PTR. While enrollment has declined significantly, the number of teachers (certified staff) has increased. The result is that the pupil-teacher ratio declined from 21.2:1 in 1969 to 13.9:1 in 1982.

Column four indicates the number of personnel needed to maintain a ratio of 21.2:1, given the changes in enrollment. The fifth column indicates the number of teachers who are in excess of the number needed to maintain the 1969 ratio. Column six presents the average teacher salary. The seventh column presents the excess salary expenditure, assuming that each of the excess teachers receives the average salary.

The key information is provided in the eighth column, which shows what the average salary could be if the salaries of excess personnel were redistributed to the teachers required to maintain the 1969 PTR. The 1982 salary in this column is 52% higher than the actual average salary paid to teachers in that year.

It might be argued that new factors such as Public Law 94-142, which required that handicapped students be educated in the least restrictive environment possible, necessitated the hiring of additional teachers. To the extent this is true, the PTR for 1969 would be inappropriate. Fewer such new conditions have appeared since 1975. Table 2 shows the same scenario if the 1975 PTR is assumed to represent an appropriate level of service. The table shows that there are more teachers in the system than are required to maintain even the 1975 PTR. The potential salary for 1982 with the excess teachers removed is 27% larger than the salary actually paid to teachers in that year.

III.2 The National Example

It might also be argued that the St. Louis metropolitan area is not representative of the U.S. situation. After all, both the region and the state have had greater than average enrollment declines. To explore this line of reasoning, national data were examined. Tables 3 and 4 replicate Tables 1 and 2 for the United States, using data taken from several years of the *Statistical Abstract of the United States*. These data generally include only teachers (including special education) and exclude certified personnel who do not teach. There is some variation in the definitions from one state to another. However, this does not change the basic trends in the results.

An examination of Table 3 indicates that the trends existing in the St. Louis metropolitan area are not unusual. Assuming the 1969 PTR is acceptable and held constant, there was an excess expenditure of more than $7.9 billion in 1981. Average salaries could have been increased by almost 24% over actual 1981 levels. However, if the 1975 PTR is a more appropriate level of service, then the mean 1981 salary could be increased 11% by redistributing the excess expenditure of $4.22 billion (see Table 4).

IV. The Impact of Reductions

Could school systems reduce the size of their teaching forces without destroying their ability to educate students effectively? It is hard to be certain, but there are clues. For instance, reductions made in the number of administrators could presumably be made with few impacts on classrooms. In addition, since administrators and support staff tend to be more highly paid than the average teacher, reductions in this area could yield comparatively greater salary gains for remaining teachers than would reductions in the number of classroom teachers.

IV.1 Administrative Reductions

Using 1969 and, alternatively, 1975 levels of support and administrative service as bases for comparison, the number of "excess" administrators in the metropolitan St. Louis area was calculated. The number of support staff and support personnel increased from 866 in 1969 to 1,643 in 1982. To maintain the 1969 ratio of students to support personnel, only 603 support personnel would have been needed in 1982. Similarly, the number of administrators increased from 1,249 in 1969 to 1,346 in 1982. To maintain the 1969 ratio of students to administrators, only 871 would have been required in 1982. On this basis, there were 1,040 support staff and 475 administrators in excess of the number required to attain 1969 levels of service. Therefore, 1,515 or 23.2% of the total of 6,542 excess personnel could be removed without directly affecting the classroom. Simply cutting back administrative staff to 1969 levels would permit a salary increase of $1,737, or 8.5%.

Alternatively, the 1975 ratios of support staff and administrators to students could be used as a basis of comparison. Doing so yields 589 excess support staff and 327 excess administrators in 1982. This excess of 916 constitutes 22.8% of the total 1982 excess of 4,024 people. A return to 1975 levels would permit a $1,005, or 4.9% salary increase for remaining teachers.

These examples suggest that more than 22% of the staff reductions required to return to either 1969 or 1975 PTR's could be achieved solely through reductions in the ranks of administrative and support personnel. Even these reductions would yield significant pay increases for teachers. Would these reductions lead to severe degradation of service to children? We think not. Indeed, evidence presented by Bidwell and Kasarda (1975) suggests that student achievement tends to decline as the number of administrators in the school system increases. If there is a cause-and-effect relationship, reductions in these staff personnel might in fact improve achievement.

IV.2 Teaching Staff Reductions

Remaining reductions in staff size might be more difficult to achieve. Many of the excess staff appear to be located in school districts which have experienced rapid enrollment declines, but have not made corresponding adjustments to the size of their staffs. It is difficult for school districts to reduce staffs in direct proportion to decreases in enrollment because enrollment decreases tend to be scattered in small numbers throughout districts. However, over time it is possible, and may now be financially necessary, to re-organize entire school districts. The closure of excess space and the resultant re-allocation of staff would enable reductions in the size of the teaching force. Closures could also result in significant reductions in the funds required to operate school plants, providing another potential source of funds to increase teacher salaries.

Staff reductions would increase class size. Work by Bereiter (nd), Haddad (1978), and Porwoll (1978) suggests that, at best, the evidence is inconclusive that class size is an important determinant of outcomes. As Bereiter states, ". . . the evidence, such as it is, gives little support to the notion that class size has a powerful effect on educational outcomes" (page 140). Haddad reaches much the same conclusion. Bereiter is careful, however, to point out that it is possible that ". . . class size can make a difference" depending on how classroom activities are conducted. Porwoll's 1978 report notes the fact that reductions in class size are very expensive (pp. 63-64), requiring extra teachers, more facilities and the like. The report further notes that except in relatively limited circumstances (e.g., students from poverty-stricken homes, children in the primary grades learning to read) the evidence on the impact of reducing class size within normal ranges was very ambiguous.

V. Conclusion

If raising teacher salaries is a worthwhile objective, either in its own right or because increases are thought to lead to improved quality in the school system, then the schools are faced with a very large financial problem. To solve this financial problem, massive amounts of new funding must be found, and/or serious changes in the organization of school staffs will be required. One such change would be the introduction of merit pay schemes. But, it has been shown elsewhere, these schemes are cumbersome, schools may not have the administrative skills required to implement them, and they won't solve salary problems unless new funds or other organizational changes are introduced. The simplest organizational change which might permit salary increases would be increases in the pupil/teacher ratio. These could be achieved by reducing administrative components and/or by increasing the work load of teachers (asking them to teach larger classes, or more classes per day).

Teachers organizations, school administrators and school boards should give serious consideration to reducing the size of school staffs as a way to find money to increase teacher salaries. Such reductions need not be achieved rapidly in order to have the desired financial outcome. Retirements, normal departures, liberal leave and early retirement policies and careful management of the allocation of personnel outside the classroom, could do a great deal to facilitate staff reductions. Such reductions, if carefully managed, might even greatly reduce the 5% to 15% of teachers reported by administrators to be performing below expected levels (Bridges, 1983, p. 2).

Staff reductions have the great advantage of being equitable to teachers. They are achievable by boards with existing resources and do not require new administrative procedures that might result from complicated proposals such as merit pay schemes. They are a simple, feasible, and fair approach to solving the problem of low teacher salaries.

References

Balfour, G. Alan. "More Evidence that Unions Do Not Achieve Higher Salaries for Teachers." *Journal of Collective Negotiations in the Public Sector*. Vol. 3, No. 4, (Fall, 1974). pp. 289-303.

Bereiter, C. "Can Class Size Make a Difference?" Mimeo, Ontario Institute for Studies in Education, (nd).

Bidwell, C. and Kasarda, J. "School District Organization and Student Achievement". *American Sociological Review*. Vol. 40, (February, 1975). pp. 55-70.

Bridges, E.M. "The Management of Teacher Incompetence", Stanford University, Institute for Research on Educational Finance and Governance, Report 83-A20, 1983.

Brown, Thomas A. "Have Collective Negotiations Increased Teachers' Salaries? A Comparison of Teachers' Salaries in States Without Collective Bargaining Laws for Public School Personnel, 1961-1971". *Journal of Collective Negotiations in the Public Sector*, Vol. 4, No. 1, (1975). pp. 53-66.

Calhoun, Frederick and Protheroe, Nancy. *Merit Pay Plans for Teachers: Status and Description*. Arlington: Educational Research Service, 1983.

Charters, W.W. "Some Factors Affecting Teacher Survival Rates in School Districts". *American Educational Research Journal*. Vol. 7, No. 1, 1970, pp. 1-27.

Haddad, W. "Educational Effects of Class Size," World Bank Staff Working Paper No. 280, June, 1978.

Holmes, Alexander B. "A Micro-Analysis of the Effect of Bargaining Units of Teachers' Salaries," Working Paper No. 75:11, College of Business Administration, University of Oklahoma, 1975.

Johnson, Susan M. *Pros and Cons of Merit Pay*. Bloomington: Phi Delta Kappa, 1984.

Koerner, J.D. "The Miseducation of American Teachers". New York: McGraw-Hill, 1963.

Mark, Jonathan and Anderson, Barry. "Teacher Survival Rates - A Current Look". *American Educational Research Journal*. Vol. 15, No. 3, 1978, pp. 379-383.

Moynihan, D.P. "Equalizing Education: In Whose Benefit?" *Public Interest*. No. 29, 1972. pp. 69-89.

Murnane, Richard. "Seniority Rules and Educational Productivity: Understanding the Consequences of a Mandate for Equality". *American Journal of Education*, Vol. 89, November, 1981, pp. 14-38.

Natriello, G. and Dornbusch, S. "Pitfalls in the Evaluation of Teachers by Principals." *Administrator's Notebook*. 29, 1982, pp. 1-4.

Plisko, V.W. "Taking Our Temperature: The Condition of Education, 1983," *Principal*, January, 1984.

Schlechty, P.C. and Vance, V.S. "Do Academically Able Teachers Leave Education? The North Carolina Case". *Phi Delta Kappan*. October, 1981, pp. 106-112.

Vance, V.S. and Schlechty, P.C. "The Distribution of Academic Ability in the Teaching Force: Policy Implications". *Phi Delta Kappan*, September, 1982, pp. 22-27.

Weaver, W.T. "Educators in Supply and Demand: Effects on Quality". *School Review*, August, 1978, pp. 552-593.

TABLE 1

POSSIBLE AVERAGE SALARIES ASSUMING 1969 PUPIL TEACHER RATIO HELD CONSTANT

YEAR*	STUDENTS	ACTUAL TEACHERS	ACTUAL PUPIL/TEACHER RATIO	PERSONNEL REQUIRED FOR 1969 PUPIL/TEACHER RATIO	EXCESS TEACHERS	AVERAGE SALARY	EXCESS EXPENDITURE ($1,000,000)	POSSIBLE AVERAGE SALARY (NO EXCESS AND REDISTRIBUTION)	POSSIBLE INCREASE IN SALARY
1969	378,682	17,873	21.19	17,873	0	9,278	0	9,278	0%
1970	380,705	18,443	20.64	17,966	477	9,879	4.71	10,141	2.7%
1971	366,631	19,282	19.01	17,302	1,980	10,280	20.35	11,456	11.4%
1972	371,226	19,941	18.62	17,519	2,422	10,626	25.74	12,095	13.8%
1973	367,687	19,890	18.49	17,352	2,538	11,282	28.63	12,932	14.6%
1974	360,459	20,084	17.95	17,011	3,073	11,955	36.74	14,115	18.1%
1975	350,878	19,909	17.62	16,559	3,350	12,777	42.80	15,362	20.2%
1976	336,893	19,998	16.85	15,899	4,099	13,628	55.86	17,142	25.8%
1977	328,420	19,704	16.67	15,499	4,205	14,423	60.65	18,336	27.1%
1978	315,120	19,643	16.04	14,871	4,772	15,308	73.05	20,220	32.1%
1979	324,003	19,411	16.89	15,290	4,121	16,456	67.82	20,891	27.0%
1980	316,018	19,605	16.12	14,914	4,691	18,469	86.64	24,278	31.5%
1981	272,438	20,642	13.20	12,857	7,785	18,628	145.02	29,907	60.5%
1982	263,353	18,970	13.88	12,428	6,542	20,325	132.97	31,024	52.6%

*In this and all remaining Tables, year refers to the first half of the school year. Thus 1969 is the 1969/70 school year.

TABLE 2
POSSIBLE AVERAGE SALARIES ASSUMING 1975/76 PUPIL TEACHER RATIO HELD CONSTANT

YEAR	STUDENTS	ACTUAL TEACHERS	ACTUAL PUPIL/TEACHER RATIO	PERSONNEL REQUIRED FOR 1975 PUPIL/TEACHER RATIO	EXCESS TEACHERS	AVERAGE SALARY	EXCESS EXPENDITURE ($1,000,000)	POSSIBLE AVERAGE SALARY (NO EXCESS AND REDISTRIBUTION)	POSSIBLE INCREASE IN SALARY
1969	378,682	17,873	21.19	21,492	-*	9,278	-*	-*	-*
1970	380,705	18,443	20.64	21,606	-	9,879	-	-	-
1971	366,631	19,282	19.01	20,808	-	10,280	-	-	-
1972	371,226	19,941	18.62	21,068	-	10,626	-	-	-
1973	367,687	19,890	18.49	20,868	-	11,282	-	-	-
1974	360,459	20,084	17.95	20,457	-	11,955	-	-	-
1975	350,878	19,909	17.62	19,906	0	12,777	0	12,777	0%
1976	336,893	19,998	16.85	19,120	878	13,628	11.97	14,254	4.6%
1977	328,420	19,704	16.67	18,639	1,065	14,423	15.36	15,247	5.7%
1978	315,120	19,643	16.04	17,884	1,759	15,308	26.93	16,814	9.8%

1979	324,003	19,411	16.89	18,388	1,023	16,456	16.83	17,372	5.6%
1980	316,018	19,605	16.12	17,935	1,670	18,469	30.84	20,189	9.3%
1981	272,438	20,642	13.20	15,462	5,180	18,628	96.49	24,869	33.5%
1982	263,353	18,970	13.88	14,946	4,024	20,325	81.79	25,797	26.9%

*Based on the 1975 PTR, there would be insufficient personnel from 1969 to 1974, and thus no excess expenditure and no money available for redistribution.

TABLE 3

POSSIBLE AVERAGE SALARIES FOR THE UNITED STATES
ASSUMING 1969 PTR HELD CONSTANT

YEAR	STUDENTS	ACTUAL TEACHERS	ACTUAL PTR	TEACHERS REQUIRED USING 1969 PTR	EXCESS TEACHERS	ACTUAL AVERAGE SALARY	EXCESS EXPENDITURES ($1,000,000)	POSSIBLE AVERAGE SALARY	POSSIBLE INCREASE IN SALARY
1969.	45472992.	1991226.	22.84	1991226.	0.	8525.	0.0	8525.	-0.00
1970.	45758000.	2032405.	22.51	2003707.	28698.	9260.	265.76	9393.	1.43
1971.	45896992.	2083108.	22.03	2009793.	73315.	9687.	710.17	10040.	3.65
1972.	45490000.	2093754.	21.73	1991971.	101783.	10121.	1030.14	10638.	5.11
1973.	45262000.	2112513.	21.32	1981987.	140526.	10677.	1500.42	11434.	7.09
1974.	44892992.	2152492.	20.86	1965829.	186663.	11505.	2147.50	12597.	9.50
1975.	44700000.	2175200.	20.55	1957378.	217822.	12523.	2727.71	13916.	11.13
1976.	44070992.	2181000.	20.21	1929934.	251166.	13294.	3339.06	15024.	13.01
1977.	43562992.	2171100.	20.06	1907589.	263511.	14233.	3750.65	16200.	13.81
1978.	42692000.	2182500.	19.56	1869949.	313051.	15027.	4704.20	17543.	16.75
1979.	41466000.	2178600.	19.03	1815763.	362837.	15987.	5800.76	19182.	19.98
1980.	40882992.	2179900.	18.75	1790234.	389666.	17262.	6726.29	21019.	21.77
1981.	40074992.	2172600.	18.45	1754852.	417748.	18987.	7931.93	23507.	23.81

TABLE 4
POSSIBLE AVERAGE SALARIES FOR THE UNITED STATES ASSUMING 1975 PTR HELD CONSTANT

YEAR	STUDENTS	ACTUAL TEACHERS	ACTUAL PTR	TEACHERS REQUIRED USING 1969 PTR	EXCESS TEACHERS	ACTUAL AVERAGE SALARY	EXCESS EXPENDITURES ($1,000,000)	POSSIBLE AVERAGE SALARY	POSSIBLE INCREASE IN SALARY
1969.	45472992.	1991226.	22.84	2212817.	-*	8525.	-*	-*	-*
1970.	45758000.	2032405.	22.51	2226686.	-	9260.	-	-	-
1971.	45896992.	2083108.	22.03	2233449.	-	9687.	-	-	-
1972.	45490000.	2093754.	21.73	2213644.	-	10121.	-	-	-
1973.	45262000.	2122513.	21.32	2202549.	-	10677.	-	-	-
1974.	44892992.	2152492.	20.86	2184592.	-	11505.	-	-	-
1975.	44700000.	2175200.	20.55	2175201.	0.	12523.	0.00	12523.	0.00
1976.	44070992.	2181000.	20.21	2144592.	36408.	13294.	484.02	13520.	1.70
1977.	43562992.	2171100.	20.06	2119872.	51228.	14233.	729.15	14577.	2.42
1978.	42692000.	2182500.	19.56	2077487.	105013.	15027.	1578.02	15787.	5.05
1979.	41466000.	2178600.	19.03	2017827.	160773.	15987.	2570.32	17261.	7.97
1980.	40882992.	2179900.	18.75	1989457.	190443.	17262.	3287.37	18914.	9.57
1981.	40074992.	2172600.	18.45	1950138.	222462.	18987.	4223.96	21153.	11.41

* Based on the 1975 PTR, there would be insufficient personnel from 1969 to 1974, and thus no excess expenditure and no money for redistribution.

Career Ladders and the Debureaucratization of Education

Arnold J. Bornfriend

Introduction

Just about a year ago (this being written in late Spring of 1984), I became aware of the master-teacher/career-ladder concept when I happened to view a lively point-counterpoint discussion between Governor Lamar Alexander of Tennessee and Don Cameron, Executive Director of the National Education Association, on a morning T.V. show. In response to my request, Governor Alexander's office sent me a copy of the bill which had been introduced in the state legislature earlier that year. From then on I have followed the rapid progress of the master-teacher/career-ladder concept in other states and school districts. By March 1984, according to Secretary of Education Terrel Bell, some 33 states were considering or had adopted a version of the concept.

From the perspective of one who has worked in both business and the public sector, and now teaches management, career-ladders is the one reform which has the greatest potential for improving our nation's schools. Providing promotional opportunities overcomes the isolation of public education from the practices followed in these other sectors. At the same time it has the promise for restructuring education by bridging the gulf between teaching and administration. The lack of career paths has sharply restricted the available pool of talent for entering the profession; and also prevents the development of the levels of motivation required to reach and sustain teaching excellence. Certainly the quality of education has suffered from inadequate financial resources and such reforms as performance-based pay, as well as substantial across-the-board salary raises, will further teacher morale and satisfaction. Yet they are not designed fully to motivate teachers to attain and sustain teaching excellence. Similarly, reforms dealing with raising competency levels, teacher training, and staff development may improve teacher's aptitudes, but cannot by themselves stimulate the commitment necessary to convert potential ability into actual performance.

Secondly, the master teacher component has the promise for helping to debureaucratize the educational system on two fronts. First, the master teacher or mentor reverse the emphasis on credentializing and towards the notion of teaching as a craft. For the master teacher is a colleague, rather than supervisor, and the craft is learned by setting standards and example rather than by the accumulation of courses and credits. Secondly, by having the master teacher assume tasks and functions formerly considered managerial responsibilities, the wide gulf between teaching and administration is bridged. Functions can then be recombined and redundant positions eliminated, leading to improved coordination and sharply reduced administrative costs.

The Non-Career Dilemma

While the notion of a career has various meanings, it invariably includes moving upward in one's chosen line of work or profession. As responsibilities increase, more money, more authority, and usually greater prestige are also acquired. The typical career path for professionals working in corporations as, for example, accountants, lawyers, scientists, and engineers coincides with four broad stages of their personal development.[1] Stage I: *Apprentice*. Emphasis is placed on becoming proficient, and connecting their own specialty with organizational routines and needs. Stage II: *Advancement*. After gaining the necessary self-confidence the individual moves away from being closely supervised, and assumes the role of independent contributor. Stage III: *Mentor*. This stage is marked by training junior colleagues and taking on responsibility for their work. Stage IV: *Sponsor*. By permitting individuals to select successors and influence them indirectly, innovative approaches are developed which shape the direction of the organization.

Of course, not all corporate professionals pass through all four stages. A few who do slip-shod work or cannot relate to the needs of the organization are washed out at Stage I. Some cannot stand the stress of supervising others so remain as independent contributors; others can't tolerate the ambiguities of sponsorship. Nonetheless, both the expectations for and the likelihood of career growth are the norm.

But for teachers as a class, stages III and IV simply do not exist; career growth is blocked at Stage II. In addition, for teachers Stage II, Advancement, becomes a Maintenance Phase, more a prolonged apprenticeship than a period for recognition as a full-fledged independent contributor. Dan Lortie, a sociologist, some years back recognized:

> Compared with most other kinds of middle-class work, teaching is relatively"career-less". There is less opportunity for the movement upward which is the essence of a career. . . . But in contrast to the larger packages of money, prestige and power usually found in other careers, the typical career line of the classroom teacher is a gently incline rather than a steep ascent . . . The status of the young tenured teacher is not appreciably different from that of the highly experienced old-timer.[2]

Ironically, the career path for teachers in recent years has been closest to the pattern of blue collar workers having little formal education. Their initial

Arnold J. Bornfriend

work stage is marked by moving from job to job, until they achieve the second stage — Stable Work. Thereafter they maintain one job until retirement, the ultimate stage. In the pungent phrase of Governor Alexander, "The school should not be a factory with assemblyline teachers." [3]

Purpose Over Technique

The common belief that most large businesses use performance evaluations as the primary tool for awarding promotions, pay increases, and other incentives is more dogma than reality. For in many situations it is virtually impossible to develop indicators of performance which meet the criteria of validity, equity and acceptability. At the upper end of the hierarchy, uncertain markets and economic conditions have more of an impact on profit and loss than the heroic efforts of key personnel. And at the lower end, studies have shown that the morale of the unit will plummet if there is a sharp discrepency in pay among employees who work together. As a result, salary schedules tend to be more closely correlated with such impartial factors as level of education, experience, and number of subordinates than with the quality of work performed. [4] Indeed corporate managers share the same reservations echoed by teacher unions over the years that merit pay can be subjective and divisive.

Recently, a group of federal personnel managers visited the sites of several national firms with reputations for management appraisal systems to investigate the possibility of transferring the technology to the new process of evaluation mandated by the Civil Service Reform Act of 1978. They observed

> Overall the performance appraisal process did not appear to receive a high degree of emphasis, and it was not particularly tied to rewards and penalties. Indeed salary decisions were, in several cases, made at quite different times of the year; relatively few people received bonuses and other inducements for performance, and there was a tendency to think in terms of group, rather than individual performance. [5]

Thus, what makes promotional and merit pay practices operate advantageously in business is not great confidence in the mechanics of performance indicators, but rather confidence in making wise and reasonable judgments with respect to personnel. This commitment to the bottom line permeates the organizational climate, particularly when there is clear-cut agreement on broad purposes and specific goals.

The Bell Model: Technique Over Purpose

When Secretary of Education Terrel Bell in March of this year issued a

---

12-page model for a "career-ladder/master-teacher/performance-pay program"[6] his intention was to provide useful guidelines for school districts implementing this approach. But instead of identifying the various features of the career-ladders/master-teacher concept, he viewed it as a minor variation of performance pay. Bell's emphasis is captured in the title itself, *Peer-Review Model for Managing Systems of Performance Pay*. Promotion from the rank of professional teacher to the new rank of master teacher is to be solely on the basis of outstanding teaching performance. By considering promotions to be *mainly* incentive awards he in effect negates the growth and responsibility features of a true career-ladder. While Bell recognizes that master teachers on occasion may work with college-student trainees and help in curriculum work, he also insists that these additional duties be carefully limited. "We don't want to identify our best teachers and then take them away from teaching. (This is what happens when our best teachers are promoted to the position of principal)."[7] Yet even though the central objective is to retain classroom teachers, he repeatedly advises that the procedure for selecting master teachers be virtually identical with those followed for filing major *administrative* positions, a highly cumbersome process given the lack of new duties and tasks to perform: posting the announcement; building a file on applicants; constituting a broadly based screening committee and making a collective decision. Secretary Bell, however, does downplay the technology of evaluation methods, thereby putting more reliance on peer judgments.[8]

While Bell finds an analog in the academic rank system of higher education, his model is more comparable to the approach used by the military for officer selection and promotion. The personnel system in the military is based on rank-in-person which makes the rank achieved contingent on the qualities and abilities of the *individual*. In contrast, the rank-in-position used in business and the civil service makes promotions dependent on the functions and responsibilities of the *position* to be filled.[9] Rank-in-person works tolerably well in the military because of the emphasis placed on qualities of leadership and command, which is congruent with the mission and purpose of the officer corps. But what are the comparable qualities specified in his model other than the dimensions of existing teaching performance? One should also be aware that, in the absence of a job description, the great weight placed on personal characteristics and traits in the military is easily abused and can result in favoritism.

Successive promotions from the rank of instructor to full professor in higher education do not constitute a career in the same sense as it does for a lieutenant who progresses to the rank of a field grade officer. A faculty member will earn more money and perhaps acquire more status when promoted, but will not have more responsibility or greater authority. Whatever command relationship that may have at one time existed between a full professor and lower ranks has long vanished. Indeed as one climbs the academic ladder, responsibilities to the institution will tend to *decrease* as evidenced by a reduced teaching schedule, fewer advisees and less committee work. For the typical faculty member, getting tenure does establish a stable base to launch a career, but the stages are more likely to be marked by individual achievements such as research and scholarship in the discipline, articles, books, major grants, and recognition from peers outside the institution than by promotional sequences. An equitable promotional system takes a range of different factors into account, such as teaching effectiveness, experience, research and publications, public and community service, and participation in governance. Depending on the goals of the college or university and the characteristics of the individual reviewed, the weight given to each of the criteria can vary widely. If in fact teaching effectiveness were always the decisive criterion, as Secretary Bell suggests in his peer-review model, the higher education system would be constantly facing the same kinds of conflicts and turmoil experienced by school districts in the controversies over evaluations.

The Current Impasse

Given the emphasis placed on the *means* of career-ladder plans rather than *ends* or purposes, it is not surprising to observe that a number of career-ladder plans enacted in 1983 legislative session became stalemated toward the latter part of the 1983-84 school year due to conflicts over evaluation techniques.[10] The key issues centering on how candidates are to be selected include what methods should be used to screen candidates, how the characteristics of a good teacher are to be measured, how valid and reliable the evaluation instruments are, and who shall conduct the evaluations. However, little attention is given to the functions and specific duties to be undertaken by master teachers. Certainly part of the problem is due to rapid spread and hasty enactment of these innovations in states and school districts. Governors, state legislatures, and educational lobbyists collaborated to get something enacted this year; next year the issue of better schools could move from center stage to the wings.

Yet, the principal cause for the present impasse is not flaws or omissions in the bill with respect to the evaluation process itself. Rarely are details of implementation spelled out in legislation because of the need to gain maximum consensus for enactment. Rather, it reflects the failure of states, school districts, and educational leaders to explore the *purposes* of having career-ladders. If career-ladders are viewed simply as a version of performance-based pay, as Dr. Bell seems to suggest, this puts an exceptionally heavy burden on selection and evaluation techniques. Since only a limited number of those eligible receive a nominal promotion, which is really a salary supplement, than the process itself will be considered unfair, regardless of the validity of the instruments used. If additional criteria were used (such as relating to students, sensitivity to parent-teacher concerns, and potential for developing new skills), the characteristics of the candidates could be more clearly differentiated, leading to more informed and relevant judgments. The emphasis on selection to the virtual neglect of

---

placement puts the cart before the horse, and ignores the needs of the educational organization itself. Also, if the tasks and duties of a master teacher are spelled out, the process of self-selection can begin to operate, greatly reducing the pressure from eligible claimants. Not all good teachers would want to take on new responsibilities or added burdens. As is the case of both business and the civil service, where career paths do exist, only a small proportion are sufficiently ambitious to climb the higher rungs.

Redesigning the Job of Teaching

Certainly a more powerful alternative for improving performance than the approach outlined by Secretary Bell is to restructure the job of the teacher to include career advancement and promotional opportunities. This would be consistent with the practices followed by business and the civil service, where promotions are given because of the need to complete more complex and challenging tasks, and not merely as rewards for performance to date.

In effect, the master teacher career concept is an extension of Frederick Herzberg's theory of motivation, which differentiates two kinds of work incentives.[11] The first type, called "satisfiers," includes such things as salary, job security, working conditions, status, and organizational policies. If these are perceived as being adequate, the work contract is maintained. When satisfiers are increased, the level of job satisfaction will rise but the employees' motivation and performance will remain unchanged. Satisfiers are not sufficiently potent to evoke the commitment to achieve. The other type of incentives, called "motivators," are directly connected with the work performed and include intrinsic aspects such as achievement, responsibility, advancement, autonomy, and personal growth. In contrast to the satisfiers, motivators will generate the increased effort and commitment which is essential to raising the motivation level.

When the first type of incentive, satisfiers, is examined with respect to teachers, it is evident that inadequate salaries, layoffs, poor working conditions, low status, and school personnel policies, instead of being satisfiers are in fact "dissatisfiers," leading to decreased commitment, poor morale, and less than maximum effort. National and state study commissions have released a stock-pile of reforms for improving teaching conditions such as across-the-board pay increases, merit, performance, and market-sensitive pay plans, new instructional policies, teacher grants and loans, and firmer codes of student discipline. Assuming that many of these measures are realized, they probably will dispel dissatisfaction and restore the level of commitment which once existed. If these incentives are substantially increased, morale will improve, fewer teachers will be absent, and turnover will be reduced. Yet performance levels are not likely to increase significantly.

Thus, pay increases and the like are *remedial* measures for bringing

Arnold J. Bornfriend

conditions up to par. But if our goals are much *better* schools, *excellence* in teaching, their attainment requires a new dimension — namely building *motivators* into the job of teaching. Some years back, Thomas Sergiovanni applied the Herzberg theory to teachers and confirmed that motivators are more powerful indicators of positive job attitudes than the satisfiers.[12] He discovered that while the routines associated with teaching were not themselves appealing, introducing achievement and recognition factors increased positive job attitudes markedly. Yet he also noted that prospects for advancement, one of the most potent motivators, was totally absent in the responses from teachers.

A well planned career-ladder can incorporate these substantial motivators through job enrichment, which is a process of job re-design. The first strategy of job enrichment is horizontal loading, which seeks to overcome the routinization of work by combining a variety of tasks.[13] This enables competencies to be developed in more than one field. In addition, it evokes a greater responsibility for outcomes. Examples of this approach which are mentioned in a number of master-teacher/career-ladder proposals include: working with both gifted and remedial students, participating in the development of curriculum plans and materials, offering adult-level education in addition to regular duties, teaching across disciplines, and combining guidance functions with teaching.

In terms of the stages of career growth cited earlier, these combinations coincide with Stage II, *Advancement*, since the role of teacher as independent contributor is enhanced by acquiring and perfecting new skills and competencies.

The second strategy, vertical loading, focuses primarily on enhancing autonomy, which is individual control of the flow of work-related activities from the planning stage on through completion, including evaluation of results. Examples of this approach as suggested in master-teacher/career-ladder proposals include supervising apprentice teachers; serving as a mentor for less proficient colleagues; conducting staff development programs; leading training sessions; assignments as department head; planning teaching schedules; selecting curriculum materials; refining the school systems programs, policies and procedures; and serving as liaison with business groups and the general community. These additional responsibilities boost teachers to Stage III, *Mentor*. Several of them, particularly the last two, contain elements of Stage IV, *Sponsor*, in helping to shape the direction of the school.

On Debureaucratizing Education

In addition to its central role in stimulating teacher performance, the master teacher plan can also help reverse the negative aspects of bureaucracies by its emphasis on restructuring the tasks and functions undertaken in the broader educational system. All bureaucracies are prone to inflated administrative structures, which produce excessive costs and lack of coordination. These factors tend to overwhelm the primary mission of the institution. School systems are particularly vulnerable to overbureaucratization due to the proliferation of supervisors and other educational specialists from within and the impact of federal and state regulations for special programs imposed from without.

To sketch one dimension of administrative costs, Peter Brimelow, in *Fortune Magazine*, points out that between 1958 and 1982 per pupil expenditures more than doubled (in constant dollars, corrected for inflation), rising from $1,123 in 1958 to $2,670 by 1982.[14] During this same period teachers' salaries — in former years the largest part of per pupil costs — decreased from 52% to 38%. As teachers lost ground, the proportional costs for administrative overhead increased substantially. Between 1950 and 1980 the number of pupils per administrator fell from 523 to 295. David Cohen, in exploring the effects of inflated administrative structures on the educational mission, observes that central offices responded to the multiplication of federal and state mandated offices by creating new levels of general management to coordinate policies.[15] But, since the subunits retained operating authority, the additional levels proved redundant and led to greater fragmentation of programs. Local school administrators were placed in the middle trying to connect their regular work with new federal programs. As a result, their primary responsibility for supervising curriculum and instruction was diverted. This "decoupling" of administration from the school's regular work meant that the primary objective of supervising instruction was not being dealt with.

While the successive waves of federally mandated special programs are a recent and dramatic example of overbureaucratization, the established practice of heavy reliance on educational specialists and instructional supervisors has also contributed to fragmentation, task redundancy, and higher costs.

Ancillary educational specialists, include guidance and counseling specialists, librarians, nutritional and health consultants, attendance supervisors, speech and hearing specialists, social caseworkers, psychology and mental health workers, and special services for exceptional pupils. The key issue here is not the value of these services, but rather who shall deliver them. Over the years, ambitious former teachers probably sought careers in several of these fields because of higher salaries and opportunities for advancement lacking in the single-salary schedule. School boards and districts would need to assess on a case-by-case basis whether using the master teacher as service-provider brings about superior performance, better articulation with the instructional mission, and cost-effectiveness. Obviously, some of these specialized areas are full-fledged professions, others are distinct occupational groupings and should retain their separate status. Additionally, if budgetary cuts have eliminated several specialized positions, the master teacher position provides a more durable base.

Basically, implementation is an extension of the horizontal loading strategy of job redesign referred to earlier.

Supervisors of instruction include subject matter supervisors, consultants in reading, foreign languages, vocational education, curriculum coordinators, special subject supervisors, and other supervisory positions generally considered staff, as distinct from line positions. It is of course appropriate to continue to maintain supervision as one of the multiple functions of line administrators, such as school superintendents and principals. But in no professional calling other than teaching is the topic of supervision so conspicuous as both a field of study and practice. Even though the current model of supervision as "human resource development" is but a vestige of its antecedents as inspector of poorly qualified teachers, the prevalence of supervision as a separate staff role is what precludes autonomy and advancement possibilities for the classroom teacher. Instead of instructional supervisors being the bottom rung of the administrative ladder, it should be a responsibility of the master teacher on the higher rungs of the academic ladder. In contrast to Secretary of Education Bell's dictum that "academic rank be distinct from special duties, responsibilities and assignments currently extant in the school system,"[16] the pursuit of accountability would be furthered by having these tasks coincide with the position of master teacher. This would also provide an impetus for school boards and districts to re-examine the nature and purpose of such titles as lead teacher, department head, and so forth, which have caused morale and coordinating problems by their ambiguous location in the zone between teaching and administration. Depending on the situation, an appropriate realignment of tasks would result. Thus, specific tasks would either be included in the job description of the master teacher or be classified under a managerial title. A job analysis of this sort, particularly when focused on instructional supervisors, could result in the elimination of redundant positions, since the master teacher would be undertaking the tasks of coaching, motivating and developing the talents of both peers and junior colleagues, which after all is the essence of supervision. In terms of job enrichment aspects, the emphasis here is on vertical loading with elements of horizontal loading included.

Federal and state mandated special programs for children include such programs as desegregation and intensive services for the disadvantaged, emotionally disturbed, hearing impaired and mutliple handicapped. While local school boards in this area do not have the discretion to consolidate offices or programs, the master teacher position is highly suitable for helping to coordinate these programs, particularly their impact on other instructional activities. In addition to their regular duties master teachers could serve as liaison persons with these program units and the central office level to help review policies and formulate guidelines applicable at the local level. No matter what specific tasks are undertaken, the position of master teacher is valuable as a bottom-up approach to achieve coordination. For it has been shown that a top-down approach of delegation through hierarchical levels leads to greater fragmentation than uniformity.

Resistance and Support

Given the potential for master teachers taking over tasks which administrators perform, it is not surprising that the strongest resistance to the career ladder concept has arisen in administrative circles. Fenwick W. English, a former director of two major differentiated staff projects, objects to the fact that teachers are paid more for supervisory tasks and curriculum development rather than for their duties as teachers in a classroom. Differential pay, he argues, is appropriate only when teachers elect to specialize in a scarce field, such as math or science. But as for master teachers, "they should remain teachers 100 percent of the time and not have to become part-time administrators with one foot in the classroom door."[17] Similarly, in a widely quoted comment, Lawrence A. Uzdell, formerly executive director of the National Institute of Education, is not inclined to reward teachers who leave the classroom to take on new and different assignments. Dismissing the notion that teachers will be paid extra for doing more work, he insists that true merit pay consists of rewarding teachers for the *quality* and not *quantity* of output.[18]

While these educators mount a direct attack on the master teacher's enroachment on administrative turf, Secretary of Education Bell's strategy is more subtle. He simply excludes the distinctive aspects of a career-ladder from his model agenda, and views it as a variant of performance pay. As noted earlier, assignments are to be temporary and limited. "We don't want to identify our best teachers and take them away from teaching."[19] In the same vein, the executive committee of the American Association of School Administrators endorsed merit pay, but omitted any reference to the career-ladder recommendations of the National Commission on Excellence in Education. Their concept of merit-pay was, furthermore, the traditional bonus for a few teachers based on classroom productivity, which must be "achieved and rewarded again and again."[20]

On the other hand, while teacher unions remain wary of merit-pay, they have tended to support career-ladders on a selective basis which combine substantial salary increases with progressive promotional opportunities. Thus after several concessions, the Tennessee Education Association backed enactment of the 1984 Master-Teacher Law, which they helped defeat a year earlier.[21] Similarly, the California Mentor-Teacher Plan enacted in 1983 was endorsed by teacher groups in the state since it provided mentors with a $4,000 bonus above their regular salaries and the opportunity to spend up to 40 percent of their time on curriculum development and counseling inexperienced teachers.[22] The now classic Charlotte-Mecklenburg model, which was under development for three years, won the approval of the North Carolina Teachers Association when it was enacted in 1984. Their earlier opposition vanished when the evaluation process was modified to include other teachers on the evaluation teams and not only principals and other administrators.[23] When neighboring Wake County, North Carolina, adopted the Charlotte-Mecklenburg Plan, it won immediate endorsement from the local teachers association, since it continued the precedent of having evaluation committees composed of both teachers and administrators.[24]

Even though several master-teacher/career-ladder plans were in limbo toward the close of the 1983-84 school year, the long run viability of this concept is assured by the increasingly positive attitudes of both union leadership and the classroom teacher. Recently, the two major national teachers associations, the American Federation of Teachers and the National Education Association, have shown a fundamental shift of doctrine and policy. Historically, both unions had insisted on a single-salary schedule, usually making allowances only for seniority and academic credentials in the interests of equity and to prevent discriminatory practices. Now both unions accept the legitimacy of the two key features of career-ladders which would likely have been rejected a year ago. First, the existence of a hierarchy of positions to be filled by teachers exercising varying degrees of authority and responsibility; and, secondly, paying differential salaries to teachers in the hierarchy. In addition, the ferment over the recommendations of the National Commission led the NEA to appoint a task force to examine other alternatives and develop a position paper for internal use. In a statement, which is strikingly reminiscent of Governor Alexander's remark ("The school should not be a factory with assembly-line teachers") that was cited in the beginning of this paper, John C. Board, chairman of an NEA committee, extends the metaphor, "The prinicpal is the equivalent of a shop steward, and teachers and students are isolated parts of an assembly line." Furthermore, he indicates the leadership of the NEA is discussing ways to *"restructure"* (emphasis supplied) schools so that teachers would have a greater role.

> Under such a system, teachers would assume much greater responsibility for organizing instruction than they now have, and there would be substantially more specialization and collaboration among teachers, and the most skilled teachers would have greater authority than their colleagues and earn higher salaries.[25]

Recent sentiments of rank-and-file teachers also indicate strong preference for career-ladder incentives and diminished support for merit-pay. In a national survey conducted by Louis Harris and Associates, which was released at the end of June, 1984,[26] 87 percent of those polled supported career-ladders "allowing teachers to take on more responsibility and receive more pay." By way of contrast, 59 percent "don't think merit-pay is an effective way to attract and keep good teachers." A year before, in a similar survey conducted by the *American School Board Journal*, 63 percent of teachers responding supported merit-pay, and agreed with the statement that teachers who are more effective in the classroom should receive larger salary increases than teachers who are less effective."[27] However, the earlier survey did not include career-ladders as an alternative choice.

Conclusion

It would be misleading to conclude that the central aim of the master-teacher/career-ladder concept is to give teachers a power base in the struggle for control between teachers and administrators. Rather, it is intended to narrow the gap which encases both teachers and administrators in separate arenas and prevents effective operation of the school. At present, there is virtually no day-to-day interaction between teachers and their peers on matters dealing with curriculum and instruction.[28] Similarly, administrators have little direct authority over work and can only marginally control the central function of instruction. Attending to environmental demands and complying with the formal rituals of educational organizations has shunted the fundamental mission aside. It is, then, the segmentation of teaching, the absence of clear standards, and the lack of coordination which leave a void that the master teacher aims to fill.

Although school districts that undertake an authentic career-ladder program will not experience immediate results, the benefits are likely to be more substantial and enduring than the returns from approaches which are superficially similar, such as merit-pay or Secretary Bell's "academic ladder." As is the case with any innovation that promotes positive change, a continuing climate of trust is needed to allay fears and suspicion. Full implementation may take a minimum of five years due to uncertainties of retirement and attrition, reclassification policies, and the vagaries of collective bargaining. Over the long run, however, career-ladders has the promise for fundamentally improving our nation's schools by attracting and motivating the performance of more talented and highly committed people who are making careers not only as teachers but as full-fledge educators.

Footnotes

1. This formulation is based on Gene W. Dalton, et al. "The Four Stages of Professional Growth," *Organizational Dynamics* 6(1977) 19-42.

2. Dan Lortie. School-Teacher (Chicago: University of Chicago Press, 1975), 84-85.

3. Commentary, "An Effort to Find Common Ground on Paying Teachers for Performance," *Education Week* April 17, 1983, 18.

4. See, for example, Arch Patton, "Why Incentive Plans Fail," *Harvard Business Review* 50 (1962) 58-66. Richard Simpson, "Performance Pay: Will It Work?" *The Bureaucrat* (Summer, 1980) 39-47. Edward E. Lawler, "Merit Pay: Fact or Fiction?" *Management Review* (April, 1981) 50-53.

5. Frank P. Sherwood, "Wrong Assumption, Wrong Strategies," *The Bureaucrat* (Winter, 1982-83), 24.

6. The entire text appears in *Education Week* March 14, 1984, 16.

7. Ibid., 16.

8. Contrary to Bell's premise that teachers have a high confidence level in Peer-Review or panels composed of both teachers and administrators, a national survey of teachers

conducted in May 1983 reveals that their own principals are the first choice of who shall evaluate — 39%. Only 25% selected peers. Even more striking, Bell's preference for a mixed panel of administrators and teachers was ranked 4th by teachers — 12%. Marilee C. Rist "Our Nationwide Poll," *American School Board Journal*, 170 (September, 1983) 23.

9. For a fuller account of the differences between rank-in-person and rank-in-position see George Berkley, *The Craft of Public Administration* (Boston: Allyn & Bacon, 1978) 154-157.

10. Thomas Toch, "Teacher Reforms Linked to Evaluation Systems" *Education Week*, March 21, 1984, 1; and Toch, "State Teacher Incentive Plans are Hitting Snags," ibid., April 18, 1984, 1.

11. See Frederick Herzberg, *Work and the Nature of Man* (Cleveland: World Publishing, 1966); and Frederick Herzberg, "One More Time: How Do You Motivate Employees?" *Harvard Business Review* (January/February, 1968), 53-62.

12. Thomas J. Sergiovani, "Factors Which Affect Satisfaction and Dissatisfaction of Teachers," *The Journal of Educational Administration* 5 (1967), 66-82.

13. J. Richard Hackman, Greg Oldham et al., "A New Strategy for Job Enrichment," *California Management Review* (Summer, 1975), 57-71; and Richard Hackman and Greg Oldham, "Development of the Job Diagnostic Survey," *Journal of Applied Psychology* (April, 1975) 159-170.

14. Peter Brimelow, "What to do About America's Schools," *Fortune* September 19, 1983, 62.

15. David K. Cohen, "Policy and Organization: The Impact of State and Federal Policy on School Governance," *Harvard Educational Review* 52 (1982), 474-499.

16. *Education Week* March 14, 1984, 16.

17. Fenwick W. English, "Merit Pay: Reflections on Education's Lemon Tree," *Educational Leadership* 41 (1983-84), 77.

18. Lawrence A. Uzdell, "Where is the 'Merit' in New Merit Pay Plans?" *Education Week* September 14, 1983, 21.

19. *Education Week*, March 14, 1984. In this connection it is interesting to note that in his *Peer-Review Model For Managing Systems of Performance Pay*, Bell cites Part 2 of Recommendation D, concerning improved teaching from *A Nation At Risk*, namely, competitive and performance-based salaries as well as Part 4, dealing with the establishment of career ladders. However, he completely omits Part 7, which states "Master teachers should be involved in designing teacher preparation programs and in supervising teachers during their probationary years." National Commission on Excellence in Education *A Nation At Risk* 30-31, (Washington, DC: US Dept. of Education, 1983). Clearly he prefers not to address the substance of the tasks to be undertaken by master teachers.

20. AASA, "Position Statement on Merit Pay for Teachers," *The School Administrator* 4, (September, 1983, 24.

21. For an account of the reasons for the Tennessee Education Association's shift see the following reports in *Education Week*: Jim O'Hara, "Tenn. Panel Approves Career-Ladder Plan," December 7, 1983; Jim O'Hara, "Union Endorses Amended Tenn. Master-Teacher Plan," February 8, 1984, 5; Charlie Eychner, "Final Passage Likely of Career-Ladder Bill," February 22, 1984; and Jim O'Hara, "Tennessee Legislature Passes Master-Teacher Legislation," February 29, 1984, 6.

22. Michael Fallon, "California Assembly Passes Sweeping Education-Reform Measure," *Education Week*, July 27, 1983.

23. Thomas Toch, "New Career Ladders For Teachers," *New York Times, Educational Supplement* (Spring, 1984), 53.

24. William Cohan, "Wake County, NC, Announces Career-Ladder Plan for Teachers," *Education Week*, April 25, 1984.

25. Thomas Toch, "NEA is Considering Major Policy Shifts," *Education Week*, March 21, 1984, 1.

26. As summarized by Barbara Zigli, "Teachers Love Jobs, Not Pay," *USA Today*, June 28, 1984.

27. Marilee C. Rist, "Our Nationwide Poll: Most Teachers Endorse the Merit Pay Concept," *American School Board Journal*, 170 (September, 1983), 23.

28. See, for example, John W. Meyer and Brian Rowan, "The Structure of Educational Organizations," ch. 4 in Marshall M. Meyer and Associates' *Environments and Organizations* (San Francisco: Jossey-Bass, 1978), 78-109.

Arnold J. Bornfriend

Career Ladders: Retaining Academically Talented Teachers

Paul R. Burden

Academically able and talented people are not being recruited as teachers, recognized once they are teaching, or retained in the teaching role. Why is this the case, and what can be done about it? This paper will look at career ladders as one way to address these issues and retain outstanding teachers.

Obstacles

Characteristics of the teaching career and conditions of the workplace greatly influence the recruitment, selection, and retention of teachers. Specifically, limitations in salary, status gains, recognition, job responsibilities, and growth opportunities affect all three areas.

One of the most prevalent complaints about teaching is that there is a lack of a career pattern for teachers (Lortie, 1975, p. 99). An examination of the teaching career shows that, by the time a teacher has reached the highest salary level and is perhaps at the peak of professional competence, there are limited possibilities for salary advancement. There is a tendency for most salary increases to occur in the first third of the career as teachers earn a master's degree and move to the top of the salary schedule within 10-15 years (Schlechty and Vance, 1983, p. 478). A survey of Kansas teachers revealed that the primary factor identified by those intending to leave the teaching profession in the next five years was financial problems (Horn, 1983). Teachers who seek higher salaries must leave teaching or go into administration; both options require the teacher to leave the classroom and stop teaching.

The lack of a career pattern also limits teachers' opportunities for recognition and status. Opportunities for making status gains rest in leaving classroom work for full-time administration, supervision, or curriculum development. There is no evidence to suggest that successfully completing a master's degree gives one added honor or responsibility in the school. Furthermore, growth possibilities and opportunities for teachers to vary their work responsibilities are limited, even though research shows that these can be important motivators for teachers (Silvers, 1982). Schaefer (1967) discussed the contradiction between the intellectual nature of teaching and the academic character of the education required to prepare for the task, on the one hand, and the isolated, nonscholarly, and non-self-renewing character of the setting in which teaching takes place on the other.

The survey of Kansas teachers indicated that teachers want more input on important changes at school (Horn, 1983). Indeed, most of the research on effective schools indicates that schools which engage teachers in job-related discussions and have them share in decisions about instructional programs are more effective than schools in which decisions are made by rule-bound bureaucratic procedures.

Schlechty and Vance (1983) contend that it is time to admit that one of the greatest crises in American education is in school management. Because of the tendency of schools to militate against shared decision-making and problem-centered analytical discussion among adults and the tendency for the informal culture of schools to be dominated by a management structure that is punishment-centered and bureaucratic, Schlechty and Vance argue that schools cannot attract the best people available (pp. 478-479).

Because of the public's perception of the characteristics of the teaching career and conditions of the workplace, some academically able and talented people may not choose teaching as a career. Vance and Schlechty (1982) reported that teaching not only fails to attract the most academically able, but also attracts a disproportionate share of the least able (p.26). Schlechty and Vance (1983) further reported that the retention rate for the least academically able teachers is higher than the retention rate for the highest academically able teachers (p. 476). Thus, a higher proportion of the career teachers are among the least academically able.

Career Ladder Plans

In an effort to address the problems of the teaching career and the conditions of the workplace, a career ladder has been proposed to aid in the recruitment and retention of teachers. A career ladder is a plan which provides a variety of stages in a teaching career with different duties and different pay at each stage.

A number of educators have endorsed the concept of the career ladder. Woodring (1983, pp. 82-84) proposed three career stages with teachers at the top stage earning as much salary as administrators. Gideonse (1982) has called for hierarchically structured teams of teachers including staff teachers and lead teachers (pp. 17-18). Schlechty and Vance (1983) proposed that the career structure of teaching in public schools should be redesigned to include high status roles that give classroom teachers with sufficient performance, commitment, and training responsibility for training other teachers and conducting research and development (p. 484). This system of differentiated staffing would give some teachers different types of responsibilities and authority than that afforded to others and would be a career structure that promotes excellence, rewards commitment, and encourages continuous growth.

Career ladder plans have also been proposed by a number of educational organizations and state education departments. Some of these reports have provided details of the proposed career ladders while others have simply endorsed the career ladder concept with no additional details. Reports with details of the career ladder plans include the: (a) Tennessee Master Teacher Plan, (b) Utah Commission on Excellence Report, (c) Wisconsin Task Force on Teaching and Teacher Education Report, (d) Florida Education Association/United Report, (e) Charlotte-Mecklenburg (NC) Career Development Plan, and (f) Shawnee (OK) Master Teacher Plan.

Organizations which have endorsed the concept of career ladders (but have not proposed details with the plans) include the: (a) Connecticut Board of Education, (b) National Commission on Excellence in Education, (c) Education Commission of the States, (d) National Association of School Boards, and (e) Forum of Educational Leaders.

While there are differences in the career ladder plans proposed in these reports, there are also a number of common features. Most of the reports include three or four career steps, predetermined criteria for advancement to a new step, objective evaluation procedures, the opportunity for teachers to accept new roles in the higher steps (including involvement in the development of preservice and inservice teachers, curriculum development, staff development programs, research, and other activities), and stipulations for certain certification and training as requirements for advancement to certain steps in the career ladder. Summaries of the career ladder plans from Tennessee, Utah, Wisconsin, and Florida are displayed in the Appendix to illustrate representative career ladder plans.

Advantages of Career Ladder Plans

Career ladders for teachers have been proposed in an effort to provide: (a) a formal procedure to recognize and use the full potential of master teachers, (b) a systematic way to provide exemplary models for beginning teachers, (c) different pay for different levels of teaching experience and expertise, (d) a system of promotion within teaching, (e) a career pattern to give teachers something to which they can aspire, (f) a means of attracting talented people to the classroom and retaining talented people in the classroom, and (g) a means of providing the profession with an avenue to improve its image and gain prestige.

There are a number of advantages of the career ladder plan for both the individual teachers and for the school districts. These advantages are listed below.

Advantages for Individual Teachers

1. More intrinsic rewards which result in personal and professional satisfaction and a desire to invest further effort by providing:

---

a. Recognition and status for excellent teachers
b. Options for diverse work responsibilities without leaving the classroom
c. Opportunities for career advancement
d. Career options within teaching and control over these options
e. Opportunities for professional growth
2. More extrinsic rewards
a. Higher pay as teachers advance into new levels on the career ladder
b. Other improved aspects of the work environment such as working conditions, effects on personal and professional life, interpersonal relationships, training assistance, and others.
3. The career ladder provides a longitudinal framework within which teachers can form their own career decisions

Advantages for School Districts

1. Enables the district to use the full potential of the teachers
2. Provides exemplary models for beginning teachers in a systematic way
3. Provides a method to reward outstanding teachers
4. Encourages teachers, through the incentive of higher pay, to meet the higher criteria for teaching and other duties at higher levels on the career ladder
5. Results in more resource people to deal with staff development, curriculum development, and a variety of other professional responsibilities
6. Provides a framework to assist individual teachers in goal-setting for professional growth
7. Provides the profession and the school district with an avenue to improve its image and gain in prestige
8. Provides a framework to aid in organizational decisions dealing with facilitating continued development (concerning issues such as supervision, travel money, and released time)

Potential Problem Areas

Problems with differentiated staffing plans in the 1960's and 1970's suggest that careful attention needs to be given to costs, role definitions, evaluation criteria and procedures, union support, and other areas (for example, see Cooper, 1972; Dempsey and Smith, 1972; English and Sharpes 1974; and Fiorino, 1972). In relation to a career ladder plan, areas to be examined carefully include the following:

1. **Role Definitions for Teachers.** Roles of teachers at each stage of the career ladder should be precisely defined.

2. **Redefinition of Administrators' Roles.** With teachers having the option of assuming some supervisory and administrative duties, the roles of principals, supervisors, and other administrators will need to be reexamined and redefined.

3. **School Management and Decision-Making.** With teachers making decisions about staff development, curriculum development, and other issues, the nature of school management and participatory decision-making needs to be examined. It would be appropriate to use one type of management system. Among those to be considered would be the Japanese management style as in Theory Z or a number of American participatory management models such as Blake and Mouton's managerial grid, Likert's System 4, Greiner's participatory management system, Tannenbaum and Schmidt's leadership continuum, and Herzberg's human relations model.

4. **Funding.** The costs for salaries of teachers and evaluators should be examined. The difference in pay at each career stage should make it worthwhile for teachers to seek advancement. Without adequate funding, the benefits of the career ladder plan would be jeopardized. The total amount of money spent on teachers' salaries would be higher than currently required in districts with single salary schedules.

5. **Evaluation of Teachers.** Evaluation criteria and procedures should be clearly described. Training for members of the evaluation team should be considered along with the logistics and costs for evaluation.

6. **Continued Training for Teachers.** School districts should carefully examine the need for personnel, time, money, and resources needed to aid in the continuing professional development of teachers.

7. **Union Support.** The involvement and support of teacher associations would affect the success of a career ladder plan. With teachers having the potential for assuming additional duties, contract negotiations might become more complicated.

8. **Legal Issues.** Conflicts with existing state laws or school district policies should be resolved, especially in the case of teacher evaluation.

9. **Tenure and Certification.** The relationship between the stages in a career ladder and the requirements for tenure and certification should be carefully defined.

10. **Released Time for Teachers.** Teachers in the higher steps of the career ladder might need some time out of the classroom to complete other professional duties such as curriculum development work. Arrangements will have to be made for someone to take the teachers' classes during these times.

11. **Performance Accountability.** To have the career ladder work successfully, it is important that teachers be held accountable for the adequate completion of any other professional duties they choose to assume.

12. **Proper Planning.** There should be careful planning for the transition

time between the time the career plan is adopted and the time it is in full operation. Once enacted, time must also be arranged for the school staff to plan and coordinate its responsibilities on a regular basis.

13. **Evaluation of the Career Ladder.** There should be on-going evaluation of all aspects of the career ladder plan so that modifications can be made to correct any problem areas.

Nationwide interest in career ladder plans is evidenced by the number of school districts, state education agencies, and other educational institutions that are now starting to develop and implement incentive-pay and career ladder plans. In 1984, the U.S. Education Department awarded over $1,-000,000 to 51 school districts, agencies, and institutions for the purpose of developing and implementing the pay-incentive plans. At least 25 of the districts or agencies receiving the awards had career ladders specifically mentioned in their proposals (Bridgman, 1984).

Many benefits can be gained through the career ladder plans for teachers. Careful thought needs to be given to the issues identified above so that the full potential of the plans can be achieved.

References

Bridgman, Anne. "E.D. Makes Grants to Help Develop Merit-Pay Plans." *Education Week* 3, 25 (March 14, 1984): 1, 14-15.

Cooper, James A., ed. *Differentiated Staffing*. Philadelphia: W.B. Saunders Co., 1972.

Dempsey, Richard A., and Smith, Rodney P. Jr. *Differentiated Staffing*. Englewood Cliffs, N.J.: Prentice Hall, 1972.

English, Fenwick W., and Sharpes, Donald K. *Strategies for Differentiated Staffing*. Berkeley, Calif.: McCutchan, 1974.

Fiorino, A. John. *Differentiated Staffing: A Flexible Instructional Organization*. New York: Harper & Row, 1972.

Gideonse, Hendrik D. "The Necessary Revolution in Teacher Education." *Phi Delta Kappan* 64, 1 (Sept. 1982): 15-18.

Horn, Jerry G. *Administrative Support and Financial Remuneration as Factors in Teachers' Decisions to Leave the Profession*. Manhattan, Kansas: Center for Extended Services, College of Education, Kansas State University, 1983.

Lortie, Dan C. *Schoolteacher: A Sociological Study*. Chicago: University of Chicago Press, 1975.

Schaefer, Robert J. The School as a Center of Inquiry. New York: Harper & Row, 1967.

Schlechty, Phillip C., and Vance, Victor S. "Recruitment, Selection, and Retention: The Shape of the Teaching Force." *The Elementary School Journal* 83, 4 (March 1983): 469-487.

Silver, Paula F. "Synthesis of Research on Teacher Motivation." *Educational Leadership* 39, 7 (April 1982): 551-554.

Vance, Victor S., and Schlechty, Phillip C. "The Distribution of Academic Ability in the Teaching Force: Policy Implications." *Phi Delta Kappan* 64, 1 (Sept. 1982): 22-27.

Woodring, Paul. *The Persistent Problems of Education*. Bloomington, Indiana: Phi Delta Kappa, 1983.

Appendix

Examples of Proposed Career Ladders

Source	Steps	Responsibilities	Pay	Other
Tennessee Master Teacher Program	Apprentice Teacher (3-year certificate)	Classroom teaching with regular observation & evaluation by senior & master teachers & administrators	District single salary schedule	Selected by completing an approved program & pass the National Teachers Exam
(In *Journal of Teacher Education*, March-April 1983)	Professional Teacher (5-year certificate)	Classroom teaching	$1,000 annually over usual increments	Apply to Master Teacher Certification Board for selection
	Senior Teacher (5-year certificate)	Additional optional summer work with gifted or remedial students; conduct inservice programs; develop curricula; observe & counsel apprentice teachers	$2,000 annually over usual increment & if on an 11 month contract, $4,000 annual supplement	Apply to Master Teacher Certification Board for selection. Renew certificates every 5 years. The state will pay salary supplements for 25% of districts' teachers.
	Master Teachers	Same as Senior Teacher	$3,000 annually over usual increments. $5,000 for 11 month contract & $7,000 for 12 month contracts.	Renew certificates every 5 years. The state will pay salary supplements for 15% of districts' teachers.

Source	Steps	Responsibilities	Pay	Other
Utah Commission on Excellence	Apprentice Teacher	Classroom teaching	Base Pay of $17,500 with yearly increments based on performance	Would hold provisional certificates and be supervised by master teachers for 2-3 years; There is no fixed ratio or percent of the district's teachers in the three steps.
(*Education Week*, Oct. 19, 1983; Vol. 3, No. 7, p. 8)	Professional Teacher	Additional responsibility for program development and for supervision of student teachers	Base pay 15% higher than that of apprentice teachers (or $20,125).	Maximum salary of 75% more than the base pay for apprentice teachers (or $30,625)
	Teacher Leaders	Responsible for the development of curriculum & instruction in their own school	Base pay would vary according to the degree of responsibilities, evaluation, and length of contract	Salary would be from about 75% more than the apprentice base salary ($30,625) and "top off" at about $40,000 Required to have a professional certificate and appropriate teaching competence as assessed by a committee of peers and other professionals including the principal.

Wisconsin Task Force on Teaching and Teacher Education (Final Report: State Superintendent's Task Force on Teaching and Teacher Education. January 1984. Bulletin No. 4250 from the Wisconsin Dept. of Public Instruction)	1. Associated Teachers	Classroom teaching	Will receive a one-year license. Advancement may occur after being positively evaluated by an evaluation team and after making progress in a planned program of professional development. Minimum salaries for each career step will be identified
	2. Professional Teachers	Classroom teaching	Will receive a five-year license renewable upon presentation of evidence of satisfactory performance and continuing professional development. May stay at this step or seek to advance to the teacher specialist or the career teachers levels.
	3-A. Teacher Specialist	At least half-time teaching. Work in specialized activities such as curriculum or staff development.	Will have an extended term of employment. Will receive a five-year license renewable upon evidence of satisfactory performance in both their classroom and specialist responsibilities and their continuing professional development.
	3-B. Career Teacher	Full-time classroom teaching.	Superlative teachers who choose to remain in the classroom. Will have an extended term of employment. Required to meet rigorous criteria. Will receive a five-year renewable license upon evidence of continuing excellent performance and continuing professional development.

Source	Steps	Responsibilities	Pay	Other
Florida Education Association/ United Career Ladder Plan (affiliate with the AFT)	Apprentice Teachers	Classroom teaching	District salary schedule	Within 5 years, in order to be eligible to be a senior teacher, apprentices would have to earn a masters degree in their field and be deemed successful by a team of evaluators from outside the school. If, after 5 years, these requirements are not met, the teacher would not be permitted to continue teaching.
(*Education Week*, Oct. 26, 1983, Vol. 3, No. 8, p. 8)	Senior Teachers	Full-time teaching, with 10 month contracts	$5,000 additional increment from the state	Can move to this level only after 3 years at the apprentice level. No limit on the number who could become senior teachers. Can stay at this level, provided they continue to pass periodic examinations.
	Associated Master Teachers	75-100% of time teaching; rest of time working with apprentices and on curriculum development. 11-month contract.	$5,000 additional increment from the state	After 3 years at the senior level, teachers would be eligible to become an associate master teacher. To move to this level, senior teachers would need to undergo an in-depth evaluation and would participate in some type of further training.

| Master Teachers | 50% of time teaching; choice of additional professional activities; 12-month contract | $5,000 additional increment from the state | After 3 years at the associated master teacher level (9-12 years after the start of their teaching career), associated master teachers would be eligible to become master teachers, again after evaluation and training. |

The Teacher Incentive Project (TIP) of the Winston-Salem/Forsyth County Schools

Linda Dockery
Marcia Epstein

In February, 1981, the State Education Agency, in response to a mandate by the state legislature, launched a project to establish uniform performance standards and criteria for evaluating teachers. The local school district served as a pilot site for field testing the Performance Appraisal Instrument (PAI) during the school year 1981-82 (see Appendix A). During the same period of time, the school district was involved in the pilot testing of the state's Quality Assurance Program (QAP) for teachers, which identifies competencies (performance standards) for teacher certification in each subject area. The Performance Appraisal Instrument was used throughout the state during school year 1982-83 as the official instrument for teacher evaluation, and the Quality Assurance Program was officially adopted by the State Board of Education in April, 1983. These instruments will constitute the foundation upon which the new incentive structure will rest.

This school district is particularly well qualified to undertake the project. In 1981, the district, in concert with institutions of higher education, teacher organizations, and the State Education Agency, established the Winston-Salem/Forsyth County Consortium for Personnel Development, this state accredited, competency-based training program not only trains teachers but also recommends them to the State Board of Education for certification in additional areas, thereby increasing their employability, reducing out-of-field teaching assignments, and reinforcing teacher skills. The Consortium is composed as follows: Representatives of the three higher education teacher training institutions in Forsyth County—Wake Forest University, Winston-Salem State University, and Salem College; representatives of the Winston-Salem Forsyth County Schools administrative staff; representatives of the local Teacher Advisory Council; and a representative form the State Department of Public Instruction.

The Consortium is completely compatible with the purposes of the project. Its existing program utilizes teams composed of three in-field professionals per team, representing and selected by higher education, practicing teachers, and school district administrators. Each team is organized to assess teacher competencies, to prescribe and arrange training, and to evaluate outcomes, as a basis for recommending certification to the State Board of in specific content or certification areas. The same training model can be used for evaluation teacher performance, with the objective of improving instruction and rewarding exemplary performance.

The Consortium team is an ideal source of technical support, assistance, and training for principals, who are legally responsible for teacher evaluation, and the expansion of its role to include teacher evaluation will objectify the evaluation process, making it more acceptable to all parties, evaluators and evaluatees alike. It is expected that improved teacher quality will be a natural outgrowth of an improved evaluation process.

It has already been pointed out that the school district participated in the pilot testing of the state's Quality Assurance Program (QAP). The Consortium, in concert with Winston-Salem State University, assumed the leadership role in this pilot project, which included an analysis and assessment of QAP certification requirements in seven areas. The objectives of the project were: (1) To correlate the major QAP competencies for certification with the functions and indicators on the Performance Appraisal Instrument in selected content areas. (2) To evaluated procedures for principals to appraise the performance of beginning teachers in selected content areas based on the QAP competencies. (3) To develop plans for professional improvement and staff development programs for beginning teachers who are working toward continuing certification. (4) To develop a plan to use the Consortium in providing technical assistance to beginning teachers. A report summarizing the results of the QAP study was submitted to the State Department of Public Instruction in June, 1983. Clearly, the Consortium is a viable vehicle of personnel development, which will assist school officials in achieving the major goal of the proposed project—the establishment of a performance-based incentive structure for teacher evaluation.

The proposed project is designed to improve teacher quality through the establishment of an incentive structure which combines teacher performance standards and a teacher evaluation system (which includes peer judgment) with a career ladder of successive levels of increasing teacher responsibility. Progression from one level to another will be determined by teacher evaluation, which in turn, will be based upon uniform performance standards and evaluation criteria. Although this school district has used teacher incentives for several years, there is no systematic structure of incentives currently in place. Moreover, incentives that have been used have not been linked to a formal evaluation system.

Local school officials and teachers now believe that something must be done about this situation. A performance-based incentive structure must be instituted—a system that utilizes incentives selectively, tying them to indicators of quality. The existing system, which links incentives to tenure, earning higher degrees, or other indicators of status, is not an indicator of teacher quality. While this system treats all teacher alike and is easy to administer, excellence goes unrewarded. Exemplary teachers and mediocre teachers receive the same rewards. The alternative is a system which used valid, objective, and uniform criteria with behavioral indicators of performance. Once in place, the new structure will enable the school district to be more competitive in recruiting better teachers and better teacher candidates, to identify and reward excellence, and to retain effective teachers in the classroom. It will also respond to a frequently articulated concern of teacher organizations—that most incentive pay plans are unfair, discriminatory, and based upon subjective assessment and favoritism. There is a consensus in this school district that an incentive structure for teachers must be based upon systematic teacher evaluation. The TIP meets the test. It also refines the evaluation process, making it more objective and therefore more defensible as a foundation for the support of an incentive structure.

Objectives

The project objectives were derived directly from the identified needs. They are: (1) By June, 1985, the local school district will have expanded the locally developed Consortium model to embrace the teacher evaluation process, making this process more objective, reliable, and acceptable to teachers, as determined by a report prepared by the project evaluation. (2) By September, 1984, the local school district will have utilized the new teacher evaluation process to identify teacher strengths and weaknesses and to prescribe effective improvement activities. (3) By June, 1985, the local school district will have established a performance-based incentive structure linking incentives to the teacher evaluation process to improve teacher quality, reward excellence in teaching, and attract and retain excellent classroom teachers.

The project will involve observation of videotapes depicting two hours of classroom teaching by each 72 participating teachers. Teachers will be responsible for videotaping approximately 12 hours of their own classroom teaching, after which they will select a two-hour segment for evaluation purposes. Because the evaluation procedure will involve observations by local team with whom teachers may not be familiar, school officials feel that the videotaping procedure is preferable to live observations.

Videotapes will be viewed by the expert Consortium teams and participating principals, and their ratings will be recorded on the Performance Appraisal Instrument. The project evaluator will then analyze and compare results, giving particular attention to areas of divergence, or disagreement. In cases where there is a lack of consensus between the principal's assessment of teacher performance and the assessment of the expert team, the team's evaluation will be regarded as a more reliable measure of actual teacher performance. The principal will then receive technical assistance from in-field consulting teachers, who will carry out their responsiblitities in close collaboration with the Consortium teams. The technical assistance will be designed to give the principal a better information base for a more

---

reliable and objective evaluation of the same teachers. Finally, post training teacher evaluations will be carried out, and the project evaluator will again analyze and compare results to determine the extent to which the technical assistance has been effective in achieving greater convergence of opinion between principals and the expert teams. Throughout the entire process, evaluation and technical assistance will be separate functions.

The plan of operation will be implemented through the following steps.: (December, 1983, through August, 1984) (1) *Identification of Principals:* Six principals, two from each division (elementary, junior high, and high school), will be identified by the superintendent of schools to participate in the pilot project. (Under North Carolina law, principals are the legally designated evaluators of teacher performance.) (2) *Identification of Teachers:* Twelve teachers will be identified in each of the six participating schools. The teachers will be selected so as to include: (a) Teachers in the same area of certification as the principals. (b) Teachers outside the principal's area(s) of certification. (c) Experienced teachers. (d) Inexperienced teachers. (3) *Identification of Consortium Teams:* Appropriate evaluation teams which correspond with the teaching areas of participating teachers will be identified from the existing reservoir of Consortium teaching area teams. (4) *Identification of Consulting Teachers:* Consulting teachers for each teaching area will be selected to work closely with the Consortium teams in providing training and technical assistance to principals to improve the evaluation function. The number of selected will be governed by need. This arrangement will ensure that the evaluation and technical assistance functions remain separate, since consulting teachers will be responsible only for technical assistance, not evaluation. The consulting teachers will also offer assistance to classroom teachers, prescribing growth activities in which these teachers may participate to improve their performance. (The qualifications of consulting teachers are described in Quality of Key Personnel.) The Consortium will be used to provide consulting teachers will specific training in procedures and skills needed for evaluation, consultation, and staff development. (5) Project Orientation: The project coordinator will be responsible for orientation and training for all project personnel—principals, evaluatees, Consortium teams, and consulting teachers—to familiarize them with all aspects of the project—its purpose, objectives, strategies, and evaluation plan. (6) *Videotaping of Classroom Teaching:* From 12 hours of self-videotaping, participating teachers will select two hours to submit to principals and evaluation teams from the Consortium to enable them to evaluate teaching. (7) *Rating of Teachers:* Using the state-adopted Quality Assurance Program as the standard of teaching excellence and the Performance Appraisal Instrument, into whose major functions the Quality Assurance Program competencies in each subject area have been integrated, principals and teams will view the videotapes and rate teachers on the appropriate functions; i.e., those that are observable in classroom teaching. (See Appendix A.) (8) *Collection and Analysis of Data:* The project evaluator will then compare and analyze evaluation reports (Performance Appraisal Instrument) prepared by principals and the evaluation teams, looking for divergence. The comparison will show the incidence of divergence between principals and Consortium teams on the basis of the certification areas of the principals and teacher evaluatees. The comparison will also center on experienced and inexperienced teachers. Following the analysis and comparison of evaluation data, the project evaluator will disseminate this information to appropriate principals and Consortium teams.

(September, October, and November, 1984) (9) *Technical Assistance:* In cases of significant divergence in evaluation results, Consortium advising teams will prescribe, and consulting teachers will provide, technical assistance to participating principals. This assistance will better enable principals to evaluate teachers outside of the principal's area(s) of certification. The Consortium team and consulting teachers will also be responsible for prescribing developmental training for teachers who have been identified as needing assistance in the functions specified in the Performance Appraisal Instrument (observable in classroom teaching, not observable). (See Appendix A.)

(December, 1984, to June, 1985) (10) *Post Training Teacher Evaluation:* Subsequent to technical assistance, the following additional procedures will be carried out: (a) Re-evaluation of teachers in cases where principals and Consortium teams failed to reach a consensus on the first evaluation, and of teachers who received technical assistance. (b) Evaluation of a new group of teachers in the same subject area fields to test the objectivity of ratings and to eliminate the possibility of bias. (c) Analysis and comparison of data from both the re-evaluations and the new evaluations. (11) *Selection of Teachers for Incentives:* Following the post training teacher evaluations, the proposed incentive structure will be instituted. This structure will be directly connected to the Performance Appraisal Instrument already in place. Teachers who receive outstanding ratings in the different functions will be provided opportunities for additional professional responsibilities, for which rewards will be prescribed. For example, a teacher who receives an outstanding evaluation in the function of managing daily instruction may be asked to provide workshops for other teachers who may need special assistance in this area.

The following diagram illustrates the levels of achievement which may be attained by teachers who demonstrate excellence. Probationary teachers automatically fall into the first category. Once career status or tenure is achieved, these teachers will advance to the second level—Career Status I.

Both the nature and the number of the additional responsibilities performed by the teacher will govern the movement from one Career Status level to the next in this incentive plan. The proposed *incentive structure* may include, but is not limited to, such *additional reponsibilities* as: selection of materials; curriculum development; demonstration teaching; conducting workshops; making videotapes of quality teaching; peer evaluations; grade level or department chair positions; twelve-month employment; summer school employment. It will include such *Rewards* as: released time; half-

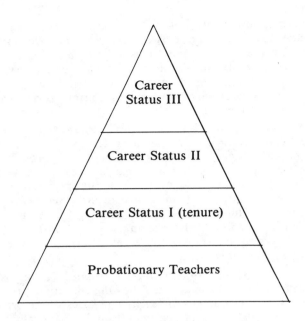

Career
Status III

Career Status II

Career Status I (tenure)

Probationary Teachers

time teaching duties; additional pay; recognition; sabbaticals; expense-paid conferences; scholarships.

The foregoing incentive structure is flexible and easily adaptable to the teaching evaluation process and needs of any school district. More importantly, the model ties incentives to excellence in teaching rather than the length of service or the degree earned by teachers. A summary of the proposed project and a timeline for implementation will be helpful in bringing together the main features of the project and its development.

Key Personnel

The personnel for the project include the Policy Board members of the Winston-Salem/Forsyth County Consortium for Personnel Development, the half-time project coordinator, a half-time secretary, Consortium advising team members, consulting teachers, participating principals, and the project evaluator.

Responsibilities and qualifications of key personnel are as follows: The *Consortium Policy Board* will be responsible for the selection of the half-time project coordinator and members of the advising teams. In addition, the policy board will evaluate the services of the advising teams and the technical assistance by the consulting teachers as well as approve the project processes and procedures. It includes representatives of higher education,

SCHEDULE OF IMPLEMENTATION

Activity	1983–1985 Timeline (D J F M A M J J A S O N D J F M A M J)
Selection of half-time project coordinator and identification of principals and teachers	
Identification of Consortium advising teams	
Selection of consulting teachers	
Project orientation for all participants	
Self-videotaping of classroom teaching	
Rating of teachers by principals and teams (review of videotapes)	
Collection and analysis of data	
Technical assistance for principals and developmental training for teachers	
Self video-taping for post training teacher evaluation	
Rating of teachers by principals and teams (review of videotapes)	
Analysis and comparison of data	
Matching appropriate incentives to teacher strengths	
Recommendation of teachers for incentives and rewards	
Design plan of replication for entire school district	

PROJECT SUMMARY

Objectives	Strategies	Evaluation
To expand the locally developed Consortium model of performance appraisal to embrace the teacher evaluation process, making this process more objective, reliable, and acceptable to teachers, as determined by a report prepared by the project evaluator	Selection of half-time project coordinator and identification of principals and teachers	Compare ratings of teachers, both before and after principals receive technical assistance, designed to respond to any divergence of opinion involving the following groups of teachers:
	Identification of Consortium advisory teams	
	Selection of consulting teachers	– Those in the principals' fields of certification
To utilize the expanded team model to identify teacher strengths and weaknesses and to prescribe effective improvement activities	Project orientation for all participants	– Those outside the principals' fields of certification
	Self-videotaping of classroom teaching	– Experienced teachers
	Rating of teachers by principals and teams (review of videotapes)	– Inexperienced teachers
To establish a performance-based incentive structure linking incentives to the teacher evaluation process to improve teacher quality, reward excellence in teaching, and attract and retain excellent classroom teachers	Analysis and comparison of data	Analyze and compare ratings of the following groups of teachers:
	Matching appropriate incentives to teacher strengths	– Teachers about whom principals and advising teams failed to reach a consensus on the first evaluation
	Recommendation of teachers for incentives and rewards	
	Design plan of replication for entire school district	– Teachers receiving technical assistance following first evaluation
		– A new group of teachers for control purposes

Analyze ratings of excellent teachers for the purpose of providing incentives appropriate to their strengths

Prepare final evaluation report by the project evaluator

teacher organizations, local school administrators, and the State Department of Public Instruction.

The *Project Coordinator* will be nominated by teachers within the school district, with the final selection being made by the Consortium Policy Board and the Superintendent of schools. The coordinator will need at least five years experience, a masters degree, tenure, outstanding evaluations, knowledge of the Performance Appraisal Instrument and Quality Assurance Program, and effective communication, consultation and organizational skills. This person will work with all other personnel in carrying out the proposed project according to the plan of operation and projected timetable.

Each of the *Consortium Advising Teams*, for each subject area, is composed of a local teacher, a representative of higher education, and a school system administrator. Chosen on the basis of their expertise, these teams will be responsible for the selection of the consulting teachers, the evaluation of teacher performance, and the prescription of appropriate technical assistance for principals and teachers.

The *Consulting Teachers* will be nominated by their peers, selected by the Consortium advising teams, and approved by both the Consortium Policy Board and the superintendent of schools. These teachers will be responsible for providing training and technical assistance to the principals and, where appropriate, to teachers. Consulting teachers must have at least five years of experience, demonstrate effective communication and consultation skills, and be familiar with the state's Quality Assurance Program competencies.

The six *Participating Principals* will be selected by the Consortium Policy Board and the superintendent. Each principal will be responsible for reviewing the videotapes for evaluation purposes, working with the Consortium advising teams in comparing and analyzing the evaluation data and, where needed, working with the consulting teachers in acting upon the recommendations of the Consortium teams. During the past two school years, each principal has received specially designed training to use the state's Performance Appraisal Instrument in the teacher evaluation process.

The *Evaluator* assigned to this project is a staff member in the school district's Division of Planning and Evaluation. The evaluator will be responsible for all phases of data collection and analysis and for the preparation of the overall evaluation report, assisted by the Division of Research and Evaluation of the State Department of Public Instruction.

Evaluation Design

The incentive structure described in this proposal is linked to a stylematic method of teacher evaluation. Evaluation efforts will focus primarily on questions concerning the objectivity of the evaluative processes, upon which the incentive structure is based. Of secondary importance will be questions

Linda B. Dockery & Marcia B. Epstein

regarding the project participants' perceptions of the technical assistance efforts and the degree to which both participants and non-participants receive the new standards for the distribution of incentives to teachers.

Constraints on the Evaluation Design: (1) *Sample Selection.* Consortium teams were originally formed to provide recertification assistance to Winston-Salem/Forsyth County teachers only for those content areas requiring more teachers. Under the guidelines of the proposed project, the duties of these Consortium teams will be expanded to include teacher evaluation. Additional Consortium teams will not be formed in other content areas solely for the evaluation of teachers until the results of this study are known. For this reason, the selection of participating teachers will be restricted to the same content areas as the existing Consortium teams. (2) *Experiences of Consulting Teachers.* In a few of the Consortium subject areas, the consulting teachers might be certified for grades K-12 and yet actually teach at the elementary level. Evaluations of teachers at different grade levels might be influenced by the degree of experience the consulting teachers have with the curricular objectives at those grade levels. (3) *Familiarity of Consortium Team with Participating Teachers.* Because the Consortium teams have been providing technical assistance to the school system since 1981, they may have to evaluate some teachers to whom they provided recertification assistance in previous years. This familiarity could influence the evaluations of these teachers. (4) *Videotapes.* The use of videotapes will allow teachers to select only cases which they feel are most representative of their teaching skills. In all probability the two hours of tapes selected will be examples of superior rather than average performances. Skills in manipulating the videotape equipment may differ by teacher. Some teachers may easily control the camera. Others may feel stifled by the intrusion of videotape equipment, unsure of whether to plan instruction around the tapings, to leave the camera's view to provide individual assistance, or lose the rhythm of instructional delivery by pausing to make technical adjustments.

Evaluation Model. Within the principals' own schools, videotapes of the teacher will be evaluated by the principal and the appropriate Consortium teams. Differences in ratings between the two groups for each evaluation category will be determined. To assess the influence of the principals' familiarity with the participating teachers on evaluation ratings, the principals will also evaluate a sample of videotapes of teachers in the same content areas teaching at different schools. Again, the degree of divergence between the principals and the Consortium team will be measured. In content areas where more than one Consortium team has been formed, at least two teams will evaluate a sample of the same videotapes. Comparisons of evaluations of the same teachers made by different Consortium teams will check the assumption regarding the objectivity of Consortium evaluations.

Technical Assistance will be provided to the principals in all areas showing divergence from the Consortium team's evaluations. Following the technical assistance activities, the principals and Consortium teams will evaluate new videotapes of the teachers in cases where there was a divergence of opinion on the first rating. The degree of divergence in evaluations will again be calculated to assess the effectiveness of the technical assistance activities for principals. When the evaluations of teachers reveal areas needing improvement, the teachers will participate in technical assistance activities to develop their skills in the problem areas. The impact of the teacher training activities will be assessed by comparing videotapes of the teachers made before and after the training activities. Feedback focusing upon the perceived effectiveness should take place between three groups — the Consortium teams and the consulting teachers, the consulting teachers and the participating teachers, and the consulting teachers and the principals.

Sample Size. Six principals will be selected from those who volunteer to participate in the project. Elementary, middle, and high schools will be equally represented with two principals selected from each. A total of 72 teachers will participate in the project. Twelve teachers will be selected from each of the six participating school. This teacher sample in each school will reflect the principal's area of certification and other areas. The teachers will be further grouped by level of experience, with equal numbers of experienced and inexperienced teachers. Each of the principals will also evaluate videotapes of four teachers from the other school representing the same grade levels. Attempts will be made to match these teachers with the participating teachers in the principal's home school in terms of the subjects they teach and years of teaching experience. Whenever possible, the groups will be equally divided into in-field/out-of-field and experienced/inexperienced groups.

The following *Evaluative Questions* will be entertained: (1) In what areas did the principal's evaluation of teachers differ from the Consortium team evaluation? (2) In what areas did the principal and the Consortium team evaluation of teachers differ for (a) teachers within the principal's school vs. teachers in other schools, and (b) teachers working in the same content areas as the principal's area of certification vs. those in other areas? (3) Was the assumption of the objectivity of the Consortium team valid? Did Consortium teams in the same content areas agree in their evaluations of the same teachers? (4) Were there group differences in evaluations between experienced and inexperienced teachers? (5) In what categories of the Performance Appraisal Instrument were the technical assistance activities between the principals and consulting teachers effective in promoting convergence of the principal's and Consortium teams' evaluations of teachers? (6) In what categories of the Performance Appraisal Instrument did teachers show excellence, adequate performance, or a need for improvement? (7) In what categories of the Performance Appraisal Instrument were teacher ratings improved following staff development activities geared at identified weaknesses? (8) What were the opinions of the project participants concerning the technical assistance activities? Did their opinions differ by the amount of time spent giving or receiving technical assistance? (9) How do both project participants and non-participants view the process of teacher evaluation developed in this project as a basis for an incentive structure?

Instruments and Reporting Methods. Pretreatment and posttreatment administrations of the Performance Appraisal Instrument will be used to address evaluative questions 1-7. During the pretreatment phase, the data will be broken down by individual participants so that necessary technical assistance activities can be prescribed. The data will also be aggregated so that group differences can be statistically analyzed. Comparisons of pre- and post-evaluations will be made to assess principal improvement in evaluative skills and teacher improvement in instructional areas.

The effectiveness of the technical assistance activities by consulting teachers for principals and participating teachers will be addressed through questionnaires and surveys. Responses to the surveys will be shared with the appropriate parties so that necessary adjustments in the training program can be made.

After all evaluation results have been reported, project participants, as well as teachers, principals, and other administrators not directly involved with the project, will be surveyed to assess their perceptions of the objectivity of the new evaluation process and its use in selecting teachers for incentives.

The Data Collection and Analysis Schedule is shown on the implementation timeline for the proposed project, including the schedule for the collection of teacher evaluations. Survey forms addressing the training sessions will be administered at various points throughout the scheduled technical assistance activities. An 'end-of-project' survey will be administered to gather opinions from participants and non-participants concerning the project's strengths and weaknesses. Data from the Performance Appraisal Instrument and the survey instruments will be analyzed in terms of frequency and magnitude of response and pre-post changes for individuals and for groups. Group differences will be assessed using Chi square tests.

APPENDIX A

WINSTON-SALEM/FORSYTH COUNTY SCHOOLS TEACHER PERFORMANCE APPRAISAL INSTRUMENT — PART I

The instrument contains the following categories and items. Each item is assessed on a six-point scale: Performs unsatisfactorily; Needs improvement in performance; Meets performance expectations; Exceeds performance expectations; Superior performance; Not applicable. There is also space for written comment under each heading.

The following are *Broad Program Functions*. They refer to planning, operating, and updating the grade level instructional program as a total program extending over the school year.

A. Major Function: Planning the Program—(1) Contributes as requested to the development of annual objectives for the school. (2) Develops an annual instruction plan that includes the formulation of objectives, strategies, timelines, and evaluation procedures consistent with annual school objectives.

B. Major Function: Overseeing the Program—(1) Applies curriculum scope, sequence, continuity, and balance in carrying out the annual instructional plan. (2) Implements learning strategies that address the needs identified in the annual instructional plan. (3) Uses appropriate evaluation methods to determine whether the annual instructional plan is working. (4) Makes changes in the annual instructional plan when evaluation indicates a need, and seeks advice and assistance if needed.

C. Major Function: Updating the Program—(1) Renews competence and keeps up with advances in child growth and development and uses this knowledge to improve the instructional program. (2) Renews competence and keeps abreast of new knowledge, research and practice in subject area(s) and applies this knowledge to improve the instructional program.

The following are *Particular Technical Functions*. They refer to the means by which the teacher adapts the broad program functions to lessons and units of study on a daily basis.

D. Major Function: Managing Daily Instruction—(1) Prepares daily lesson plans, makes classroom presentations, conducts discussions, encourages practice, and corrects student work in a manner that demonstrates subject area competence. (2) Correlates subject matter to students' interests, needs, and aptitudes. (3) Uses resources, materials, and enrichment activities that are related to the subject(s). (4) Employs instructional methods that are appropriate to the instructional objectives. (5) Involves

Linda B. Dockery & Marcia B. Epstein

students, parents, and others as needed to help insure that students keep up with daily lessons.

E. Major Function: Differentiating Instruction—(1) Identifies students' strengths and weaknesses in relation to objectives to determine if grouping is required because of different skill levels. (2) Groups students as needed for effective teaching and learning. (3) Uses the school's media center to support and supplement instructional activities. (4) Provides instructional activities that aid students in becoming independent learners.

F. Major Function: Individualizing Instruction—(1) Monitors individual student achievement of objectives as teaching occurs. (2) Provides individual students with prompt feedback on their progress and provides necessary remediation. (3) Adjusts instruction to objectives and individual student needs on a daily basis. (4) Arranges to have appropriate materials and equipment available to satisfy individual needs.

G. Major Function: Supervising—(1) Manages the daily routine so that students know what they are to do next and are able to proceed without confusion. (2) Keeps student talk and movement at a level that lets each student attend to his or her instructional task without interruption. (3) Maintains a pleasant working atmosphere that does not stifle spontaneity and warmth.

The following are *Indirect Facilitating Functions.* They refer to a moderately related set of activities that do not involve direct teaching between teacher and student, but have important effects on the success of that direct teaching. *Noninstructional Duties* refer to the teacher's essential role in the logistics of administering a program to a large social group of several hundred students in a limited space.

H. Major Function: Human Resources—(1) Uses student talent as a resource in instructing, developing materials, and operating equipment. (2) Makes appropriate use of volunteers and resource teachers with special skills and knowledge. (3) Makes use of appropriate community resources to extend classroom learning. (4) Makes effective use of other professional personnel to improve instruction and classroom management.

I. Major Function: Human Relations—(1) Shows respect for the worth and dignity of all students. (2) Is aware of and encourages respect of cultural differences. (3) Establishes rapport with parents.

J. Major Function: Noninstructional Duties—(1) Carries out noninstructional duties as assigned or as need is perceived. (2) Adheres to established laws, rules, and regulations.

At the end of the instrument, space is provided for summary comments by the evaluator and for the teacher's "Reactions." Each party signs the instrument, the teacher's signature indicating "that the written evaluation has been seen and discussed."

APPENDIX B

A representative subject-specific instrument for the evaluation of teaching is the "Addendum to the *Science* Performance Appraisal Instrument." This instrument assesses additional "competencies" that are "required in the teaching of science," such as the following, reproduced here in condensed summary form:

Under Planning the Program: (1) Demonstrate knowledge and understanding of basic science conceptions and process skills, and of the social implications of science. (2) Demonstrate ability to identify and integrate science process skills into all science activities. (3) Demonstrate an understanding of the interrelationships among various disciplines of science. (4) Demonstrate an understanding of the interrelationships between science and other academic areas. (5) Demonstrate an awareness of the economic and technological importance of the application of science. (6) Know of the contributions of major scientists in biology, chemistry, physics, and earth science.

Under Overseeing the Program: (1) Demonstrate an understanding of the investigative nature of science.

Under Updating the Program: (1) Be familiar with contemporary issues such as abortion, birth control, venereal disease, and genetic engineering. (2) Be familiar with moral and ethical issues such as world hunger, population control, alternate energy sources, pollution control, world resource allocation, and endangered species. (3) Understand the implications of physics application to new and emerging technologies such as computers, robots, nuclear reactors, space vehicles, and sources of energy. (4) Have thorough knowledge of measurement including knowledge of the SI system of measurement. (5) Know how to use appropriate measuring devices. (6) Know how space exploration has resulted in increased information about the earth.

Under Managing Daily Instruction: (1) Demonstrate a positive attitude toward teaching science. (2) Demonstrate knowledge and application of the scientific method in teaching science. (3) Demonstrate the ability to plan and conduct a laboratory lesson which includes concept(s), appropriate activity(ies), science process skills, science materials and equipment, and evaluation procedures. (4) Demonstrate an understanding of the investigative nature of science.

Under Human Resources: (1) Demonstrate the ability to plan and execute lessons that make use of resources outside of the school environment such as field trips, speakers, special events, and community resources. (2) Understand how people affect the process of change.

Linda B. Dockery & Marcia B. Epstein

Under Human Relations: (1) Understand the implications of social/ethical biology. (2) Understand the consequences of the use of drugs including alcohol, narcotics, and tobacco. (3) Understand the nature of populations, communities, and ecosystems. (4) Understand patterns of interaction with an ecosystem. (5) Understand how changes in people's behavior could improve life's chances for survival in the future. (6) Understand how human activities have modified the environment both deliberately and inadvertantly.

APPENDIX C

The "Carolina Teaching Performance Rating Scale— Adapted for Teacher Incentive Project"

This instrument examines six areas of "practice," rating each teacher on the project's six-point rating scale (given in Appendix A). Space is provided for informal comment by the evaluator (only). The categories and items are (in their entirety) as follows:

(1) INSTRUCTIONAL TIME: Materials Ready; Class Started Quickly; Gets Students on Task; Maintains High Time-on-Task.

(2) STUDENT BEHAVIOR: Rules—Administrative Matters; Rules—Verbal Participation/Talk; Rules—Movement; Frequently Surveys Visually; Stops Inappropriate Behavior.

(3) INSTRUCTIONAL PRESENTATION: High Rate of Success; Begins with Review; Introduces Lesson; Summarizes Main Points; Lesson Understandable; Assignment Clear; Provides Relevant Examples; Speaks Fluently, Precisely; Transition Between, Within; Brisk Pace.

(4) INSTRUCTIONAL MONITORING: Assesses Performance—All; Checks During Independent Work; Maintains Deadlines, Standards.

(5) INSTRUCTIONAL FEEDBACK: Immediate Feedback—In-Class; Affirms Correct Answer Quickly; Sustaining Feedback; Prompt Feedback—Homework.

(6) INSTRUCTIONAL CONTENT: Presents Accurate Content Material; Demonstrates Knowledge of Content Material.

ABOUT THE AUTHORS

Barry D. Anderson is Executive Director, Division of Educational Finance Research and Economic Analysis in the British Columbia Ministry of Education.

Arnold J. Bornfriend is Professor of Management, Worcester State College in Massachusetts.

Paul R. Burden is Assistant Professor in the Department of Curriculum and Instruction at Kansas State University.

Linda Dockery is Coordinator of the U.S. Office of Education Teacher Incentive Project, Winston-Salem—Forsyth County (North Carolina) Schools.

Marcia B. Epstein is Director of Staff and Organizational Development in the Winston-Salem—Forsyth County (North Carolina) Schools.

Dan S. Green is Director of Academic Affairs at the Beaver Campus of The Pennsylvania State University.

Willis D. Hawley is Dean of George Peabody College for Teachers at Vanderbilt University.

Terry Herndon, former Executive Director of the National Education Association, is Chairman of the National Foundation for the Improvement of Education.

Philip W. Jackson is David Lee Shillinglaw Distinguished Service Professor of Education and the Behavioral Sciences at the University of Chicago.

Henry C. Johnson, Jr. is Professor in Education Theory and Policy at The Pennsylvania State University.

Jonathan Mark is Systems Analyst, Computer Service Division, City of Vancouver, British Columbia.

Richard J. Murnane is Associate Professor, Harvard Graduate School of Education.

Gary Natriello is Assistant Professor of Sociology and Education at Teachers College, Columbia University.

Robert E. Rumery is Associate Professor of Psychology at Illinois State University.

Wayne J. Urban is Professor of Educational Foundations and History at Georgia State University.

David Wood is Associate Professor of Business Information Systems at Robert Morris College, Coraopolis, Pennsylvania.